LIVING POORLY
IN
AMERICA

LIVING POORLY IN AMERICA

Leonard Beeghley

PRAEGER

New York
Westport, Connecticut
London

Library of Congress Cataloging in Publication Data

Beeghley, Leonard.
  Living poorly in America.

  Bibliography: p.
  Includes index.
  1. Poor—United States. 2. Economic assistance,
Domestic—United States. 3. Public welfare—United
States. I. Title.
HC110.P6B4   1983   362.5'0973   83-9467
ISBN 0-275-90945-X (alk. paper)
ISBN 0-275-91564-6 (pbk.: alk. paper)

Library of Congress Catalog Card Number: 83-9467

ISBN: 0-275-90945-X
       0-275-91564-6 (pbk.)

First published in 1983

Praeger Publishers, One Madison Avenue, New York, NY 10010
A division of Greenwood Press, Inc.

Printed in the United States of America

∞

The paper used in this book complies with the
Permanent Paper Standard issued by the National
Information Standards Organization (Z39.48-1984).

10 9 8 7 6

For MAH

Preface

No matter how much we may try to deceive ourselves or the public, very little social scientific research is value-free. This is especially true in applied areas, such as the study of poverty, in which findings have significant political implications. For no matter how precisely concepts are measured, no matter how elegant the statistical models used, and no matter how rigidly the rules of logic are followed, the meaning that findings have is nearly always dependent on one's own values.

Here are two examples. The first is a straightforward question: At what level of income is a family poor? As will be seen in Chapter 2, whenever Americans are surveyed, they give a practical answer—one that is well above the poverty line. The government's official definition of impoverishment provides a different response to the question. Yet some academicians criticize the poverty line for being too high, mainly because it does not take into account the effects of in-kind income. For these observers, then, there is another answer: The true poverty threshold is well below the official definition. In fact, there is no scientific way of resolving this issue. Athough I shall suggest some common-sense criteria that can be used, the peoples' answer to the question posed is ultimately a matter of their values, goals, and positions in society.

The second example comes from Chapter 5 and deals with an empirical generalization: the lower the social class, *then* the lower the rate of political participation. Now this is a fact; no one familiar with the research literature would disagree with it. Its meaning, however, is another matter. For some, it is a good example of the lethargy of the poor, who have no one to blame for their situation in life but themselves. For others, however, it reflects the extent to which the poor are disenfranchised. Although I shall suggest a reasonable way of interpreting this finding, the meaning of this fact ultimately depends on one's values.

For this reason, there is merit to an explicit statement of the political orientation underlying this book: I believe the United States should be less unequal than it is today. If America were to become more egalitarian, it would be a more just society, more true to its heritage, more economically productive, and a more enjoyable place to live. While I have tried to present the evidence fairly and (more or less) without polemics, this value orientation underlies my interpretations, and readers have a right to know about it.

In presenting a number of provocative arguments, I have tried to write clearly and, at the same time, show how sociological insight can be useful in understanding what it is like to live poorly in America. I reject the stereotype that understandable prose must also be superficial.

I would like to acknowledge the suggestions and encouragement of several persons. Mary Anna Hovey read the entire manuscript and made many helpful comments. In addition, several of my colleagues at the University of Florida, especially Ronald L. Akers, Benjamin Gorman, John C. Henretta, Gerald R. Leslie, and Gordon F. Streib, helped me to improve the exposition. Joseph S. Vandiver kindly passed me his copies of various Census Bureau documents, for which I am most appreciative. Finally, several friends, especially members of the Men's Lunch Group, reacted to the text in useful ways. I hope they approve of the result.

Leonard Beeghley

Table of Contents

List of Tables

1

INTRODUCTION

This is a book about living poorly in America today. It is intended to correct some of the myths about poverty, to describe how those with very little money live, and to explain the correlates and causes of impoverishment. In performing these tasks, it is my hope to provide readers with a realistic view of the vexing problem of poverty in the United States and a humane understanding of those individuals who must survive in the margin of our society. In general, neither public debate nor public policy has been informed by these characteristics in recent years.

Any book about the poor in the 1980s must confront the legacy of Lyndon Johnson. In 1964, President Johnson observed that "we are not content to accept the endless growth of relief rolls and welfare rolls. We want to offer the forgotten fifth of our people opportunity not doles."[1] He then declared a war against poverty. Unlike the other war fought during those years, the American people overwhelmingly supported this struggle. In 1964, at the beginning of the war on poverty, 72% of the population agreed that the federal government should do away with impoverishment. In 1974, 82% of the people agreed that it was very important for the government to help the poor.[2] Despite this level of support and the optimism permeating that period, the war against poverty has been over for some time now and, to paraphrase a popular bumper sticker, poverty won. One indicator of this result is that the extent of pauperism in our society expanded rather than contracted: More people became dependent on public aid than ever before. Thus, rather than eliminating impoverishment, the war against poverty alleviated some of its worst aspects by expanding the system of public assistance. Although this result represented significant progress, it did not signify victory. It is important to keep this fact in mind because some commentators have suggested that public aid, especially in the form of in-kind assistance, has "antipoverty effects." The perverseness inherent in this assertion will be noted in the following.

Herbert Gans has observed that it is the beginning of wisdom to understand the functions of poverty in America, for phrasing the issue in this way provides some preliminary insight into the intractable nature of this problem.[3] The notion that poverty has positive consequences for some segments of society implies that the existence of a class of poor people, some of whom receive public aid, provides many benefits for those who are more fortunate. When this fact is recognized, then the persistence of poverty and the expansion of public assistance programs become intelligible, the possibility for self-deception is lowered, and several myths about the poor can be addressed. Hence, I would like to begin by briefly reviewing some of the ways in which the nonpoor benefit from the persistence of impoverishment.

The first function of poverty is to supply a cadre of low-skill workers who can and will perform vital tasks that others do not wish to do. Such jobs come easily to mind: making cloth and clothes, picking and cooking food, cleaning buildings and streets, and all the other dirty, menial, dangerous, low paying, and short-term occupations that must be filled in any industrial society. What these facts mean is that the pervasiveness of poverty ensures that a class of persons is available to fill positions nobody else wants. I know it sounds odd (not to mention cynical), but an unexpected implication of an analysis of the functions of poverty is that while the task of the public school system is primarily to educate, one of its unintended consequences is to weed out a sufficient number of individuals who will then be available for jobs in what has been called the secondary labor market.[4] Thus, by systematically failing to educate a certain proportion of students, mostly those who come from lower socioeconomic backgrounds and have fairly limited aspirations, the school system helps to create and perpetuate a class of poor people who make up the cadre of low-skill workers that our society needs. The interesting thing about this process is that it really is unintended: It occurs despite the efforts of dedicated teachers. The inability of such persons to affect the lives of most of the impoverished students they teach ought to suggest both the vulnerability of poor people and the influence of social facts on individual behavior. I shall return to these topics subsequently.

The second function of poverty is to keep prices down. Because their wages are so low, the existence of an indigent class subsidizes the consumption activities of the more affluent. The result is that clothes are cheaper, food is less expensive, rent is kept down, and taxes are lower. What these facts mean is that the life-style of the middle and upper classes in American society is dependent on the existence of a low-paid work force, many of those members are also dependent on public aid for survival. Nonetheless, many people persist in believing that the poor do not work, that they are lazy. Sometimes myth is easier to accept than reality.

The third function of poverty is to create jobs and income for people 3) who would regulate, serve, or exploit those who are less fortunate. For example, the poor guarantee work for police officers, lawyers, court clerks, judges, probation officers, and all the other persons connected to the criminal justice system. In addition, widespread dependence on public aid guarantees jobs for social workers, clerks, and administrators employed in social service departments of government at all levels. Less obviously, but just as importantly, the existence of a class of persons which does not earn an adequate living provides work for grocers, clerks, liquor store dealers, pawn shop operators, service station attendants and owners, doctors, nurses, pharmacists, and many other individuals. What these facts mean is that the jobs of millions of relatively affluent people are dependent, directly or indirectly, on the existence of poor persons. To this list must be added those social scientists (such as myself) who study the poor and obtain tenure as a result.

Job and income creation illustrate one of the less obvious implications of the public aid system. While the expansion of assistance rolls in the 1960s and 1970s has been widely recognized and lamented, the "trickle up" effect that is intrinsic to spending on public aid rarely has been noted. Thus, although it is not recognized very often, assistance actually serves two purposes: on the one hand, cash and in-kind services meliorate some of the wretched social conditions associated with poverty and, on the other hand, the money goes—directly or indirectly—to those who serve and exploit needy people. Thus, while the system of public aid is often seen as a means of redistributing income from more affluent to less affluent people, this is not what actually occurs. In reality, public assistance programs buttress the status quo. From another angle, it is my suspicion that the trickle up effect of public aid expenditures results in far greater economic benefit to society than the "trickle down" effect posited by supply side economists and politicians.

Poverty has a fourth function: The poor subsidize the economy, 4) creating both jobs and profit by purchasing goods and services more affluent people do not want. Indigents are the people who are forced by their circumstances to buy deteriorating or shoddily constructed merchandise, who patronize second-hand stores and give new life to old products, and who provide a market for stolen or "hot" goods of all sorts. In addition, it is destitute people who are forced by their circumstances to obtain services from badly trained or malevolent individuals who cannot make a living from middle-class customers. This is not just another way of saying that poverty creates jobs, for what these facts mean is that the poor are more likely to be exploited and have less legal protection than any other segment of the population.

The exploitation of the poor illustrates the perverse consequences of planning ahead for people without much money. For example, when purchasing discount or aging merchandise, they are trying to save money, to be frugal, to live the values that guide American society. In so doing, impoverished people often become trapped into paying for goods well after they have lost their usefulness. And because they have little recourse, one of the lessons that poor people learn frequently is that there is no solution to their problems. I shall return to this topic and discuss the social consequences of coping with pervasive unsolvable problems in Chapters 4 and 6, for what is at issue here is the myth that poor people can get ahead if they only try harder.

As a caveat to this fourth function, however, it should be recognized that some highly qualified persons do choose to serve or work for the poor, our most vulnerable citizens. Thus, while the impoverished population can be exploited readily, and this is one of its functions, it also provides an outlet for those with a more altruistic orientation.

The fifth function of poverty has been quite obvious during the past few years: The poor are made to absorb the economic and political costs of change in American society. For example, over the past 15 years the nation has come to accept higher levels of unemployment as normal, as necessary for curbing inflation. Although this policy has not stopped the upsurge in prices, it has caused much needless suffering among those who are impoverished. In addition, in recent years, the plight of the poor has become even worse because high inflation and high unemployment have been combined with decreases in public assistance benefits and restrictions on eligibility. These facts mean that because the poor do not, indeed cannnot, participate in the political process, they rarely benefit when political change occurs. I shall return to this subject in Chapters 3 and 5.

When the functions of poverty are recognized, it is easy to see why the war against poverty was lost, even without a detailed analysis of the programs created during the 1960s (this issue will be dealt with in Chapter 3). Before leaving the present topic, however, it is important to understand that an analysis of the functions of poverty does not imply a plot on the part of middle-class people to exploit the poor. The existence and stability of an impoverished population, as well as its functions, result from the relatively impersonal operation of social forces that are usually not perceived by the public. This statement is neither an apologia nor a confession of impotence. Rather, it is simply an assertion that we live in a society whose parts are interdependent—be they persons, classes, corporations, or levels of government—and this interdependence means that individual and collective actions in one part have consequences for other parts. This is a common sociological view. Its political significance is that some aggregate of people usually benefits from ongoing social arrangements. Thus, when well-intentioned public policies fail to eliminate a problem, as is the case here, it is often because some group of people has an economic stake in continuation of the status quo. Although this is not always true, of course, it is correct often enough that analysts who fail to raise the issue are omitting an important area of inquiry.

I noted that an awareness of the functions of poverty can lessen the possibility for self-deception. This is not always the case. For example, Martin Anderson, who was Ronald Reagan's Domestic Affairs Advisor for 2 years, has argued not only that the war on poverty has been won but also that the results have been disastrous for American society.[5] Despite the puerile and contradictory nature of this argument, it forms the intellectual basis for the public policies pursued for the past few years. For this reason, I have chosen to outline the major elements of Anderson's sketch of the problem of poverty in order to use it as a background for presenting my own, rather different interpretations in subsequent chapters. In effect, this description represents the conservative analysis of what it means to live poorly in America.

The conservative argument involves four claims, each of which is described in turn. First, it is asserted that "the 'war on poverty' that began in 1964 has been won" and, as a result, poverty has been "virtually eliminated in the United States."[6] This victory is said to be due to an increase in the number of jobs in the private sector coupled with an expansion of public assistance programs. This argument is deeply flawed. While many new jobs have been created in the private sector over the past 20 years, nearly all of them have gone to skilled workers, a fact that any good economist knows. Poor people, who are generally both unskilled and uneducated, got very few of these jobs. In addition, although the expansion of public assistance has been useful in alleviating the immediate problems people without money face, it has not eliminated poverty. Simply providing families with food stamps or Aid for Families with Dependent Children (AFDC) benefits does not change their life situation. Such provisions merely allow households to survive—albeit poorly—on public aid. As such they are paupers; that is, they are dependent on public aid. It is ludicrous to describe public assistance benefits as lifting people out of poverty. It does not make sense to assert that an increase in pauperism signifies a decrease in poverty, for the two are inextricably linked.

In order to argue plausibly that the war on poverty has been won, the fact that government figures showed virtually no change in the poverty population during the 1970s must be confronted. According to the Census Bureau, about 12% of the American people lived below the poverty line throughout this period. The conservative view, however, is that government data fail to show a decline in the proportion of poor people because (a) underreporting of income is greater among the poor than among other segments of the population; and (b) the Census Bureau does not count the value of noncash (or in-kind) income in making its calculations. The implication of this second point is that the poor receive more benefits from in-kind and other governmental transfers than do the nonpoor. The result, according to this argument, is that public–aid recipients are not poor.

While both of these rationales are incorrect, a fact that will be shown in Chapters 2 and 3, the issue of in-kind income is worth a brief review here because it reveals not only the aura of unreality pervading many academic studies of poverty but also the irrational suspicions that many conservatives have about poor people and public policy oriented toward them.

A number of analysts have attempted to show that the "real" incomes of individuals receiving in-kind public assistance (such as food stamps and Medicaid) are actually living above the poverty line and, hence, are not poor. This is done by using a variety of computer simulations and statistical procedures which calculate the economic value of noncash benefits and arbitrarily add this figure to the incomes of those who are poor, whether they actually receive the aid or not. Such exercises, and Chapter 2 will show there are now quite a few of them, require a large number of heroic assumptions, most of which are not tenable. In general, when policy-oriented research must resort to complex mathematical or statistical models it is often not very useful. This is not only because neither the public nor policymakers understand such work, although that fact is obviously important, but also because the authors' political orientations are so easily (and so often) smuggled into the analysis under the guise of quantitative precision.

This problem is especially acute in the studies of the presumed "antipoverty effectiveness of in-kind transfers," for the effect of the statistical legerdemain characteristic of such work is to obscure the true dimensions of the problem of poverty. For example, analyses which purport to demonstrate that people who receive public assistance are not really poor do not add to the public's understanding. This is because the eligibility requirements for assistance stipulate that applicants must be destitute in order to qualify for aid and must stay destitute in order to keep receiving it. Similarly, such interpretations of the effect of public assistance programs do not allow administrators to better identify those individuals who require help and to assign benefits. Finally, these studies do not help policymakers to design programs or to evaluate whether they are fulfilling their purpose. More prosaically, it is programmatically useless to assert that those people who must have food stamps in order to get enough to eat are not really poor. Nonetheless, and with a conspiratorial air, conservatives argue not only that "there has been a deliberate 'cover-up' of the true extent of poverty in the United States," but also that millions of people who are called poor are really pretty well off.[7] Despite the substantive irrationality of this point of view, it becomes possible on this basis to justify dismantling a large part of the current welfare apparatus while claiming to preserve a "safety net" for the "truly needy." This is precisely what recent public assistance policy has tried to do. The lesson here is that social science and political action often go hand in hand, and that statistical sophistication is no guarantee of objectivity.

The conservatives' second claim is that "the virtual elimination of poverty has had costly side effects": The expansion of public assistance over the past 20 years has meant "the almost complete destruction of work incentives for the poor on welfare."[8] The main reason for this presumed decline in paupers' desire to work is that assistance carries with it what economists call high marginal tax rates. This term refers to the additional taxes one pays on earnings above a specified level. In the case of public aid recipients, as job-related income increases, public assistance benefits go down. The lost benefits are, in effect, taxes on income. Hence, the conservative argument is that people who receive public assistance have had an incentive to remain on relief in order to retain their aid and that they have worked less as a result.

The problem with this point of view is that it has little basis in reality; it is a myth. One of the main reasons why public aid costs rose so much between 1965 and 1980 is that paupers were able to combine low-wage work and assistance. Thus, although the tax rates (lost benefits) associated with employment were fairly high and the programs were cumbersome to administer, reducing aid on a graduated scale depending on income, child-care needs, job expenses, and the like often avoided forcing households to choose between assistance and employment when they had a chance to increase their wages. Recently, however, a different strategy has been adopted: The size of the pauper population has been restricted by eliminating various deductions from gross income. The result is that low-wage workers are now often forced to choose between public aid and employment. Nearly all have chosen the latter. Although these facts will be described in some detail in Chapters 3 and 4, the perverse aspect of this change in public assistance rules should be recognized here: A policy that could have had adverse effects on the work orientations of the poor was sponsored and implemented by conservative politicians.

There is an underlying political reason for raising the issue of work incentives. Conservatives nearly always imply that paupers are siphons at the public trough and use the public's fear that a person will get something for nothing as a political weapon. (Here is another function of poverty, by the way; the poor serve as a sort of negative political reference group.) "Why should someone work," it is asked, "forty hours a week, fifty weeks a year for, say, $8,000 when it would be possible not to work at all for, say, $6,000?"[9] This is a common question among economists, one they seem incapable of dealing with in any meaningful way. The answer has nothing at all to do with marginal tax rates on public assistance. In reality, as will be seen in Chapter 4, most poor people choose to work; this is partly because it is necessary at this economic level because assistance benefits are so low and partly because employment is the fundamental source of status in our society. In general, it is short-sighted to discount the social force of prestige in any society, and in America it is better to have a job than not to have one. Furthermore, what must be remembered about family economics, and what some economists cannot seem to understand, is that while a difference in income of $2,000 is significant for a suburban family, for a poor household it is imperative. This fact can be easily demonstrated by simply calculating budgets that would allow a family to live at income levels of $6,000 or $8,000, a task that will be done in Chapter 2. Nonetheless, in the past few years the rich have been given something for nothing in the form of tax breaks while eligibility for public aid has been sharply restricted.

The conservatives' third claim reveals the peculiarly misleading and shortsighted character of their thought. "The majority of Americans favor government welfare programs for those who cannot care for themselves, while at the same time [they favor] large cuts in welfare spending because of their strong belief that many welfare recipients are cheating."[10] Phrasing the issue of public assistance cheating in this way is terribly misleading, since nearly all the fraud in these programs is white-collar crime committed by relatively affluent people who have both the skills and the opportunity to engage in it. Paupers generally have neither of these traits. It is not realistic to formulate public policy in these terms, yet that is just what has happened in the past.

The assertion is shortsighted in that, while it reflects the ambivalent view many people have toward those who are dependent on public aid, it does not help them to resolve the dilemma. Americans are ambivalent toward paupers because, on the one hand, they are humane toward those who cannot help themselves and, on the other hand, they are terribly vindictive toward those who are perceived (correctly or not) as lazy or unwilling to provide for themselves. Thus, apart from individuals who are obviously physically incapacitated, able-bodied people who happen to be poor are often judged as deserving their fate. If they would only work harder, or so the belief goes, they could make it; they must prefer leisure.

I have always thought that Americans, as a people, are so imbued with the work ethic that we are often unable to enjoy our leisure. For many individuals, work does not bring much intrinsic pleasure, although it may produce economic security and social status. But neither does leisure bring relaxed pleasure. Particularly for the middle class, leisure is often the time to "work" in the yard, "work" on the house, or "work" on other activities designed to improve the self, the family, or perhaps the community. Because of this orientation, our dreams and fantasies about what it is like not to have to work are projected onto those who do not appear to labor: the rich, who are perceived as having earned their free time, and the poor, who are seen as inherently undeserving. Idleness, laziness, pleasure, and being taken care of constitute the fantasy of leisure time. Because most nonpoor Americans cannot live this fantasy and resent those who seem to be able to do so, paupers are viewed with much suspicion and harshness. The unrecognized flaw in this projected fantasy is that living poorly on public aid is not leisure, especially in a wealthy and competitive society.

The conservatives' fourth claim is that "a small group of committed ideologues" has tried for years to institute a guaranteed annual income plan under the guise of public assistance reform. It is argued further that most Americans do not understand why they should work to support those who wish to loaf rather than be employed, that "there has been a conspiracy" to implement some form of guaranteed income since 1965, and that such a policy would inevitably result in a massive reduction in the work effort of millions of low income people—most of whom do not currently receive public aid.[11] The logic behind this argument is not altogether clear, especially when it is juxtaposed with the assertion that poverty has been "virtually eliminated in the United States."

Apart from the undue suspiciousness inherent in this claim, its political significance lies in a cynical awareness of the functions of poverty: Poor people provide the affluent with a low-wage work force and the withdrawal of such individuals from the labor market would have untoward consequences for the economy. In fact, it is argued that such a decline "is fraught with dangers for our society" and that "the potential for social disaster is large."[12] Surprisingly, as noted previously, recently enacted public assistance policies have restricted households' ability to combine low-wage work and public aid. To the extent that these policies stimulate a withdrawal from the labor force, conservatives will get precisely what they fear most. Like the paranoid, conservative social planners have irrational attitudes toward certain kinds of persons. One wonders who they will blame when their policies fail.

The conservative analysis is a siren song; that is, it constitutes an alluring and deceptive appeal to people's prejudices and values. It is incorrect to argue that poverty no longer exists "in any meaningful sense." It is incorrect to state that past public assistance policies caused a decline in work incentives among the poor. It is incorrect to assert that paupers are the main source of public assistance fraud and to justify cutting back programs on this basis. And it is puerile to insist that a "conspiracy" underlies recent efforts at reform of public aid programs.

This book is an attempt at correcting myths such as these. It is organized in the following way.

Chapter 2 outlines the extent of poverty in America in strictly economic terms and critically evaluates those studies that purport to show that the rate of poverty has declined. Thus, the chapter begins with an examination of the history and purpose of the official poverty line, a discussion that shows trends in the number of poor people in the United States and some of the characteristics of those who live poorly when the government threshold is used as the measure of poverty. The chapter then describes what it is like to live at or below the poverty line by constructing a hypothetical budget and compares living poorly at that level with other measures of poverty. In these sections, I shall argue that the official poverty threshold identifies those who are impoverished in an absolute sense: People who live below the cutoff are not merely poor relative to the rest of the population, they have great difficulty surviving. Chapter 2 then explains the decisions that go into setting the poverty line, with special attention to the definition of income, and demonstrates the many problems afflicting analyses of the "antipoverty effectiveness of in-kind income." I shall show here that it is simply nonsense to claim that poverty has been eliminated or that the war against it has been won. Actually, one of the ironic results of that battle is that there is now a relatively precise method of measuring the number and characteristics of those who live poorly.

After identifying the extent of poverty, it is necessary to examine the public aid system, and that is the topic of Chapter 3. Large segments of the population and some policymakers believe that welfare recipients have a comfortable, even luxurious, existence. This is partly because the term welfare connotes well-being and good fortune, as in the notion of a welfare state. Thus, people who do not live poorly often view public aid recipients as the undeserving beneficiaries of society's largesse, as living a good life while being lazy and dependent. Indeed, even social scientists (who should know better) fall into this trap: The literature on long-term welfare use describes the "settling-in effect," as if people are settling into an easy chair. Chapters 3 and 4 will show that such an image is completely inaccurate. In order to avoid self-deception, it is important to use terms that accurately depict people's social situation. For this reason, I have chosen to avoid use of the term welfare and to label those programs providing benefits to poor people as public aid or public assistance. According to the dictionary, individuals who are dependent on public aid for survival are paupers. This is an odd term because it connotes times past; people conjure up visions of beggars asking for alms in medieval societies. Nonetheless, use of such terminology should jar readers into rethinking their suppositions about the characteristics of those who live poorly in America. In addition, of course, pauperism is a very precise way of describing the status of those who receive assistance, since eligibility requires a public declaration of destitution and a plea for help.

Chapter 3 begins by describing the differences between antipoverty and public assistance programs, and comparing the cost of such policies with other income maintenance programs. Surprisingly, it will become clear in this context that public assistance does not cost very much money when it is compared to the total federal budget, to outlays for social insurance, and to expenditures for other income maintenance programs, nearly all of which go to benefit the nonpoor. The chapter then reviews four public aid programs, two of which are cash and two of which provide in-kind benefits: Aid for Families with Dependent Children, Supplementary Security Income, Food Stamps, and Medicaid. This sketch of the requirements of each program and the characteristics of the participants in each one will show clearly that paupers live poorly. The chapter concludes with a brief discussion of some of the problems and contradictions in the system of public assistance in the United States. It will be seen in this chapter that public aid cannot eliminate poverty even in principle, for it is not designed to do so. Rather, pauperism perpetuates poverty. Recent changes in public aid programs have not improved this situation; in fact, they have made it worse. These alterations illustrate the extent to which the poor are made to absorb the costs of change in American society.

Chapter 4 is an examination of the relationships among poverty, public assistance, and work. This topic is important because many people believe that the poor, especially paupers, do not wish to have jobs. Hence, the chapter begins by exploring the attitudes of poor and nonpoor people toward work, and shows that there are no differences in adherence to the work ethic or any other measure of attitudes toward employment. This is true, by the way, when both quantitative and ethnographic data are used. Then overall rates of employment and unemployment are assessed, along with the results of the work incentive programs, negative income tax experiments and other policies designed to encourage wage earning. I shall argue that, in general, impoverished people work whenever there is opportunity to do so. All the data suggest that poor persons' lives reflect the salience of dominant values, especially the importance of employment.

The qualifying phrase used—in general, poor people work whenever they can—is important, however, because there is considerable concern over the effect of public assistance on wage-earning activity. Thus, I shall evaluate the available data on this topic and argue that, in the past, most paupers (between 75% and 90%) have either received assistance for a relatively short time or used public aid as a means of supplementing their low incomes. For most of these people, wages provide the largest share of the income they receive over the long run. There is a minority of recipients, however, who seem to have given up, since they are on the assistance rolls for long periods and are totally dependent. I shall begin a discussion here as to why this process occurs and continue it in Chapter 6. One last note: I stated that most paupers are short-term recipients or using public aid as an income supplement. It will be shown throughout Chapters 3 and 4 that the policies enacted in recent years may produce a significant increase in the proportion of long-term, totally dependent paupers. The irony is that conservatives will blame this tragedy on everyone but themselves.

Chapter 5 depicts some of the correlates of poverty. While living poorly and being dependent on public aid are usually thought of in economic terms, it is important to remember that lack of income is also reciprocally related to many other aspects of people's lives. In order to produce the sort of synthetic analysis that is necessary to take this fact into account, I have adopted a specifically sociological point of view: People choose among socially structured alternatives.[13] This angle of vision is useful because it stimulates understanding of the vulnerability and limited choices available to impoverished persons in a variety of social contexts.

On this basis, the chapter begins by showing how, underlying the pluralist dictum that there is open access to the political arena and, hence, that people should only act within the law to influence public policy, is the reality that the poor are politically disenfranchised in the United States. In effect, the people who benefit from participation also dominate the political arena. This is why the poor absorb the costs of change. The ironic result, then, is that their only realistic alternative for influencing public policy is to become unruly in some fashion. Since this option is also restricted by a variety of social constraints, the poor are nearly always politically apathetic.

A similar argument is made when the relationships between crime and poverty and between health and poverty are examined. In general, those who benefit also dominate. This is why poor people commit the specific crimes they do and why other destitute persons are ordinarily the victims of street crime. It is also why the criminal justice system fails. For there are ways, effective ways, of reducing street and property crime. It is because these alternatives are not pursued and because the organization of the criminal justice system makes the dangerousness of street crime and street criminals especially salient, that the equally serious crimes committed by the rich are ignored.

The chapter continues by showing that, despite the impact of Medicaid and Medicare, there is a yawning health gap between the poor and the nonpoor in the United States. I shall argue that higher rates of all forms of ill health among the poor result from the organization of the health-care delivery system. This is because it is designed to benefit the providers of health care rather than the recipients.

Chapter 6 evaluates the hypothesis that many poor people have deviant values. There are two versions of this proposition, one positing that such values are transmitted across generations and the other postulating that they are merely situational adaptations. This is the continuation of the discussion previously alluded to.

Thus, in common-sense terms, it seems reasonable to attribute deviant values to people who behave differently than is normal, than they should. For example, when hard-living poor persons display a present time orientation, appear to have given up on the ideal of working in order to subsist on public aid, and exhibit other nonconforming characteristics (alcoholism, marital instability, etc.), then it is often assumed that they have deviant values. This is a very beguiling idea and, although they proceed in somewhat different ways and arrive at rather different conclusions, both conservative and liberal social scientists have found support for the idea that poor people have values which are different from those held by middle–class persons. My own guess is that this is another area in which scholarly work seems to substantiate the political preconceptions of those doing the research.

After showing that the behaviors in question cannot reflect deviant values, regardless of their presumed origin, I shall offer a tentative interpretation that accounts for the actions of hard–living poor people in a more plausible way. Based on a review of the literature in experimental psychology, it will be suggested that the issue for many impoverished persons is not adherence to nonconformist values but their vulnerability and limited choices. It is the social and psychological significance of this fact which must be taken into account: for the result is that frustration is pervasive in every facet of poor people's lives and they adopt a variety of analgesic behaviors designed to blunt awareness of their situation and avoid pain. Thus, the need for social and psychological (and sometimes medicinal) analgesia reflects the salience rather than the absence of dominant values in the lives of impoverished persons. Over the long run, such behavior becomes rewarding, I will suggest, because what poor people learn is that the problems they have cannot be solved. Now this analysis is admittedly tentative. Nonetheless, it will be seen that it provides a more reasonable account of the behavior of the poor than does the notion of deviant values.

Chapter 7 analyzes the causes of poverty in structural terms, an angle of vision that most nonsociologists do not understand and most sociologists do not systematically employ. Hence, it is worth taking some space here at the beginning of the book in order to explain what is involved.

When Americans are asked to account for the existence of poverty by survey researchers, they generally focus on individualistic explanations. Thus, the nonpoor tend to say that the most important reasons for being impoverished are (in order) lack of thrift and poor money management, lack of effort, lack of ability or talent, loose morals (especially drunkenness), and sickness or some other physical handicap.[14] Yet these explanations are really statements of certain cultural values that permeate American society: People ought to be thrifty and manage their money so as to avoid waste, they ought to work hard for occupational advancement, they ought to avoid pleasure (especially when stimulated by alcohol or other, more basic, desires), and they ought not to be weak. Thus, as described in Chapters 4 and 6, it is often assumed that individuals who are poor do not have such values, and they are, therefore, regarded as deserving their fate. It is often easier to blame the victim than to think problems through systematically.

It is important to ask the right questions about poverty. Thus, in order to understand the causes of impoverishment it is less useful to ascertain why certain individuals are poor than to discover why there exists a class of poor persons in American society. Almost any answer to this latter query will get at the way social forces systematically produce poverty. This is a structural explanation.

In Chapter 7, I focus on four characteristics of American society that cause the existence and persistence of impoverishment:

1. The way in which the correlates of poverty create a vicious circle that often traps the poor and prevents them from changing their situation
2. The manner in which the class system reproduces itself
3. The organization of the economy
4. The continuation of institutionalized discrimination against blacks and women.

The dual characteristics of these social processes make them especially interesting. On the one hand, they operate more or less independently of the individuals caught up in them. As Michael Harrington observed more than 20 years ago, "The real explanation of why the poor are where they are is that they made the mistake of being born to the wrong parents, in the wrong section of the country, in the wrong industry, or in the wrong racial or ethnic group. Once that mistake has been made, they could have been paragons of will and morality, but most of them would never even have had a chance to get out of the other America."[15] On the other hand, however, these social processes are malleable. For once the structural causes of poverty are clearly understood, then public policies designed to combat them can be instituted.

2

THE RATE OF POVERTY

According to Census Bureau data, there were 32 million people living below the poverty line in 1981; 25 million of these persons were members of families while the remainder were single individuals. Overall, 14% of the U.S. population was officially poor in 1981. As will be seen, the official rate of poverty has increased over the past few years after being stable for about a decade.

There has not always been a precise measure of the rate of poverty. When Michael Harrington wrote *The Other America* in 1962, a book that some believe helped to spark the war on poverty, there was no official definition; that is, no explicit threshold clearly separated the poor from the nonpoor.[1] So Harrington had to work out his own interpretation, and he did a pretty good job. In effect, he focused on a combination of economic and psychological characteristics: low income along with a low level of self-esteem, a restricted view of personal effectiveness, and a sense of separation from the society. Thus, although there was no formal poverty line, there were data showing millions of people with very low incomes, and Harrington observed that these individuals had great difficulty providing for themselves. For example, in the days before food stamps were available, he saw starvation in America because families did not have enough money to purchase food, a fact that was subsequently confirmed by the now famous Citizens' Board of Inquiry.[2]

The way in which the rate of poverty is measured has become a topic of some controversy in recent years. As noted in Chapter 1, some observers have argued that there is really far less poverty in the United States than Census Bureau figures show. This chapter refutes this argument. It begins by describing the poverty line and those who live below it, showing that the threshold provides a realistic count of the rate of poor living, and enumerating some of the issues involved in measuring poverty. The chapter concludes with an evaluation of recent studies of the "antipoverty effectiveness of in-kind transfers." This literature, and there is now an abundance of it, attempts to show that households having incomes so low that they qualify for food stamps, Medicaid, public housing, and the like, are no longer poor as a result. I shall demonstrate that this line of reasoning is misbegotten.

THE POVERTY LINE

The creation of President Johnson's war on poverty in 1964 meant that an index of poverty was necessary to identify the poor. In order to be useful for practical purposes, such a measure had to be quantitative; that is, it had to focus on income. People's psychological states and other characteristics are often relatively difficult to measure and—with the exception of a few groups, such as college students—income levels can generally serve as a simple indicator of how much poverty exists. Some of the noneconomic correlates of poverty will be examined in Chapter 5.

The initial measure of poverty was developed in 1964 by the President's Council of Economic Advisors (CEA).[3] It identified families with incomes below $3,000 and individuals living alone on less than $1,500 as poor. Underlying the selection of these thresholds was a Social Security Administration study which estimated that a nonfarm family of four needed an income of $3,165 to provide for itself in 1961. While these first benchmarks seemed reasonable—they identified about 19% of the population as poor, or 36 million people—they had a number of peculiar problems. For example, an elderly couple with an income of $2,900 was defined as poor while a family of six with an income of $3,100 was not.

Because results like these were illogical, subsequent researchers, the most important of whom was Molly Orshansky in the Social Security Administration, set about constructing a more practical measure of poverty. Their essential goal, it must be remembered, was simply to count the poor, and the reason for enumerating them was to identify the number and kinds of people toward whom public policy ought to be directed. As Orshansky noted retrospectively "There is no particular reason to count the poor unless you are going to do something about them," and Lyndon Johnson intended to do just that.[4] Given this goal, it should be recognized that the establishment and use of a measure of poverty are inherently political acts. Thus, when a threshold is used to indicate the point below which people are in poverty, it must be politically and socially credible. That is, it must identify a sufficient number of individuals as poor, but not too many, and it must focus on persons whose characteristics are such that both the public and the Congress will recognize that they are really poor and, hence, deserving of attention. Otherwise a measure of poverty will be useless.

What has come to be called the poverty line is, therefore, not intended to be scientific or comprehensive. It is merely designed to identify those who are living poorly in America. For this reason, although the Social Security Administration originally developed two indicators of need, President Johnson's advisors selected the lower of the two and labeled it the poverty line, the index which is still used today. This decision was obviously made because the lower threshold was judged to be politically realistic; it identified about the same number of people in poverty as the original CEA measure did but without the latter's peculiar results. The reason for this difference is that the poverty cutoff varies in terms of the size and age composition of the family. It should be noted here that until 1981 the threshold also varied in terms of location (rural–urban) and sex of family head. These distinctions have been eliminated in favor of weighted averages that take into account the location and family characteristics of the poor population. The current levels of the poverty line and the manner in which they vary are illustrated in Table 2.1.[5]

TABLE 2.1: **Official Poverty Levels by Selected Characteristics, 1981**

Size of household	Poverty level
	(in dollars)
1 Person	4,620
15–64 years	4,729
65 years and over	4,359
2 Persons	5,917
householder, 15–64 years	6,111
householder, 65 years and over	5,498
3 Persons	7,250
4 Persons	9,287
5 Persons	11,007
6 Persons	12,449
7 Persons	14,110
8 Persons	15,655
9 Persons or more	18,572

As indicated in the table, the poverty standard for a family of four was $9,287 in 1981. The yearly indicator for a four-person household is the single figure that is most commonly used to denote those who are poor and it will be the major point of reference here and in the remainder of the book. It should be recognized, however, that the poverty line also takes into account the manner in which age combines with family size to affect economic well-being. Thus, the threshold is lower for aged individuals and families because older people are presumed to have some assets that reduce their expenses.

When seen in the aggregate, the income levels shown in Table 2.1 seem high to many people, primarily because their notion of what a poverty threshold income is has not caught up with price increases caused by inflation. This is one reason why the measurement of poverty has become so controversial in recent years. As will become clear, however, households with incomes below the levels specified in the table are poor by any reasonable definition.

The poverty line as it is currently constructed was first used in 1965. Updated each year, the threshold was only quasi-official until 1969, when the Census Bureau designated it as an official statistical series to be published annually. In addition, because of the need for the trend data, the poverty line was extrapolated back to 1959, the earliest year for which appropriate census information was still available. It is thus possible to count the number of people who have been identified as poor from 1959 to the present. These data are depicted for selected years in Table 2.2.[6]

TABLE 2.2:   **Persons Below Poverty Level, Selected Years 1959–1981**

Year	Number (in millions)	Percentage of Total Population
1959	39	22
1960	40	22
1962	39	21
1964	36	19
1966	30	16
1968	25	13
1970	25	13
1972	25	12
1974	23	11
1976	25	12
1978	24	11
1980	29	13
1981	32	14

As seen in the table, at the beginning of the 1960s decade, between 39 and 40 million people were officially poor, or about 22% of the total population. These figures dropped steadily throughout the next 10 years, stabilizing at about 24 million, or 11–12% of the population in the 1970s decade. In 1980 and 1981, however, the rate of poverty began to increase and it seems probable that this trend will continue. It appears, then, that while some progress against poverty was initially made, the problem proved to be more intractable during the 1970s and, in fact, has recently become worse. Of course, those observers who think Census Bureau data are inaccurate dispute this whole analysis. Before turning to that issue, however, it is necessary to identify those who live poorly in the United States as indicated by the official measure.

What kinds of people live poorly in America? The data in Table 2.3 provide a preliminary answer to this question, one that will be elaborated in later chapters.[7] Despite stereotypes that the nonpoor may have gained from watching the nightly news or traveling in some large cities, the figures in the table show clearly that most poor persons are white, about 22 million individuals in 1981 or 11% of the total white population. However, while a much smaller number of blacks and people of Hispanic origin are poverty stricken, such persons are more likely to be poor; that is, 34% of all blacks and 27% of all Hispanics are living in poverty. (It should be recognized here that Hispanic surname individuals represent a mixture of Chicanos, Puerto Ricans, Cubans, and several other nationalities, each of which has come to the United States under different circumstances and has had rather different experiences in this country.)

Table 2.3 also shows that women of any ethnic or racial group are much more likely to live poorly than are men. This fact is especially true when women are heads of families. As seen in the table, 6% of all white married couples are poor, compared to 15% of all black and 15% of all Hispanic couples. But when women without husbands are family heads, the figures jump dramatically: 27% of all white female-headed households are poor, and more than half of all blacks and Hispanic female-headed households are impoverished. The number of men heading families without the help of women is still very small. Further, as is well known, the table shows that age is related to poverty in that youths and old people are more likely to live poorly. Thus, 21% of all children under 15 years of age, about 10 million young people, are living in families without money. At the other extreme, 15% of those persons over 65 are poverty stricken.

TABLE 2.3: Selected Characteristics of Persons Living Below the Poverty Line, 1981

Race	Number (millions)	Percentage of population
White	21.5	11
Black	9.2	34
Hispanic[a]	3.7	27
Couples and sex of family head		
White married couple	2.7	6
Black married couple	.5	15
Hispanic married couple	.4	15
White female head (no husband)	1.8	27
Black female head (no husband)	1.4	53
Hispanic female head (no husband)	.4	53
Age		
Under 15 years	10.6	21
15–24 years	6.3	15
25–44 years	7.0	11
45–54 years	1.9	9
55–59 years	1.0	9
60–64 years	1.2	11
65 and over years	3.9	15

[a] Persons of Hispanic origin may be of any race.

While the data in Table 2.3 compare those living poorly with the rest of the population, it is also useful to look at the distribution of impoverished people along certain significant dimensions.[8] Most indigent persons live in families in which the head is either relatively unskilled or engaged in those occupations that are most susceptible to fluctuations in the economy. Thus, 54% of all poor household heads have less than a high school education, while another 32% have only a high school diploma. At the same time, 75% of all poverty-stricken families are headed by a person who works in a blue-collar occupation. These figures are in accord, of course, with common-sense views of American society. But they have an unexpected implication: People who are uneducated or in unstable occupations are our most vulnerable citizens; that is, they are most likely to be affected when change occurs and they are least likely to advance through hard work alone. A hard-working dishwasher or machine operator or waitress who retains a job for, say, 5 years, is likely to be a hard-working dishwasher, etc., at the end of that time. In chapters to follow, I shall note repeatedly the vulnerability of impoverished persons and how limited their choices are.

LIVING POORLY AT THE POVERTY LINE

The poverty line seems awfully high to many people. After all, they think, a family of four can live pretty well on $9,287—if it has the will. It should be recalled from the first chapter that one of the stereotypes people have about the poor is that their poverty results from lack of thrift and poor money management. In this section, I intend to show that this stereotype is incorrect and that the poverty line is a realistic indicator of impoverishment. In order to do this, I am going to proceed by constructing a poverty threshold budget for a hypothetical family of four, comparing this budget to others that have been devised, and describing why expenses are so high in the United States as compared to other nations. On this basis, then, it will be possible to evaluate the assertions of those academics who argue that the poverty line is set too high and that very few people are really poor.

One way of ascertaining whether the poverty line is realistic is to show that families with incomes at or below this level have difficulty surviving. The issue here is whether such households can make ends meet in an absolute sense. A poverty-level budget for an intact family of four illustrates the problems such households have.

In constructing a budget at the poverty threshold, it is necessary to specify a few assumptions. Let us assume that the family consists of two adults and two children, an infant and an elementary-school child. This family thus has all the medical, dental, school, and potential child-care expenses that accompany the presence of young children. Let us also assume that one parent works full time—that is, 40 hours a week, 52 weeks per year. (Contrary to the implicit assumption of conservative ideologues, there are no 2-week paid vacations at this economic level.) Now if the employed adult earns the minimum wage, $3.35 per hour, his or her income will be only $6,968 yearly. Hence, let us assume that the person receives $4.46 per hour, a pay scale that will place the family at the poverty line. In addition, let us assume that this family does not receive public assistance of any sort. This is a viable assumption: As will be seen in the next chapter, an intact family in which one parent works full time is rarely eligible for AFDC benefits and would receive only a small amount of food stamps. In addition, such a family will be ineligible for Medicaid in many states. Finally, let us assume that the family spends one-third of its income on food. As will be indicated, this assumption is built into the poverty line. Here is the household budget: $3,093 for food and $6,194 for everything else.

The food budget for this family of four translates into $59.48 per week, or $2.12 per person per day. More prosaically, for this sum of money one can purchase a Big Mac and a small coke (but no french fries) each day. And that is it. Now it is possible to obtain an adequate, if bland, diet when spending this amount of money and eating at home, but it would take a family of nutritionists with perfect knowledge to do so. In addition, obtaining a balanced diet on this budget also requires a high degree of motivation, shopping around, transportation, and time. Finally, of course, some food is consumed away from home at all income levels, simply because it is impossible to plan every meal.[9] Besides, it is fun to eat out. In most families someone goes to the store, usually the nearest one, purchases a mixture of junk food and more nutritious food along with other necessities, and tries to keep the cost down. Poverty-stricken people, of course, often pay higher prices than do the nonpoor because nearby stores are usually either mom-and-pop operations or franchised small stores. Nonetheless, their shopping habits are not much different than those of the more affluent, for the exigencies of everyday living in American society force a similarity of lifestyle on all social classes. The overall result, then, is that a family making do at the poverty line finds it nearly impossible to stay within the food budget specified here. This is why food stamps are so important; it is also why such households actually spend much more than one-third of their income on food, regardless of their efforts at being thrifty.

The nonfood budget translates into $516.17 per month to cover the cost of rent, utilities, taxes, automobile maintenance and other transportation costs, medical and dental bills, clothing, educational expenses, entertainment, and all the other things necessary for life in the United States. Dividing this sum up is difficult; however, let us assume that monthly rent is $200, utilities (electricity, gas, telephone) are $100, taxes (Social Security at 6.7% and federal withholding at 10%) are $120, and transportation costs $60. While none of these amounts is very high, and there is considerable variation from one location to another and from one family to another, the budget for this household now has $36.17 left for medical and dental bills, clothing, incidental purchases necessary for a school-age child, entertainment, and all other expenses. As a result, a family making do at the poverty line finds it nearly impossible to stay within the nonfood budget specified here, especially when all the normal expenses not accounted for in this example are considered. Such a family does not simply have cash-flow problems, a predicament that households at all economic levels sometimes find themselves in; such a family does not, on its own, have enough money to meet the basic, fundamental expenses inherent in living in the United States. A family with an income at the poverty line is not only objectively poor, it is desperate. This is why Medicaid and other forms of in-kind income are so important.

Now the scenario portrayed here can be altered. For example, a person can work "off the books" and thereby avoid having taxes withheld. However, such jobs, which many poor people hold, are often highly exploitative and do not last very long. (It is my impression that most individuals who work off the books also earn significantly less than the minimum wage; they certainly do not earn $4.46 per hour.) In addition, if impoverished families are sufficiently aware, they can recover nearly all their income that is withheld for federal income tax purposes, plus a low-income allowance. However, many poor families do not file income tax forms at all and, as a result, do not know about these facts. Finally, of course, the unemployed parent can also go to work outside the home—providing that adequate child care can be obtained at a less than prohibitive cost and that a job for a person without skills is available. Both of these provisos are questionable for many, if not most, poor families (see Chapter 4). Essentially, none of these options can really alter the economic situation of a poor household.

Families living at the poverty line have a very difficult time making ends meet. They are poor absolutely, not just in relationship to the rest of the population. They are poor in terms of their ability to obtain the minimum necessities necessary for surviving in the United States. It should be recognized, however, that the scenario described here contains an additional unmentioned and unrealistic assumption: that the employed parent never gets sick, never has an accident, and is never laid off from work—even for one day. For loss of just a single day's income can mean that there is no food in the house, or the utility bill does not get paid, or the rent goes into arrears. Thus, even when they succeed, families living at the poverty line are one emergency, one mistake, one accident away from truly dire straits. Yet, as will become clear in Chapters 4 and 5, such conditions are very common among poor households.

Finally, it is also important to remember that the example used here has been for a household living at the poverty line. As noted at the beginning of this chapter, 14% of the population is poor, or 25 million family members and more than 6 million single persons. However, it is sobering to realize that the average poor family had a cash income $3,511 below the poverty threshold in 1981. Put differently, imagine the problems a household of four would have in trying to live on an income of about $5,776 in 1981. Yet many families did just that: More than 3.5 million households had incomes of less than $5,000 in 1981.[10] By any objective standard, the individuals making up these families are poor.

Another way of ascertaining whether the poverty line is realistic is to compare it with other, more relative, definitions of poverty and with public perceptions of the amount of money it takes to support a family. In effect, this exercise shows the gulf between the absolute definition of poverty used by the Census Bureau and practical indicators of the minimum amount of money families need.

The U.S. Bureau of Labor Statistics (BLS) reports a budget each year that identifies the minimum income necessary for a family of four to fully participate in American life at a "lower level." In the autumn of 1981, this income was $15,323.[11] This figure is a practical, albeit relative, measure of poverty in the sense that it indicates the lowest cost of a more or less complete market basket of goods and services. For example, the BLS budget for food is $4,545 a year, or $87.40 per week for a four-person family. It should be recalled that the family food budget at the poverty line was only $59.48 per week. As an aside, the BLS formulates annual budgets at three levels: low, intermediate, and high. Thus, in 1981 the cost of an intermediate life-style was $25,407, while the amount for a high standard of living was $38,060.

The budgets calculated by the Bureau of Labor Statistics are based on a detailed analysis of prices. Even though the public does not have such precise information available, most people have a pretty realistic sense of what it takes to participate in this society. Thus, each year the Gallup organization surveys the American people in order to ascertain their perception of the "smallest amount of money a family of four (husband, wife, and two children) needs to get along in this community."[12] The average figure given by respondents was $277 per week in February of 1981, which translates into a yearly income of $14,404; while this figure is less than what the BLS reported as necessary for a lower standard of living, it is still considerably above the official threshold.

When these relative definitions are juxtaposed with the poverty line, $9,287 for a four-person family, it becomes clear that the official cutoff point identifies millions of people who are separated from the rest of the nation by an economic chasm. The noneconomic effects of living in such straits are innumerable, as will be seen in Chapter 5. Although the standard for a household of four has been used throughout this chapter, the same point is applicable to all poor families, regardless of their size. Thus, while Table 2.1 shows that the poverty index for a family of seven was $14,110 in 1981, and this seems like a fair amount of money at a first glance. But when budgets are calculated that take into acount the actual expenses such a household faces, then the squalidness of its life–style becomes apparent. People who have cash incomes below the poverty line are poor by any reasonable definition. Attempts by conservative analysts to obfuscate this issue are not very useful either in helping the public to understand the problem or in the formation of public policy.

Despite the situation portrayed here, some Americans want to view poverty in comparative terms by observing that an income of, say, $9,000 would place a family in the middle class in many other societies or that Americans who live poorly possess amenities—such as running water and other utilities, automobiles, and televisions—which only elites have in other nations. This view fails to recognize that in many ways it is harder to be poor in America, partly because low-income people in the United States are literally forced to consume items they cannot afford and partly because the fixed cash costs are so much higher in this country than in other nations.

The use of an outside privy, for example, is not legal in any American city, although it was a common practice only a few decades ago and is still frequent in many areas of the world today. Similarly, people must have electricity to provide light and preserve food, neither of which is true in many places. In short, urban dwellers in America must be hooked up to and pay for the utility system. Yet the utility bills of many poor families are often much higher than those of the nonpoor, mainly because the houses, apartments, and trailers in which impoverished people reside are so badly insulated and inefficient.

Having a telephone is not of much use in those societies where communication systems are undeveloped, and in such a context, possessing one is a symbol of luxury. However, being without a telephone in the United States deprives people of the ability to deal with emergencies, conduct business, and interact with friends and relatives. Thus, in a realistic sense, a telephone and the fixed costs it brings with it are necessary prices for participation in American society.

Reliance on the automobile is still not characteristic of many countries and, hence, the cost of buying, running, and maintaining a care is not intrinsic to being a part of life in those nations. In most American cities, however, one cannot either shop or work without an automobile, a fact that was not true just a short time ago.

Finally, in places where popular entertainment occurs in the streets and where news is not so vital for participation in society, television is obviously less important. But in this country television is the chief means of entertainment and information, and as a result, possessing one is necessary in order to share in American life.

All of these examples (there are others) are designed to show that while the incomes of poor people are higher in the United States than in some other countries, this fact is not relevant for understanding their predicament in America because costs are so much higher. What must be kept in mind is that most poor families have to make do at income levels well below the poverty-line budget previously outlined, and they are not somehow less poor because incomes in some other societies are even lower.

The blunt fact is that people who survive at the poverty line or below it live poorly, and they do so in an absolute sense as well as relative to the rest of the population. This reality forms the backdrop against which studies of the "anti-poverty effectiveness of in-kind transfers" must be evaluated. For such analyses purport to show that many, if not most, people living at the poverty line or below it are not really poor at all because they receive public assistance.

ISSUES IN MEASURING THE RATE OF POVERTY

As just described, the poverty line is an attempt at counting the number of poor persons in the United States. Underlying this effort is the presumption that public policy ought to be directed toward those vulnerable families and persons who have difficulty surviving. Thus, the poverty threshold is, quite simply, a subjective attempt at identifying the poor in terms of the minimum income households must have in order to obtain the necessities for living in this country. This fact can be seen in the formal definition of the poverty line: It "is based on the amount [of money] needed by families of different size and type to purchase a nutritionally adequate diet on the assumption that no more than a third of the family income is used for food."[13] The result, as shown in the last section is a very realistic count; for households living at or below the poverty cutoff have great difficulty making ends meet in an absolute sense.

It should be apparent that the establishment of a poverty standard involves a number of decisions: for example, the use of food rather than some other criterion as the basis for determining need, the multiplier relating food and nonfood costs, the means by which the poverty index is updated each year, and—perhaps most importantly—the definition of income. The basis for and potential problems with each of these four decisions are reviewed in the next few paragraphs.

The first decision that had to be made in setting the poverty line was to determine the criterion for need. Although there are a number of ways of doing this, the best criterion is one that is readily understood, easily measured, and has an aura of objectivity. Food meets all these requirements. Thus, even though some obstacles do exist in assessing people's nutritional needs—primarily because of differences in taste, inadequate knowledge of nutritional requirements, individual variation in nutritional needs, and changes over time in the nutritional value of food—there are relatively precise Recommended Dietary Allowances (RDA) available for the various food groups. These recommendations have some scientific and, by extrapolation, some political justification.

This is why the poverty threshold is based on the minimum cost of a nutritionally adequate diet. Between 1965 and 1974 the U.S. Department of Agriculture's least costly economy food plan was used in calculating the poverty line. Since that time, the cost of the Agriculture Department's Thrifty Food Plan has been the basis for determining the level of poverty.[14] The most that can be said for such a diet is that a family of four which spends $3,093 (one-third of the poverty index in 1981) can, if it considers its purchase wisely, have reasonably palatable meals that will be nutritionally adequate. Just how wise such a household has to be has been shown.

The second decision that had to be made in setting the poverty cutoff dealt with the ratio between food and nonfood costs. The multiplier used in setting the poverty level was originally determined by means of a 1955 consumer survey which found that the average family spent 1 out of every 3 dollars on food. For the purpose of establishing the poverty index and identifying the poor, it has been assumed that the food to nonfood ratio is the same for those living on the margin. This judgment is completely arbitrary; its only usefulness lies in the fact that a politically acceptable number of poor people is identified as a result. The essential problem is that the proportion of income spent on food varies by income level. Many poor households actually spend up to half their income on food, while the average family today probably spends a fourth or a fifth of its income on food, and a family with an income in excess of $100,000 can hardly spend more than one-tenth of its income on food. For this reason, the use of higher multipliers has been suggested by many observers so that poor people's total incomes would provide adequate amounts for shelter, clothing, and other expenses. However, using higher multipliers would expand the number of persons defined as poor to a quarter or even a third of the total population; that is, instead of 32 million poor people in 1981, there would be between 50 and 70 million poverty-stricken individuals.[15] Such a result would not only be politically unacceptable, it would also be useless programmatically, for the public would not accept such a definition and public assistance programs based on it could not be passed by the Congress.

The third decision that had to be made in setting the poverty line was how to update it each year in light of changing prices. (As will be seen in the next chapter, this is called indexing.) Updating the threshold is necessary because the fixed cost of living in the United States changes from one year to another. Thus, until 1969, the poverty standard was altered every year in light of increases in the cost of food. However, over time it became obvious that an increase which included changes in the cost of nonfood items was better than one that did not, so the Consumer Price Index (CPI) has been used since 1969 in updating the poverty threshold.[16] It was observed previously that the poverty cutoff in 1981, which resulted from using the Consumer Price Index over the past 13 years, is a very realistic indicator of who is poor. Nonetheless, it is common for critics to assail the use of the Consumer Price Index as a measure of the cost of living, especially for the poor. In reality, however, each of the available alternatives has many problems as well.[17] What must be recognized here is that there is no scientifically justifiable way of indexing federal income programs, whether they be for the poor or the nonpoor (and there are many programs for the latter, as will be seen in Chapter 3). This is why the mode of indexation favored by commentators usually corresponds to their political orientation.

Historically, using the Consumer Price Index as the means for updating the poverty line has meant that the threshold is raised each year as prices increase. Some observers have become confused by this fact into thinking that the poverty cutoff is a relative definition. Table 2.4 shows that this is not true.[18] In 1960, the poverty standard was set at about one-half of the median income. However, since the real income of the population as a whole expanded during the decade of the 1960s, the poverty level fell steadily farther until, in 1970, it was 36% of the median income. Finally, since the real income of the population has remained more or less stable in relationship to prices during the last decade, the poverty threshold has also remained at roughly one-third of the median income. Should real income rise during the decade of the 1980s, then, following current procedures, the poverty line will fall still further from the median income.

What this analysis means is that even though the poverty standard is indexed to prices, it still constitutes a survival budget. Because of indexing, it keeps pace with the minimum cost of living in the United States but not with prevailing standards of living. The poverty line is an absolute rather than a relative definition of impoverishment.

The fourth decision that had to be made in setting the poverty threshold dealt with the definition of income. Income data on the United States population are gathered each year by the Census Bureau's

TABLE 2.4: A Comparison of the Official Poverty Line with the Median Income, Families of Four, Selected Years

Year	The poverty line	Median income	Poverty line as percentage of median
	(in dollars)	(in dollars)	(percentage)
1960	3,022	6,295	48
1970	3,968	11,167	36
1980	8,385	24,410	34

Current Population Survey. These data are obtained by means of extensive interviews with a very large random sample of citizens (in excess of 50,000 people), and they are used not only to identify the poor but also to assess the economic and social characteristics of the entire population.

Here is the formal definition of income used by the Census Bureau in the Current Population Survey: Income is total money received; that is, it is the sum of all amounts obtained from wages, Social Security payments, cash public-assistance benefits, dividends, interest, rent, unemployment and workers compensation, pensions, and all other periodic cash received by an individual. This total is gross money income before payment of income taxes (federal or state), Social Security taxes, union dues, Medicare premiums, and the like. Thus, the Census Bureau's definition of income does not reflect the economic value of noncash transfers a person may obtain. This means that the value of food stamps, public housing, school lunches, Medicare and Medicaid, business transportation, subsidized student loans, tax subsidies, employer payments (for such things as retirement, medical insurance, or educational expenses), expense accounts, and all other economically valuable forms of noncash transfers are not counted as income.[19]

The question, then, is whether the Census Bureau is able to accurately count the poor using this definition. As was pointed out in Chapter 1, the measure of income used in identifying the poor is an issue of some controversy. Conservatives argue that Census Bureau data do not show a decline in the number of poor people because (*a*) underreporting of income is greater among those who live poorly than among other segments of the population; and (*b*) because the Census Bureau does not include the value of noncash benefits in calculating income. I shall deal only with the first argument here, postponing the second issue for the next section.

As everyone knows, income is a sensitive issue for most persons and some underreporting occurs even in the best surveys, such as the CPS.[20] Overall, the Census Bureau estimates that it records about 89% of all cash income. This includes virtually all wage and salary income, 97%, undoubtedly because such income is subject to federal withholding. Most underreporting occurs with income that is not subject to federal withholding. It turns out, however, that underreporting of income is positively related to class rather than inversely, as the conservatives claim; that is, the higher the socioeconomic status, *then* the higher the rate of underreporting. For example, when Current Population Survey data are analyzed in light of those obtained from independent sources, the Census Bureau estimates that while it records about 77% of public assistance income, it registers only 44% of income from dividends and only 42% of income from interest on bonds and other items. It should be noted that while the Internal Revenue Service records a somewhat higher percent of income from dividends and interest than does the CPS, the IRS still fails to collect billions of dollars each year because of underreporting by the rich. This is why withholding of dividend and interest income is a good idea. The notion that the number of poor people has not declined because of underreporting of income by the poor is false.

AN EVALUATION OF STUDIES OF THE "ANTIPOVERTY EFFECTIVENESS OF IN-KIND TRANSFERS"

In this chapter, I have tried to show that the poverty line is a realistic indicator of impoverishment: People who have cash incomes below that threshold are really poor. While this point of view is neither very exciting nor very original, I have emphasized it throughout the chapter mainly because there is now a sizable literature which purports to show that when the value of both cash and in-kind income received by the poor is taken into account, then there is a significant decrease in the rate of poverty, a decline that is not revealed by Census Bureau data because they are based only on cash income. As this finding has been used to provide an intellectual patina for the public policies pursued in recent years, it is particularly important to understand the logic underlying the poverty reduction literature.

The argument advanced in these writings is very beguiling. In syllogistic form, it can be expressed in the following way: (*a*) The poverty line identifies the level below which a household is poor; (*b*) when the value of both cash and in-kind welfare benefits is taken into account, many households are seen to have incomes above the poverty threshold; (*c*) therefore, such families are no longer poor. When sophisticated researchers link this artifice with formulae, diagrams, and complex statistical arrays, the result is persuasive to many readers—as long as they do not reflect on the subject for very long.

In practice, then, observers have estimated the value of food stamps, Medicaid, and other in-kind benefits to the poor, arbitrarily (*i.e.*, statistically) added these amounts to the cash income of households living below the poverty line and eligible for public assistance, and concluded that the rate of poverty is considerably lower than previously thought.[21] Edgar Browning, for example, asserts that "in a meaningful sense poverty had become virtually nonexistent by 1973." Similarly, Roger Freeman contends that many people "have a money income below the poverty level [who] may not be poor in any meaningful sense." And Morton Paglin, the most creative scribe, states that only 3% of the U.S. population was "really" poor in 1975, compared to the Census Bureau's figure of 12%. Most recently, Timothy Smeeding contends that, depending on how the various in-kind programs are "valued," the poverty rate would be reduced to between 9% and 6% of the population if the effect of noncash income were counted. In this way, a social problem is made to disappear—like magic.

In the remainder of this chapter, I am going to show that these findings reflect illusion rather than reality and that no amount of methodological and statistical sophistication can hide the blunt fact that the rate of poverty has not declined. Rather, as indicated in Table 2.2, it has incrased in the past few years.

This literature is characterized by four problems that make it completely misbegotten in origin and purpose. First, the research in this tradition does not acknowledge that public assistance programs require continuing destitution in order for households to retain their eligibility. Second, income is counted twice in the poverty reduction literature, once as cash and then in the form of in-kind benefits. Third, the results obtained by these researchers are unrealistic and illogical. And fourth, the poverty reduction literature counts in-kind income when it is obtained by the poor but not when other segments of the population get it. Each of these problems is described in the following paragraphs. Except where otherwise noted, I am going to focus on Timothy Smeeding's recent study, partly because it is the most detailed and sophisticated effort to date and partly because it was conducted under the aegis of the Census Bureau. This latter point has important political implications.

First, the poverty reduction literature ignores the fact that continual destitution is required in order to be eligible for public assistance. The unexamined premise underlying the syllogism described previously is that public assistance functions to eliminate poverty. This is not true. Actually, as will be seen in grim detail in Chapter 3, public aid functions to alleviate some of the problems associated with being indigent. For example, a family that has assets totalling less than $1,500 and income, after certain expenses, well below the poverty line is eligible for food stamps. On the average, the combination of cash income plus food stamps puts a household at the poverty line or a little above it.[22] Because such families have great difficulty making ends meet and because continued eligibility is dependent on not acquiring either additional assets or additional income, it does not make sense to describe a household that is so impoverished that it receives food stamps as no longer poor after receiving them. Yet this is precisely what the poverty reduction literature argues.

Second, the research in this tradition counts income twice, once on an in-kind basis and once as cash. That is, when measures of poverty reduction are estimated, in-kind income is imputed to the poor (via statistical assumption) without any recognition that the money actually goes to vendors who provide services. This problem is most acute with Medicaid, and that is what will be focused on here, but it also occurs with public housing and various food programs.

In studies of the "anti-poverty effects of in-kind tranfers," Medicaid is by far the single most important factor reducing the rate of poverty.[23] For example, Smeeding says that the official poverty rate is "reduced" to 9.4% when the market value of in-kind food and housing benefits is considered and to 6.4% when the market value of Medicaid is included. Since, as he observes, "It is nearly impossible to identify actual amounts of medical care consumed by recipients," he treats Medicaid as insurance, imputing the value of the premium and adding it to the cash income of those who are eligible for this program. Thus, at market value, an AFDC mother with two children (the average size of an AFDC family, by the way), is said to have "received" an additional $1,287 in 1979 because she was covered by Medicaid.[24] This is a phantom figure, of course, as the money went to doctors, pharmacists, and others in the health industry, whereas the care may or may not have been obtained by this mother.

It is illogical to assert that a household is not poor on this basis. Although medical care is vital to the well-being of all families, poor households cannot afford to pay for it, as the budget described earlier shows. Poor people receive medical services not income, which goes to providers.

Third, the substantive findings in the poverty reduction literature are unrealistic and illogical. It was noted previously that the market value of Medicaid to an AFDC family of three was presumably $1,287 in 1979. But the problem with this figure is that Medicaid is not for sale on the open market, with the result that its meaning is unclear because there is nothing with which to compare it. Recognizing this point, Smeeding and Moon, along with several other researchers, argue that it is necessary to calculate the value recipients place on noncash benefits such as Medicaid. This figure is the most useful measure, the authors in this tradition argue, because it indicates the amount of cash people would take instead of in-kind transfers.[25] In performing this exercise, Smeeding argues that the "cash equivalent" value of food stamps increases with household income, an assertion that is common in the poverty reduction literature.[26] Thus, families with an income of less than $2,500 presumably place a cash value on food stamps that is 89% of their in-kind (or face) value, while families with an income of $7,500 presumably place a cash value on food stamps that is 97% of their face value. Translated, this argument means that lower income households, which presumably need food stamps more, value them less and would take less cash as a substitute. This result does not make sense and is not credible.

Here is another example of the unrealistic and illogical nature of the findings in this research. In addition to market value and cash equivalent value, it is also possible to calculate "the poverty budget share value." This figure is an estimate of the "funds released at the poverty income level as a result of the receipt of in-kind benefits."[27] Smeeding asserts that a family of four which lives at the poverty line and receives Medicaid had $547 "released" (or available) to spend on goods other than medical care in 1979. This figure translates into $45.58 per month. This assertion is not credible, as a glance at the poverty-level nonfood budget described earlier in this chapter shows.

In my opinion, findings like these result from the fact that researchers are either so concerned with showing that poverty is no longer a problem or so interested in displaying their methodological virtuosity that they have not thought through the implications of their results. For example, Smeeding and Moon observe that one of the most important issues facing poverty researchers today is "the choice of techniques" for placing a value on in-kind income received by the poor. As they see it, "The problem is not whether to count the anti-poverty effects of medical care [and other noncash] transfers, but how to measure this effect."[28] As a result, attention is directed away from the crucial problem of logic (and fairness) and toward a consideration of sterile methodological issues. The syllogism just outlined is simply assumed to be true.

Thus, the figures cited previously for the market value of Medicaid and for the "cash equivalent" and "poverty budget share" values of food stamps were arrived at by a continuous sequence of adjustments to the data and a large number of assumptions about the U.S. population. It was decided, for example, to define as Medicaid recipients all those who were eligible for the program, regardless of whether they received services or even if they did not know they were covered.[29] Similarly, at every stage of the analysis and for every program dealt with (food stamps, public housing, Medicaid, and Medicare), estimates and assumptions had to be made. The following quotation suggests how elaborate the procedures were; it is a simple example:

> The estimates of the number of persons covered by Medicaid within State and risk class were made by combining the CPS [Current Population Survey] and HCFA [Health Care Finance Administration] information. First, the CPS estimates were adjusted to include the institutionalized and decedents by State. Next the HCFA estimates were adjusted to exclude beneficiaries in Puerto Rico and the Virgin Islands. The final estimates were derived by choosing the CPS estimate of covered or the HCFA estimate of "ever-received," whichever was greater, for each State and risk class.

If the goal is to ascertain people's economic circumstances, would it not be easier to just ask them how much money they make?

Fourth, even though it is premised on the notion that the Census Bureau's definition of income is inadequate, all of the studies in the poverty reduction literature measure the value of in–kind income for the poor but not for the rest of the population. In effect, their argument is that the value of both cash and noncash income should be used in determining the poverty rate but not in assessing the economic status of the remainder of the population. This point of view assumes that noncash benefits change the economic situation of the poor but not the nonpoor. Although, this position is illogical, most researchers do not even mention this issue. Smeeding is one of the few who does. He observes that "it would have been preferable to estimate the value of all types if in-kind benefits from both public and private sources [in order] to assess their effect on poverty and on the entire income size distribution."[30] This procedure is not possible, he says, because adequate microdata are not available. Nonetheless, like all the others, he estimates the value of food stamps, school lunches, public housing, Medicaid, and Medicare; then he arbitrarily adds these figures to the incomes of poor households and observes a reduction in the rate of poverty.

In pursuing this strategy, it is often implied that most in-kind transfers are received by the poor. This may be due to the fact that noncash transfers obtained by the nonpoor are less publicly visible because they occur mainly in the form of tax expenditures and employee fringe benefits. As noted, Smeeding estimates the value of food stamps, school lunches, public housing, Medicaid, and Medicare. But unlike most researchers, he also contrasts the cost of these in-kind benefits with that of other programs, most of which benefit the nonpoor. Interestingly, he labels the welfare programs "major" and the remaining programs "other," despite the fact that those falling in the "other" category are two to three times as expensive, depending on where Medicare is placed. These data are presented in Table 2.5.[31]

The table suggests an obvious conclusion: Most in-kind income goes to people who are not poor and it decisively effects their economic situation. Given the relative political power of the poor in comparison to other social classes, this judgment is intuitively plausible. It is further reinforced by a study that shows that for every 5-dollar increase in cash income, people receive 1 dollar more in noncash transfers from the government; private subsidies, such as employer payments for expense accounts and the like, were not tabulated.[32] While the authors of this study rightly emphasize its tentative nature, the findings make sense.

My own methodological orientation should be made clear at this point. As described previously, the Census Bureau assesses people's

TABLE 2.5:   Contrast between the Cost of "Major" and "Other" In-kind Transfers, 1980 (in Billions)[a]

	"Major" transfers covered in Smeeding's study		"Other" transfers not covered in Smeeding's study	
Means Tested	Food stamps	$9.2	Tax Expenditures[b]	$32.0
	School lunch	3.3	Other government subsidies[c]	27.8
	Public housing	5.4	Private subsidies[d]	83.5
	Medicaid	26.2		$143.3
		$44.1		
	Medicare	$28.4		
		$72.5		

"Major" programs as a percentage of total: 33.6%
Means-tested programs as a percentage of total: 20.4%

[a] Cited in Smeeding, 1982.

[b] Tax expenditures are revenue losses incurred by the government when it decides not to collect money it might otherwise be due. For example, homeowners can deduct mortgage interest from their tax obligation.

[c] Other government subsidies are medical payments to the military and veterans, housing subsidies, and minor amounts for school milk program and the Supplementary Food Program for Women, Infants, and Children (WIC).

[d] Private subsidies are generally employer benefits that are not taxed, such as payments for medical insurance, retirement plans, or expense accounts.

economic characteristics in terms of cash income. This means, of course, that cash income is a proxy for their "true" standard of living. It does not seem either useful or fair, at least to me, to compare the economic situation of the poor with that of the nonpoor by using two different definitions of income. Rather, if observers wish to include the economic impact of noncash income in determining the level of poverty, and I do not think this is a very good idea, then two steps should be taken: (a) the value of in-kind income accruing to all segments of the population ought to be measured; and (b) the poverty line and all other indicators of people's economic situation should be recalculated upward so as to reflect the amount of cash and noncash income that is necessary for living at each status level. When faced with this suggestion, conservative academics immediately note that it would make the poverty line relative rather than absolute. But this is not true, as the preceding analysis of the relationship between the poverty line and the median income makes clear, for the poverty cutoff would still be adjusted in light of changes in the cost of living rather than the standard of living. The problem with this suggestion is not that it would make the poverty threshold relative, but that measuring in-kind income is too difficult, too imprecise, and too unclear — not only to the public but to policymakers as well. The first three problems cited here will not go away.

Although it would be nice to think that there are very few poor people in the United States and that the war on poverty has been won, such claims are an illusion. They are based on methodological sophistry. In the real world where people must obtain food, shelter, and all the other necessities of life, the only way to eliminate poverty is for people to become economically independent. Families whose incomes are above the poverty line and who no longer need government aid in order to survive are also no longer poor. Individuals who are paupers are poor, and no amount of obfuscation can hide this blunt fact. If such persons cannot obtain medical care, they will be poor and sick rather than just poor. If they do not live in public housing, they will be poor and living in sub-standard housing rather than just poor. And if they do not obtain food stamps and other nutritional aid, they will be poor and hungry rather than just poor. This is how public assistance programs alleviate some of the problems associated with poverty.

Now ordinarily, social scientific literature that is misbegotten is ignored and eventually discarded. But when the political implications are great, which is the case here, then this result is less likely. Thus, the arguments advanced in the poverty reduction literature have been used by public officials in order to justify their policies. Thus, as described in Chapter 1, Martin Anderson has reviewed these studies and concluded that the War on Poverty "has been won." After arriving at this conclusion, it was easy for him to extrapolate that many welfare recipients would rather receive public aid than work, that many of them are cheating, and that it is reasonable (indeed necessary) to drastically reduce public assistance while preserving a "safety net" for the "truly needy."[33] Although none of these extrapolations is correct, a fact that will become clear in subsequent chapters, and while the effects of academic research on public policy can be overrated, the analyses cited here have been used to justify recent changes in welfare programs.

But these changes are based on a pattern of reasoning that is highly dubious. What must be recognized is that, although there is no inherently correct way of measuring poverty and even though the official poverty line cannot be defended on scientific grounds, the poverty threshold is a very useful indicator of the extent of impoverishment in the United States because it identifies people who live in dire economic straits and because it is simple to understand. In addition, since it has been in use for some years, the poverty line has a sense of legitimacy with the public. I see no indication that the poverty reduction literature offers a viable alternative to the present means of measuring impoverishment.

3

PUBLIC ASSISTANCE

There are 32 million poor people in America, about 14% of the population, and millions more live at the brink of poverty. Pauperism is a constant specter for these individuals. This chapter explains the characteristics of the nation's most expensive and controversial public assistance programs: Aid for Families with Dependent Children (AFDC), Supplementary Security Income (SSI), Food Stamps, and Medicaid.

In the process of explication, I shall make three arguments. First, public assistance cannot eliminate poverty because it is not designed to do so. This fact is suggested initially by distinguishing between the creation of antipoverty programs and the expansion of public assistance, both of which occurred in the 1960s, and demonstrated later through a detailed analysis of the characteristics of the aid programs just cited. Second, and this is really surprising, public assistance does not cost very much. This fact is shown by comparing the cost of assistance to the total federal budget, to outlays for social insurance, and to special interest subsidies. In addition, it is also argued that the cost of public assistance is mitigated by the fact that it provides income support for both the poor and the nonpoor. Third, the problems inherent in public aid programs, of which there are many, have not been resolved by the changes made in the past few years; rather, they have been made worse.

ANTIPOVERTY AND PUBLIC ASSISTANCE PROGRAMS

One reason why so many people are confused about poverty and pauperism today is that they have not thought through the essential differences between the creation of antipoverty programs and the expansion of public assistance.

The antipoverty programs enacted during the Johnson administration were explicitly designed to eliminate both poverty and pauperism in America. The titles of these programs show their intent: Head Start, the Job Corps, the Neighborhood Youth Corps, the Community Action Program, Upward Bound, Volunteers in Service to America (VISTA), and several other initiatives. These programs were youth oriented and stressed a social-work strategy: rehabilitative services rather than income or jobs. From this angle, the long-term solution to the problem of poverty was seen as helping people to obtain education and skills so they could qualify for jobs and become economically independent. While this seems like a reasonable goal, these programs both misperceived the causes of poverty and engendered unrealistic expectations. As a result, they met with many problems and, with the exception of VISTA and Head Start, both of which limp along, all of them are now defunct.

In contrast, the public assistance programs enacted and expanded during the Johnson administration constituted an increase in the federal government's role in guaranteeing the welfare of the population. The philosophy then was that only Washington could protect America's least powerful citizens, not only because the states were too prone to influence by idiosyncratic and parochial interests but also because they did not have either the desire or the fiscal capability to enact the necessary programs.[1] As such, the federal government's assistance initiatives — while imperfect — functioned to alleviate (not eliminate) the squalidness and wretchedness of poverty. This result can be seen in the nature of the relief that paupers received: increased AFDC benefits, the expansion of AFDC to cover intact families (optional to the states), the enactment of income disregards that allowed public aid recipients to work, the implementation of the food stamp and other nutrition programs, the passage of Medicaid and Medicare, the extension of the eligibility period for unemployment compensation, the expansion of public housing, the increase in coverage of basic social insurance programs, the replacement of state-run programs for the blind, aged, and disabled with a single national program (Supplementary Security Income), and several other initiatives. While these enactments are impressive, it is important to remember that not one of them will eliminate poverty in the sense of allowing an independent existence. They are consumption subsidies, which means that they help people to survive at a subsistence level but do nothing to change their station in life. This is because welfare, despite its connotations, leaves recipients just as poor at the end of the month as they were at the beginning. When paupers become independent it is due to factors other than public assistance programs as they are currently constructed.

What should be clear, then, is that it is a misnomer to label public assistance programs as antipoverty efforts. The war on poverty cannot be won through pauperism and those who make such assertions are dissembling. The primary purpose of public aid is to enable poor persons to survive each month, while antipoverty programs were intended to obviate the need for monetary support. In its shortsightedness, America has not only abandoned the goal of eliminating poverty, it has also chosen to restrict the public aid available to poor people while enhancing that available to the nonpoor. The resulting misery will undoubtedly cost a great deal over the long run.

THE COST OF PUBLIC ASSISTANCE

Without thinking about it, the argument that public assistance does not cost very much seems outrageous, especially in light of the figures thrown out in newspapers and on the nightly news. But it is true. Here are two empirical generalizations that give some perspective to this assertion. First, the higher the social class, *then* the greater the economic benefits received from government. Such benefits flow from political power, of course, and the poor constitute the least powerful social class. Once this fact is recognized, it makes intuitive sense to suggest that, despite the publicity given to assistance costs, the nonpoor receive more economic benefits than do the poor. Second, public assistance has dual functions: It not only provides income support for the poor but also for the nonpoor. This is because paupers either cannot keep the money they receive or get services instead of cash. In either case, the charge commonly made by economists, that public assistance is a means of redistributing money from the nonpoor to the poor, is inaccurate. Rather, the dual functions of public aid mean that it results in maintenance of the economic status quo. The remainder of this section should be read with these ideas in mind.

In order to begin analyzing the cost of public assistance and comparing it to the subsidies provided to other persons, it is necessary to mention two characteristics of income maintenance programs as they affect people at all socioeconomic levels. A large number are entitlements and many of them are indexed to the cost of living. Each of these terms, entitlements and indexation, is defined in the paragraphs that follow.

Entitlement programs are those in which statutes dictate payments to all individuals who meet eligibility requirements. Thus, the Congress cannot reduce the cost of such programs simply by appropriating less money for them, since funds to pay benefits constitute a prior legal obligation. This is why expenditures for entitlement programs are so difficult to control. What Congress can do, however, is prescribe eligibility requirements that beneficiaries must meet. As will be seen, the Reagan administration has exploited this capacity with a vengeance, especially

with regard to public assistance. Nonetheless, because the term entitlement has been bandied about in the press, in Congress, and by the
President without much explanation, many people have gotten the
impression that assistance programs are the only entitlements. This is
incorrect; entitlement programs support people in all classes. Some
examples will be offered later in this section.

Indexing is a means of raising benefits in accordance with price
increases. Although it has some weaknesses, the Consumer Price Index is
the most common indicator of prices that is used in government programs, primarily because other indicators are either difficult to measure
or have additional disadvantages.[2] The major purpose of indexation is to
hold beneficiaries' purchasing power constant and, hence, to protect
their standard of living. At least 90 federal income-maintenance programs are indexed and most of them support the incomes of nonpoor
persons.

Everyone knows that public assistance costs a great deal of money.
What everyone does not know, however, is that expenditures for public
aid are a very low proportion of the federal budget, less than 9%. This
fact is shown in Table 3.1, which displays federal outlays for various
public assistance programs in 1981 and 1982.[3] While conservative rhetoric would lead one to believe that assistance eats up the budget and that
our economic problems could be solved if the programs identified in Table
3.1 could be cut, this is obviously not the case now and will not be the case
in the future. Sonewhat surprisingly, the table leads to the inescapable
conclusion that, even though the sums involved are very great, public
assistance does not cost very much money — when it is seen as a proportion of all federal spending.

The big buck items in Table 3.1 are entitlements (Medicaid, AFDC,
and SSI) or are treated as though they are entitlements by the Congress
(food stamps and housing subsidies). In addition, many of them, with the
notable exception of AFDC, are indexed. This is why there was little
change in the cost of most programs between 1981 and 1982. Despite
budget cuts, rising prices automatically triggered benefit increases for
those left on the rolls. This is why the administration has emphasized
tightening eligibility requirements.

In considering the cost of public assistance, it should be remembered
that the poor do not receive any of the money spent on Medicaid, the
most expensive program by far. It goes directly to hospitals, physicians,
nursing homes, pharmacists, and all the others in the medical industry.
As will be seen when this program is discussed, one reason it is out of
control is that the hidden beneficiaries — middle- and upper-class people
— control costs. This is why Medicaid is one of the few programs in which

TABLE 3.1: Federal Outlays for Public Assistance, Fiscal 1981 and 1982, in Billions

Cash programs		1981	1982
Aid for Families with Dependent Children[a]		$8.5	$8.0
Supplementary Security Income[b]		7.2	7.7
Earned Income Tax Credit		1.3	1.2
Low Income Energy Assistance		1.8	1.7
Refugee Assistance		.7	1.0
Other		.2	.2
In-kind programs	Subtotal	$19.7	$19.8
Medicaid		$16.9	$17.4
Food stamps[c]		11.3	11.0
Other Nutrition[d]		5.0	4.6
Housing subsidies[e]		6.9	8.0
	Subtotal	$40.1	$41.0
	Total public assistance	$59.8	$60.8
	Total federal budget	$678.2	$745.7
Public assistance as a percentage of federal budget		8.8%	8.2%

[a] Includes AFDC-UF.

[b] Aid to aged, blind, and disabled.

[c] Includes aid to Puerto Rico.

[d] Includes school lunch and breakfast programs, milk programs, WIC, etc.

[e] Includes rent subsidies, public housing, etc.

expenditures increased significantly between 1981 and 1982. A similar explanation accounts for the rise in housing subsidies, although this program is not analyzed here. Furthermore, a large percentage of the money spent on food stamps, AFDC, and other programs also goes directly to administrative costs (that is, to middle-class bureaucrats), due to the necessity of documenting and redocumenting people's eligibility. Finally, as noted in Chapter 1, all the money actually spent by paupers trickles up to those middle- and working-class persons who serve the poor in various ways. For these reasons, then, public assistance functions to maintain the life-style of both the poor and the nonpoor. The economic status quo endures as a result.

Before leaving Table 3.1 and comparing public assistance expenditures with social insurance and special interest subsidies, it should be emphasized that the figures given in the table are for federal outlays only. State moneys are also part of the cost of welfare, social insurance, and other income maintenance plans. While the inclusion of state expenses would strengthen the analysis presented here, primarily because state governments are financed by regressive taxes and are even less oriented to the needs of the poor, they would also make comparisons less systematic and more difficult to understand. Hence, the focus of this sketch is on federal costs. Until recently, the federal government has paid about 70% of public assistance expenses and about 85% of social insurance expenditures, with the states making up the remainder.[4] I shall argue in the following that the states have not taken up the slack with the decline in federal outlays for public assistance, primarily because they are both unwilling and unable (in fiscal terms) to do so. Historically, only the federal government has been able to protect the powerless.

Now that the cost of public assistance is clear, I want to compare it to expenditures for social insurance, which benefit members of all social classes. Table 3.2 displays federal outlays for various social insurance programs in 1981 and for 1982.[5] When Tables 3.1 and 3.2 are compared, it becomes clear that social insurance expenditures are more than four times (453%) those for public assistance. By itself, social insurance amounts to more than one-third of all federal expenditures, $245 billion in 1981 and about $276 billion in 1982.

Table 3.2 also shows that, unlike public assistance, outlays for social insurance rose substantially between 1981 and 1982 despite the administration's emphasis on cutting the budget. There are a number of reasons for this increase. Nearly all of these programs are indexed entitlements, which makes costs difficult to control. In addition, and much more important, there is overwhelming public support for social insurance; bene-

TABLE 3.2: Federal Outlays for Social Insurance, Fiscal 1981 and 1982, in Billions

Cash programs	1981	1982
Social Security[a]	$138.9	$154.1
Federal Employee Retirement	17.3	19.6
Veterans Income Security[b]	16.0	16.5
Veterans Hospital and Medical Care	7.0	7.5
Railroad Retirement	5.3	5.7
Unemployed Compensation	19.7	23.8
Disable Coal Miners	1.8	1.9
In-kind programs Subtotal	$206.0	229.1
Medicare	$39.1	$46.6
Total social insurance	$245.1	$275.7
Total federal budget	$678.2	$745.7
Total Insurance as a percentage of federal budget	36.1%	37.0%
Social Insurance as a percentage of public assistance	409.9%	453.5%

[a] Includes both OASDHI and disability.

[b] Includes pensions, insurance, education, housing, and training.

ficiaries are perceived as deserving the money they get, either because they "paid into" the program, as with social security, or because they have made sacrifices that make them eligible, as with veterans' programs. Finally, those who receive social insurance benefits are active voters who are represented by powerful and persuasive lobbying organizations. The result, then, is that most social insurance programs have not been cut.

In thinking about the cost of social insurance, it is worth remembering that people who try to live on these benefits often find it very difficult. For example, it will be shown later in this chapter that aged persons who must survive only on Social Security payments cannot do so. This is why millions of people in such circumstances also rely on Supplementary Security Income. It is also one reason why, alone among public assistance programs, SSI has been relatively immune to cutbacks.

The cost of public assistance should also be compared to the special interest subsidies nonpoor people get. This task is important because many persons believe that paupers get something for nothing while other segments of the population do not. Implicit in this point of view is the stereotype that while middle- and upper-class people are earning a living and being productive members of society, the poor are living on the dole and reaping the benefits of other people's hard work. In fact, however, the actual situation is quite opposite. Despite the expansion of public assistance during the 1960s, most income maintenance projects undertaken by the federal government have little to do with the poor: They benefit middle- and upper-class people. The main difference between income maintenance for the impoverished and for those who are better off is that people without money must declare their destitution in order to get help whereas those who already have money exercise enormous political power to obtain aid. For this reason, they are called special interest subsidies. Because of the higher socioeconomic status of most recipients, special interest subsidies involve not only governmental outlays but also tax expenditures.

There are nearly 200 income-maintenance programs funded by the federal government, most of which are intended to aid the nonpoor.[6] In 1977, it was estimated that these programs cost about $250 billion and that nearly 80% of this money went to projects that were not income conditioned; that is, it went to support the incomes of middle-class people. Here is one example.

Agricultural price supports provide farmers with guaranteed incomes by making up the differences between the actual market price of commodities and specified target prices.[7] Growers of goods such as wheat, corn, grain, sorghum, barley, cotton, soybeans, tobacco, rice, wool and mohair, sugar, milkcows, and even bees are eligible for income support under certain conditions. In most cases, however, payments to one farmer are limited to $20,000 per year from all programs combined. What is important to remember here is that these benefits are added to other wages. Thus, a farmer can have an income from selling crops of any amount, even $50,000 or $100,000 yearly, and then add up to $20,000 more in government subsidies because these programs are not income conditioned. In comparison, it should be noted here that the total of wages and subsidies provided to farmers is generally far greater than the average of $5,400 in disposable income available to AFDC recipients (see Table 3.3). Yet price supports are not considered to be welfare and are never described as guaranteed incomes, although that is how they function.

The total cost of guaranteeing the incomes of farmers was $3.3 billion in 1979, but rose to $13.3 billion in 1982, an amount greater than federal expenditures for food stamps, as indicated in Table 3.1. These income maintenance subsidies for farmers not only protect them from low prices but also mitigate the effects of natural disasters and their own mistakes. Because the establishment and maintenance of agricultural income guarantees depends on the political power of farmers and farm organizations, small farmers see little of this money. Poor people, of course, see none of it. Despite recent efforts at cutting the federal budget, farm price supports have continued to be indexed entitlements. This is why the programs have grown so much in the past few years.

One last point: In considering the cost of income guarantees for farmers, it should be recognized that they are not evil, that they are not trying to rip off the government or the American people. Rather, like any other special interest group, farmers are merely trying to assure their economic security in a context where prices fluctuate widely from year to year. The hypocrisy lies not in this effort but in denying the legitimacy of similar efforts by others, such as the poor or those representing the poor.

It will be recalled from Chapter 2 that tax expenditures are revenue losses the government incurs because it decides not to collect money it would otherwise be due.[8] Such losses take the form of income exclusions, tax deductions, and tax credits built into the internal revenue statutes and, as such, they are the same as payments to individuals.

For example, taxpayers are allowed to exclude from their taxable income any employer payments for pension and profit-sharing plans; accident, life, and medical insurance; unemployment compensation; and many other items. In this form, tax expenditures are in-kind income for recipients. In addition, of course, taxpayers are also allowed to exclude from their incomes many of their own payments for the items mentioned above; to exclude or deduct many kinds of interest, capital gains, and other types of unearned income they receive; and to exclude or deduct interest, taxes, and many other payments they make. In these forms, tax expenditures constitute cash retained by recipients rather than paid to the government. Most people, however, do not recognize these benefits as income support or as welfare, although they clearly function to maintain the economic well being of recipients. Rather, tax expenditures are seen as benefits connected to a job or as just rewards for investment activities.

The total cost of tax expenditures was estimated to be $143.4 billion in 1981, nearly all of which went to the nonpoor. Thus, only $.4 billion consisted of the exclusion of public assistance benefits from taxable income, while $14.7 billion resulted from not counting employer payments to pension funds of employees (in-kind income) and $16.1 billion resulted from excluding employer payments for medical insurance and employee medical deductions (cash retained). There are, of course, many other examples of each form of tax expenditure. It can be safely concluded, then, that tax expenditures are a haven (or perhaps heaven) for the middle and upper classes. In comparison, it will be recalled from Table 3.1 that federal outlays for public assistance amounted to only $59.8 billion in 1981, or only about 40% of the cost of tax expenditures.

In considering tax expenditures, it should be remembered that — like public assistance — they have a dual function: on the one hand, they provide income support for affluent people and, on the other hand, benefits trickle down to the rest of the population because this money is spent (ideally, it is invested) and thus creates jobs. The result, then is to maintain the economic status quo: Poor people remain poor and affluent people remain affluent.

Because tax expenditures are revenues forgone by the government, many people have difficulty visualizing how they work and how they combine with outlays. An example is provided in Table 3.3, which displays the cost of health care by income group in 1977.[9] This example is especially useful, even though the data are not as recent as one would like, because here is a context in which tax expenditures and outlays combine to show that the government spends just as much on health care for the rich as it does for the poor. Health care is thus a deviant case, or at least it was in 1977.[10] In addition, the example is also useful because it shows clearly how tax expenditures and outlays benefit different segments of the population.

As seen in the table, tax expenditures for health care (such as employer payments for employee health insurance) go overwhelmingly to the nonpoor, like nearly all such benefits. Medicare outlays, which are designed to aid all aged people regardless of their income level, are spread more or less evenly across all groups. And Medicaid services, of course,

TABLE 3.3: Federal Tax Expenditures and Outlays for Health Care, 1977, by Income Group, in Billions

Income level	Tax expenditures for health	Medicare outlays	Medicaid outlays	Total tax expenditures and outlays	Percentage of total to each group
< $10,000	$.1	$4.3	$5.6	$10.0	29
$10,000–$15,999	.5	3.1	2.0	5.6	16
$16,000–$31,999	3.5	4.7	1.3	9.5	27
> $32,000	6.2	3.3	.2	9.7	28
	$10.3	$15.4	$9.1	$34.8	100

primarily benefit the poor (although it should be remembered that the income goes to the nonpoor). The reason Medicaid services can sometimes go to patients who have higher incomes is because the Congress enacted certain provisos in the legislation to cover catastrophic and highly expensive medical problems. Thus, a middle-class family can have kidney dialysis paid for under Medicaid because, even though it has a relatively high income, the price is so incredible.

In summary, public assistance does not cost very much money. It is only 9% of the total federal budget. It is only one-fourth as expensive as social insurance. It is only a small proportion of those special-interest subsidies that are cash outlays. And almost no tax expenditures go to the poor. In addition, when it is recognized that the money paupers spend supports not only themselves but also middle-class people, maybe public assistance is a good economic investment. I want to turn now to a detailed consideration of four assistance programs.

PUBLIC ASSISTANCE PROGRAMS TODAY

Table 3.1 shows that most of the money spent on public assistance goes to four programs, two of which distribute cash and two of which provide in-kind benefits: Aid for Families with Dependent Children, Supplementary Security Income, Medicaid, and Food Stamps (along with other nutrition programs). As these programs form the core of the welfare system in America, each of them is examined in the next few pages in terms of their overall design and purpose, the determination of the need and eligibility, the number of people obtaining assistance and the amount they get, and the social characteristics of the recipients. Since many paupers receive more than one form of aid, the implications of obtaining multiple welfare benefits are also discussed. This last topic is important because some observers have argued that many paupers are not poor because they receive aid from several different programs, a point of view that provides a rationale for conservative social policies.

Aid for Families with Dependent Children is often called the nation's primary public assistance program. Yet the first essential fact to remember about AFDC is that it is antifamily in orientation, primarily because eligibility is restricted. Despite the existence of the unemployed father's component of the program (AFDC–UF), which will be commented on later, just being poor does not necessarily qualify a family for relief. Rather, because the basic eligibility requirement is the death, continual absence from the home, or the physical or mental incapacity of a parent, the program is directed mainly at broken families. Thus, in 1981 about 8 million children received AFDC payments averaging about $97 per month and 89% of them lived with a single parent, their mother.[11]

This emphasis has important implications for family stability among paupers. While millions of households do not obtain aid simply because they choose to remain husband–wife families, it is probable that AFDC requirements are important factors in the decision to marry or divorce. Although the effect of AFDC on family breakup cannot be demonstrated with certainty, it is apparent that the program does not encourage family stability and, to that extent, can be considered antifamily in orientation. From this point of view, then, it would seem that those who favor strengthening the family would also be in favor of a nationwide public assistance program that covered intact households. Unfortunately, this is often not the case.

AFDC was passed almost as an afterthought to the Social Security Act of 1935. At that time, Congress decided to provide support for the "deserving poor," families without male breadwinners, while forcing men in intact households to remain in the labor force at whatever wages they could get. It is worthwhile to remember that in the 1930s there was little expectation for females (especially white widows, to whom the program was directed) to be self-supporting; women without men were viewed as in need, almost by definition. AFDC is seen in a different light today partly because sex-role expectations have changed and partly because blacks are now about 40% of all recipients. From this angle, it is ironic that the same conservatives who oppose the Equal Rights Amendment and, by extrapolation, would deny women the opportunity to work at equal wages, also decry "welfare mothers," especially black "welfare mothers," as lazy. The hypocrisy in this orientation is evident.

The second essential fact to remember about AFDC is that even though the federal government pays most of the cost of the program, it is controlled by the states because they determine need levels and other eligibility criteria while also setting benefit rates. Thus, AFDC is actually 50 programs rather than one, each of which is administered differently, defines eligibility differently, and sets benefit levels differently. As a result, there is great variation from one state to another in the number of paupers and the extent of their assistance. This chaotic situation greatly increases the cost of AFDC.

AFDC is an entitlement program; that is, the federal government is required to make payments to all individuals who are eligible. But unlike many other income-maintenance projects funded by the federal government, such as agricultural price supports, state requirements determine federal funding levels. Thus, while AFDC is financed jointly by federal, state, and local governments, Washington is obligated to pay up to 78% of each state's payments to recipients and half of the administrative costs. The extent of local outlays varies widely, depending on each state's funding formula. This arrangement means that the federal government is hostage to state policies, since state appropriations and caseloads determine the amount the federal government will spend on AFDC. The historical reason for this situation is that the framers of the original legislation believed that public assistance ought to be primarily a state function. The fact that Washington must fund a program over which it has no control is one reason why the Reagan administration offered to federalize Medicaid in exchange for state takeover of AFDC (both programs are currently financed jointly). This proposal died, however, because state governors opposed it. They believe that all public assistance programs should be a federal responsibility, a point of view that is consonant with most recommendations for welfare reform. I shall return to this topic in the concluding section of the chapter.

Although the federal government cannot control expenditures, it does impose certain minimum standards of AFDC eligibility on all the states. Thus, children must be without the support of one or both parents, less than 18-years-old, U.S. citizens, and residents of the state in which the application is made. Parents who want assistance to meet their own needs must be single, U.S. citizens, and participate in the Work Incentive Program (see Chapter 4).

In addition to these requirements, however, the federal government has made several AFDC options available to the states, most of which are designed to make public aid available to all those who really need it, including intact families. Thus, if the states took full advantage of the available options, AFDC would not be restricted to broken families. There is, however, considerable variation in both acceptance of these options and in requirements established by the states. Here are two examples among many. Although 32 states allow a pregnant woman to apply for AFDC on behalf of her unborn child, there are enormous differences in the eligibility standards such women must meet. For example, in some states women are eligible only if it is their first child, in others they are eligible after the fourth month or the sixth month of pregnancy, and so forth. In addition, while 25 states allow needy intact-families to apply for aid under the AFDC–UF program, only 5% of all AFDC children are in husband–wife households under this provision because the requirements these states have imposed are so restrictive.[12] Hence, the major thrust of AFDC remains as it was initially: to provide succor to broken families. It is not a generalized public assistance program.

These variations may decline, although not because any reform of AFDC has occurred. Thus, one way the states can react to recent budget cuts is by eliminating AFDC options. This response will have serious long-term costs, both economic and social, since it will restrict the scope of AFDC even further. For example, states can choose to prevent pregnant women from entering the rolls. The inevitable result will be that such women will not eat as well during their prenatal period and will not get medical care, since AFDC is the primary means by which poor people become eligible for food stamps and Medicaid. These sorts of changes are unavoidable because state and local officials generally will not be willing to raise taxes to cover the shortfall in federal money that they are now experiencing. The likelihood that the progeny born under such circumstances will require public aid in the future means not only that the number of paupers and their economic cost to the government will increase, but also that the social cost to our society will be enormous.

The third fact to remember about AFDC is that potential recipients must be destitute before they are eligible to be paupers and must stay destitute in order to retain their eligibility. This circumstance can be seen when the property resources families can retain are considered. In addition to low income, AFDC beneficiaries are required to dispose of all real property and liquid assets, including insurance policies and savings accounts. In the past, there has been considerable variation in the asset thresholds used in the different states. The Reagan administration simplified this situation by placing a $1,000 limit on allowable family resources, excluding an occupied home and one automobile worth not more than $1,500.

However, certain aspects of the asset limitations are worth noting because, although they were passed under the guise of restricting eligibility and thus reducing costs, they could have the opposite effect. For example, the new rules require that "detailed assessments" (*i.e.*, home visits) be made to verify applicants' lack of assets. But this rule is apparently being ignored by most states because welfare officials say it would increase costs without discovering any cheaters. They assert that it is more efficient to take an applicant's word and investigate only when there are grounds for thinking that fraud is occurring.[13] In addition, the new rules also allow each state to place liens against houses on the grounds that "many recipients of AFDC own a valuable home." The rules permit a family of paupers to continue living in its home but require that "upon the sale of the house the state would be able to recover some of the benefits paid during the period of need."[14] Like the requirement for detailed assessment of assets, the lien rule is silly: 90% of all AFDC families rent and the value of homes owned by the remainder is so low that this policy will probably involve more administrative costs than any state will ever get back. It is not clear whether the states are using this rule.

These new rules were passed by the Congress at the behest of the Reagan administration in order to reduce AFDC costs. Yet, perversely, if the states were to vigorously enforce them, then administrative expenses would rise and much of this increase would be borne by the federal government. This is not the way to reduce public assistance expenditures.

Nonetheless, the point of this section should be clearly understood: In order to be eligible for AFDC, households must be without practically everything of value. Those who qualify for public aid are completely without material and financial resources, a state of affairs that inevitably drives them to pauperism. Recognition of this fact is important because, as was noted in Chapter 1, a number of observers have argued that paupers are not poor, primarily because they get "welfare."

The fourth essential fact to remember about AFDC is that the way income is calculated is crucial in determining both eligibility and the extent to which paupers work. In the past, federal law has required that certain items be disregarded (or subtracted) from wages in order to obtain a family's net income for AFDC purposes and thus determine both its eligibility and level of aid. The function of these disregards was to encourage paupers to work; the logic being that it is better to combine employment and pauperism than to be totally dependent. Even though these disregards have been very effective, as will be seen in Chapter 4, they have been eliminated and the rules have been tightened in several other ways as well. The rationale underlying these changes is that low-wage workers who supplement their earnings with public aid are not destitute, not "truly needy." As a result, many paupers are being forced to choose between employment and public assistance. Although there has been a large number of changes in AFDC rules, I shall describe only two of them here.

In the past, net income after subtracting such work-related expenses as travel costs and child care was the main criterion for AFDC eligibility. But the requirement has been changed such that any family with an income more than 150% of a state's need level is automatically ineligible, even if the result cannot provide a minimal standard of living. (Each state's need level is usually, but not always, the same as its maximum benefit level; see Table 3.4. Both need and maximum benefit levels are typically well below the poverty line.) Thus, a woman with three children who gets a full time job at the minimum wage, $6,968 yearly, is automatically ineligible in 27 states, since her monthly income will be above the 150% of the need standard. For example, her monthly income is 235% of Mississippi's need standard and 175% of Illinois'.[15] Her income, by the way, is only three-fourths of the poverty line and, in most states, she will be ineligible for Medicaid.

Clearly, then, impoverished persons living in these states have an incentive not to work, even at the minimum wage. They have an incentive to become and remain paupers. Yet the 150% rule was justified because "families with such high incomes have resources on which to rely and should not draw on public assistance that should be reserved for those unable to support themselves."[16] Such political legerdemain is not sound public policy.

As an aside, at least two states, North Carolina and Florida, have dealt with the 150% rule by raising their need standards while keeping their maximum benefit levels the same. As a result, few families (at least in these states) have been purged from the rolls.[17] This practice, of course, will prevent AFDC costs from declining and the federal government can do nothing to stop it. This example illustrates why Mr. Reagan proposed giving total responsibility for AFDC to the states. Unfortunately, it will be seen in the next section that even when the value of food stamps and energy assistance is counted, paupers in such states still live well below the poverty line.

The other alteration in AFDC I want to explain involves the $30 plus one-third rule, for it also affects poor people's ability to work.

In the past, after job-related expenses were subtracted from wages to determine eligibility for AFDC, two additional deductions also occurred: $30 plus one-third of the remainder. Because it worked a little like a negative income tax — higher wages meant lower AFDC benefits, and vice versa — this practice allowed low-income workers to combine employment and pauperism. They were thus able to be productive members of the society even though dependent on public aid as an income supplement. This is a good indication, by the way, that despite stereotypes to the contrary, paupers want to work (see Chapter 4). In general, this rule allowed employed paupers to live near or at the poverty line.[18]

Unfortunately, the $30 plus one-third rule disregard now terminates after 4 months, a policy that attempts to cut public assistance expenditures by drastically increasing the penalty (the marginal tax rate) for working. In effect, AFDC mothers are now unable, by law, to combine work with public aid in order to survive at the poverty line. Yet the administration justified termination of the $30 plus one-third benefit because "it is not reasonable to continue to substantially increase welfare families' income indefinitely once they are capable of meeting their own needs through employment."[19] This is social planning at its most illogical: Families that are able to be self-supporting by combining public aid and employment are cut off from assistance because they are self-supporting. As a result of this change, it is now the case in 12 states that AFDC families in which the head chooses to work will have less disposable income than if she decides to depend entirely on public aid. In another 18 states the effect of employment will be to increase total income by less than $25.[20] In such contexts, one of the most important questions facing a poor mother will be whether her wage income will cover the increased cost of medical care that she will have to pay our of pocket if she remains employed (low-wage workers do not have access to private health plans). Although recent evidence does not indicate that people have quit jobs to remain on public assistance, the fact is that the AFDC program is now organized in a way that gives poor persons an incentive not to work, an incentive to be totally rather than partially dependent.

The fifth fact to remember about AFDC is that benefit levels are abysmally low and vary widely from one state to another. For example, as seen in Table 3.4, the average monthly AFDC payment to nonworking families of three was $277 in 1982, a figure that is only 46% of the poverty line for a family of that size.[21] This is why poor people often try to combine work with assistance. The manner in which AFDC varies from state to state is also displayed in the table. As shown, Mississippi has the lowest benefits in the nation, $96 per month, while California has the highest, $506 per month.

It is well known, however, that public aid recipients receive disposable income from other programs in addition to AFDC, mainly food stamps but also energy assistance. The payment levels for AFDC make it clear why such additional assistance is necessary. Hence, Table 3.4 gives examples of the total disposable income available to nonworking families of three. The main source of variation in disposable income is AFDC, since the states set both standards of need and benefit levels (only the latter are shown in the table). While the food stamp program will be analyzed in detail subsequently, its impact on AFDC recipients can be seen in the table: It reduces the state to state variation in disposable income because the value of coupons received is a function of cash income (regardless of source). The energy assistance levels are typically higher in the North because heating is seen as costing more there.

The inequities displayed in Table 3.4 arise because federal law only requires that need levels be determined and applied equally statewide.[22] There is no requirement that benefits relate to the actual cost of food, rent, clothing, and other commodities, or that they be adjusted to changes in the prices. In 1969, the federal government did obligate the

TABLE 3.4: Monthly AFDC and Other Public Assistance Income for Non-working Families of Three in Selected States, FY 1982, Compared to Poverty Line, CY 1981

State	AFDC	Energy assistance	Food stamps	Total disposable income	Disposable income as a percentage of poverty line [a]
Mississippi[b]	$96	$8	$183	$287	48%
Alabama	$118	$6	$183	$307	51%
North Carolina	$192	$9	$167	$369	61%
Florida	$209	$6	$162	$377	62%
Indiana	$255	$16	$149	$419	69%
Illinois	$302	$13	$134	$449	74%
New Jersey	$360	$23	$117	$500	83%
Massachusetts	$379	$27	$111	$518	86%
New York	$424	$15	$98	$537	89%
California[c]	$506	$5	$73	$584	97%
Vermont	$477	$37	$82	$596	99%
Average monthly	$277	$18	$128	$450	74%
Average yearly	$3,324	$216	$1,536	$5,400	

[a] The poverty line for a family of three was $604.17 per month in calendar year 1981. Fiscal year 1982 began in October, 1981.

[b] Lowest AFDC payment in nation.

[c] Highest AFDC payment in nation.

states to raise payment levels in light of price changes that had occurred since need standards had been established, but this was a one-time occurrence. Nearly all the expansion in AFDC costs over the past decade has come from increases in the number of participants rather than changes in benefit levels. Put differently, the economic value, in terms of purchasing power, of AFDC has declined precipitously over the past few years, a period during which inflation has been very high. Thus, the Department of Health and Human Services has calculated that the value of AFDC benefits declined between 10% and 16%, on the average, between 1975 and 1979.[23] Among those who are not poor, inflation is a terrible burden because it forces a constriction in life-style; for many people, increases in income have not kept ahead of rising prices and this is a very frustrating experience. Among paupers, however, especially those receiving AFDC, inflation is a catastrophe, for they often must make terrible choices: between paying rent or utilities, between rent or food. What should be recalled in this context is that income maintenance programs for the nonpoor are indexed, which means that levels of assistance go up each year. AFDC payments do not.

In sum, the data in Table 3.4 clearly show that paupers are poor: They not only have no assets, they must use up all their disposable income in order to survive each month. Once this fact is recognized, it becomes very hard to visualize AFDC recipients — who are bereft of assets and skills — using public assistance to escape from poverty, even when AFDC is combined with food stamps, Medicaid, and other programs. As noted earlier, public assistance is a treadmill; those who step off of it are the lucky beneficiaries of changes in the economy or public policy.

The sixth fact to remember about AFDC is that its meager benefits are obtained by individuals who are on the borderline of American society: They are young children of young and unskilled parents who are usually on the rolls for fairly short periods of time. These facts have unexpected implications for the analysis of pauperism.

Despite the stereotypes many people have of public assistance families, most AFDC households have relatively few children in them: 40% have only one child, 27% have two, and 16% have three. There are only 2.2 children in the average AFDC family. Yet when asked, most nonpoor Americans believe that public assistance households are much larger.[24] Further, the children receiving aid are young: 35% are less than 6-years-old, while 34% are between ages 7 and 11. Thus, more than two-thirds of these young people clearly require either parental supervision or some sort of day care; that is, if they are to be cared for properly. These figures suggest that those who are serious about putting welfare mo-thers to work ought to consider funding day-care programs, such as Head Start. The Head Start program, however, enrolled less than 400,000 children in 1980 and has been cut back even more since that time. In addi-tion, federal funding for most other forms of day care also has been reduced drastically. There is a certain perverseness in the common indict-ment of public assistance mothers as lazy and unwilling to work, when many of them are performing important jobs: raising their children the best they can in a context in which few provisions for child care are available.

In addition, a large proportion of AFDC mothers are young; 8% are teenagers and 43% are between 20- and 29-years-old. What this means is that many AFDC households are headed by girls and young women who have not had much chance to develop skills and succeed occupationally before they must care for small children by themselves. These facts immediately suggest a partial but important solution to the "AFDC problem:" preventing unwanted pregnancy and births by making young people aware of the obligations that go along with having children, acquainting them with birth control alternatives, providing them with access to contraceptive devices, and funding abortions through Medi-caid.[25] It is ironic that many of those who express disdain and anger at AFDC mothers having children are also instrumental in both preventing family planning among the poor and limiting the level of public assistance. It is hypocritical to prevent poor people from controlling procreation for religious reasons while also preventing them from feeding, clothing, and otherwise caring for the children that result. I find little that is moral or religious in such attitudes. Although no one should be forced to prevent a birth, sound public policy dictates an investment in family planning.

As might be supposed from the preceding analysis, most AFDC mothers, about 42%, are needed at home and are not employed. However, about 14% have full- or part-time jobs, and another 11% say they are actively seeking work outside the home. Most of the remainder have become so discouraged that they have dropped out of the labor market altogether. However, what is surprising to many people is that 60% of all AFDC recipients are on the rolls for less than 3 years, while another 15% obtain aid for between 4 and 5 years.[26] The picture that emerges, then is that of young children of young parents who receive public assistance for relatively short periods in their lives. The implication of this fact is that poor people work most of the time and only resort to AFDC for short periods. This scenario is lent credence by studies of welfare dependency and the relationship between pauperism and work. This topic will be dealt with in some detail in the next chapter.

As noted in Chapter 1, some observers have argued that the war on poverty has been won, primarily because of the effect of "welfare." This summary of the AFDC program makes the ludicrousness of that claim clear. AFDC does not and cannot eliminate poverty; what it does do is alleviate a few of the consequences of being utterly without assets and money. This is why recipients live poorly. None of the changes introduced since 1980 have altered the basic problems with the program. In fact, in some cases they have been exacerbated. AFDC is antifamily in orientation, it is administratively inefficient, its benefits are distributed inequitably, and it contains work disincentives. The rationale underlying the current direction of this program is difficult to fathom, for it is hard to see how either costs will decline or how it can effectively serve as a "safety net" for the poor.

I want to turn now to the other major cash-assistance program, Supplementary Security Income (SSI).[27] Like AFDC, SSI is aimed at a specific population group: poverty-stricken aged, blind, and disabled persons. Thus, this mode of relief is directed toward those whom many consider "deserving" of public aid because their ability to help themselves is limited. The title of the program makes its purpose clear: to supplement the income of aged and handicapped people so they can have a minimum standard of living. Virtually no recipients of AFDC also get SSI, since each of these cash programs is aimed at different population groups. It is possible, however, for families to obtain aid from both programs; for example, a handicapped father may qualify for SSI while his children also receive AFDC. But this is very rare.

In 1981, an average of 3.7 million persons received SSI payments each month; of that amount, 1.5 million were aged, 2.1 million were disabled, and the remainder were blind.[28] As noted in Table 3.1, federal outlays for this program totalled $7.7 billion in 1982. Some states have chosen to supplement SSI payments with additional benefits, and a few states have been required to do so because of variations in payment levels prior to the implementation of SSI. In most cases, the federal government disburses state funds and covers the cost of administration.

Prior to 1974, the year SSI went into effect, aid was provided by each state with matching funds supplied by the federal government. In other words, public assistance for poor aged and handicapped persons used to be run in a way similar to AFDC today. As a result, there was enormous variation from one state to another in the definition of eligibility, the amount of assets people could have, payment levels, and many other characteristics. For example, in 1973, just prior to the imposition of SSI, monthly benefit levels for old-age assistance ranged from a high of $121 in Massachusetts to a low of $38 in New Hampshire. The new Supplementary Security Income program was designed to eliminate that chaotic situation. It is ironic that SSI was enacted in the same year, 1972, that Congress defeated Richard Nixon's Family Assistance Plan, a guaranteed annual income for all poor persons.

SSI is a federally run guaranteed annual income for aged, blind, and disabled poor people. Operated by the Social Security Administration, SSI imposes a set of uniform eligibility, asset, and income requirements; provides a nationwide minimum monthly income for most aged, blind, and disabled persons; results in financial assistance without stigma; and reduces administrative costs.

Under SSI, eligibility standards are uniform nationwide. Apart from the obvious requirement that recipients must be over 65, blind, or physically or psychologically disabled, such persons must also be destitute and stay that way. Thus, a single individual can have assets worth up to $1,500, while a couple can own things valued to $2,250. Unlike AFDC, homes do not count regardless of their value because the Social Security Administration found that the costs involved in trying to enforce a value provision were prohibitive. Actually, people who have homes of great value nearly always have other assets and, hence, are ineligible for SSI anyway. This is because SSI recipients cannot have personal effects worth more than $2,000. Those receiving SSI may own a car as long as it is worth less than $4,500. If, however, the auto has been modified to meet a medical problem or is necessary to get to work or to obtain medical care, then its value is disregarded. In general, then, SSI is like AFDC in that people must exhaust their assets in order to become eligible. SSI is unlike AFDC in that these requirements are applied nationwide. It is interesting to note that these limitations were established in 1974 and have not been changed. This means that, because of inflation, people have to be much poorer to qualify for SSI today than they had to be in 1974.

SSI provides a nationwide minimum monthly income that is the same for all recipients. The maximum SSI payment level for an individual with no other income was $265 per month in fiscal year 1982, or $3,130 a year. This figure was 74% of the poverty line for a single person. For a couple, the maximum payment was $357 per month, or $4,284 a year. This figure was 75% of the poverty line for two individuals. Although these assistance standards are very low, they reflect the decisive differences between AFDC and SSI. Supplementary Security Income is a uniform minimum income guarantee for poor aged and handicapped persons and, as such, there is no state-to-state variation in benefits.

Rather surprisingly, SSI has not been altered very much in recent years. The only changes have been the implementation of a variety of procedural changes designed to prevent overpayments to clients and produce more efficient operation of the program. It is estimated that the resulting savings will be about $60 million annually.[29]

As noted, SSI is designed as a supplement for other income. Here is how it works. The first $20 a month of income from any source (*e.g.*, either Social Security or wages) is disregarded. In addition, $65 per month earned income (wages) plus half the income over that amount are not counted. Food stamps and Medicaid or Medicare are disregarded. Two examples can illustrate what these requirements mean in terms of a household budget. The first example is for an aged or disabled person whose only income is from Social Security.

Monthly Social Security benefit	$200
Less $20 disregard	20
Countable Social Security benefit	$180
Basic SSI payment	$265
Less countable Social Security benefit	180
Monthly SSI payment	$85
Monthly Social Security benefit	$200
Plus monthly SSI payment	85
Total monthly cash income	$285

This monthly amount translates into a yearly income of $3,420, or

79% of the poverty line. In many cases, but not all, the combined effect of the income disregards, state supplements, and food stamps is to bring such individuals' disposable income up to the poverty line. In addition, SSI recipients are also eligible for Medicaid or Medicare, which are necessary if they are to obtain even minimal medical attention. Although this additional aid is obviously vital to the well-being of such households, health care does not add to people's disposable income.

The second example is for an aged couple, one of whom works part-time.

Husband's Social Security benefit	$200.00
Plus wife's Social Security benefit	100.00
Less $20 disregard	20.00
Countable Social Security benefit	$280.00
Wages from part-time job	$100.00
Less $65 disregard	65.00
Less ½ remainder ($35/2)	17.50
Countable wages	17.50
Countable Social Security benefit	$280.00
Plus countable wages	17.50
Countable SSI income	$297.50
Basic SSI payment	$357.00
Less countable SSI income	297.50
Monthly SSI payment	$ 59.50
Monthly SSI payment	$ 59.50
Husband's Social Security benefit	200.00
Wife's Social Security benefit	100.00
Wages from part-time job	100.00
Total monthly income	$459.50

This monthly figure translates into a yearly income of $5,514, just a few dollars above the poverty line. Although this couple would qualify for Medicare, it would not receive food stamps unless it had extraordinary expenses. As in the preceding example, households trying to survive at this level — that is, trying to pay rent or mortgage, utility bills, food, clothing, automobile upkeep, and all the other expenses that must be met — do not live gracefully. Rather, they lead a shabby disconsolate existence; they live poorly in the richest nation on earth. There are millions of people existing in such circumstances. Nonetheless, the income disregards function to allow recipients to be productive members of the society even though they receive public aid. In this way, SSI contrasts sharply with AFDC.

In general, most recipients feel that less stigma is associated with SSI than with previous programs to aid the poor aged and handicapped.[30] This is primarily because the Social Security Administration has tried to employ "a matter-of-fact, non-manipulative bureaucratic [approach] that simply certified eligibility and proceeded to make a regular payment." For example, many aged and handicapped people live with relatives. Rather than assuming the applicants receive an equal share of total household income or trying to assess the actual support they may (or may not) receive from those they live with, a procedure that would be expensive, time consuming, and very annoying, the Social Security Administration simply deducts one-third of the monthly payment. This more impersonal orientation has meant a lot less prying into the private lives of applicants and less appearance of subjectivity in the payment process. It has also increased efficiency and reduced the cost of administration. These characteristics make SSI unlike both AFDC and food stamps.

In sum, even for the "deserving poor," many of whom cannot work, the purpose of public assistance is not to eliminate poverty. Like AFDC, SSI alleviates some of the consequences of impoverishment, with the result that recipients live poorly. What distinguishes SSI, however, is the way the program is organized: It is administratively efficient; its benefits are equitably distributed; and it contains some work incentives (albeit inadequate ones). I would like to suggest that the Supplementary Security Income program is a good model of how public assistance should be organized.

Neither AFDC nor SSI exists in a public assistance vacuum. As just seen, the average AFDC payment to all families was $277 per month in 1982, while the maximum SSI payment was $265 for individuals and $357 for couples. What these figures mean is that most paupers cannot make ends meet with just their cash benefits, for their incomes are well below the poverty line. It should be emphasized once again that what is at issue here is not the cash-flow problems which middle-class people face perpetually, nor is it a relative restriction on life-style, also a fact of life for many middle-class persons; rather, AFDC and SSI recipients have great difficulty surviving on these budgets. The in-kind programs, Food Stamps and Medicaid, provide vitally important additional help to poor individuals and families. The following paragraphs will show, however, that in-kind public assistance does not eliminate poverty.

The Food Stamp Program aids many of the poor, mainly because AFDC and SSI recipients are automatically eligible. The program is designed to help low-income families obtain a more nutritious diet. Thus, in 1981 about 10% of the population received food coupons with an average value, over the entire year, of $498 per person. Thus, the total of food coupons and income is, on the average, well below the poverty line.[31] Without nutritional assistance, many of these individuals would be malnourished. Some would starve. What should be recognized, however, is that while most paupers receive food stamps, many nonwelfare poor people do not. There were 32-million poverty-stricken persons in the United States in 1981, which means that about one-third of those who are eligible for food stamps do not get them, usually because they are unaware they qualify or unable to assert their rights with the public assistance bureaucracy. This is one reason why starvation is still a reality for many individuals in the United States.[32]

The current Food Stamp Program began in the 1960s when it became clear there was hunger in America. As originally organized, the program suffered from many of the same problems that AFDC still does: unequal benefits across the nation along with gross variations in the way eligibility was determined. For example, the 1964 Food Stamp Act allowed each county to choose between dispensing surplus food or stamps. By distributing excess commodities, local governments aided farmers a great deal without helping the poor very much. This is because relief depended on the availability and perishability of food, which meant that nutritional requirements were not satisfied or were met for only brief periods. In some locales, poor people would eat well for a week after commodities were distributed and starve for 3 weeks after food ran out or spoiled. In principle, coupons allow families to spread their purchases and, hence, have a more stable and nutritious diet. However, it was not until 1974 that every country in America actually had a Food Stamp Program, and this occurred only because the federal government required it. Over the same period, Washington imposed national standards of eligibility and payments in place of disparate state and local regulations. As shown in Table 3.4, these changes had the effect of reducing some of the state-to-state variation in disposable income.

For individuals and families who do not receive either AFDC or SSI, eligibility for food stamps is determined by a combination of low assets and low income. Like the cash assistance programs, food stamp clients have to be destitute and stay that way in order to get relief. Applicants must have less than $1,500 in assets, not including their homes and personal effects. As with AFDC, the way income is calculated is crucial in determining eligibility, so recent changes in the program have focused on this factor in an effort at restricting the food stamp rolls.[33] First,no family with a gross income above 130% of the poverty line is eligible to receive coupons, even if it has extraordinary expenses. In addition, the deductions from income have been changed: The standard deduction is now $85; the deduction for work expenses is now 18%; and the maximum deduction for child care is now $115. Aged or disabled applicants are also allowed to deduct medical expenses over $35 that are not covered by insurance, Medicare, or Medicaid. Finally, there is now a family unit requirement; that is, "parents and children who live together shall be treated as a group of individuals who customarily purchase and prepare meals together for home consumption even if they do not do so, unless one of the parents is sixty years of age or older." This last rule will prevent many families from being eligible because it is often the case that parents sometimes let young adults who have children reside with them. The avowed purpose of these changes is to purge about 40,000 people from the rolls and avoid any significant budget increases for this program through fiscal year 1986.[34]

Although food stamps have increased the nutritional adequacy of poor people's diets because their effect is to increase families' disposable incomes, the results have not been as great as was hoped for at the time of the program's inception, primarily because indigent people are often poorly educated and, hence, not very wise shoppers.[35] The original expectations were probably too high, however, for the reality underlying the common indictment of recipients for misusing coupons is that they are nutritionally ignorant; like many of us, they often buy what tastes good rather than what is nutritious. Partly because the health of the population is a national concern, the federal government also operates several other nutrition programs in addition to food stamps. Two of them are briefly discussed here, primarily because recent changes have been so shortsighted.

The Supplementary Food Program for Women, Infants, and Children (WIC) provides about 1.5 million persons with an average of $24 per month in additional food coupons.[36] Thus, the program supplies limited but highly significant dietary supplements to people who are needy and especially likely to benefit, both immediately and in terms of preventing future health problems. A typical package includes coupons for such items as iron-fortified formula, milk, fruit, eggs, and cheese. Although this program cost less than $1 billion in 1981, it has been cut back. It should have been expanded; for not only does the program fail to reach thousands who need help, it is also cost effective. That is, there is considerable evidence that the money spent on food for pregnant women and infants in the first year of life prevents the development of long-term physical and mental health problems, which would cost a great deal more to deal with later.[37] Apparently, the federal government intends not to interfere with the suffering of such individuals.

The national school lunch program is an attempt at providing children with one-third of their recommended daily allowance of vitamins and minerals.[38] The federal government pays about one-half the cost, while state and local governments and children's payments make up the rest. Since the price of these lunches is subsidized, it represents in-kind income for everyone who eats at school, including children from middle-class families. In the past, about 38% of all lunches have been served free to children from poor households. However, this situation has changed.

The School Lunch Program was cut by 30% in 1982, mainly by changing eligibility rules under which children received meals and altering the subsidy paid to school districts. The rationale for this latter change is that middle-class children should not be getting reduced price lunches. While this may seem reasonable, at least ideologically, it is shortsighted fiscally because the viability of a school lunch program at the local level is usually dependent on the participation of a sufficient number of children from all social classes. When the price of lunches is raised, as it must be when the federal subsidy is lowered, then middle-class children tend to stop purchasing them. But the fixed costs of running a program are such that it is difficult to operate if lunches are only served to poor children. As a result, nearly 1,000 schools dropped out of the lunch program between 1981 and 1982. Similar cost reductions have affected the other food programs for children: the School Breakfast Program, the Special Milk Program, the Child-Care Food Program, and the Summer Food Assistance Program. Thus, Americans are faced with the spectacle of increasing malnutrition among the children of poor people so that the federal budget deficit will be less and rich persons can get tax deductions. One has to wonder about the priorities of an administration that would limit dietary supplements for children that are cost effective over the long run.[39]

One basis for the conservative argument that "welfare" eliminates impoverishment is the presumed "antipoverty" effect of food stamps. While the logical and methodological problems inherent in this argument were shown in Chapter 2, the data presented in this chapter (e.g., Table 3.4) and the requirements of the programs show clearly that cash benefits along with food stamps and other nutritional aids cannot eliminate poverty. People who receive some combination of cash and coupons do not become economically independent as a result. Nonetheless, the importance of food assistance cannot be overstated, for it helps to alleviate some of the consequences of poverty. There is considerably less hunger in America now than there was just a few years ago, primarily because of the implementation and expansion of food and nutrition programs. Yet the really sad fact is that hunger and malnutrition remain a specter for millions of people.[40] Thus, the shortsightedness of current policies regarding food stamps and other nutrition programs is not only economic, although the cuts in these programs now will increase costs in later years, but also social and human; the quality of life for all American citizens will decline because we have made human sacrifices out of people who have little political power.

The final public assistance program to be analyzed in detail is Medicaid, which is the primary source of health-care coverage for the poor in America. Passed in 1965, Medicaid is designed to assist the states in providing medical care to people who are also eligible for the cash assistance programs. The phrasing used here suggests Medicaid's similarity to AFDC: There are enormous variations from one state to another in both coverage and services, and recipients must be destitute in order to receive help. The major difference between AFDC and Medicaid, of course, is that the latter is an in-kind public assistance program, and this is the topic I wish to focus on initially.

The first and most important fact to remember about Medicaid is that, like AFDC, the federal government does not control the cost of the program. Medicaid is financed jointly by federal and state governments; Washington pays between one-half and three-fourths of the cost in each state, depending on the state's *per capita* income. As seen in Table 3.1, federal payments to health vendors under the Medicaid program totalled nearly $17 billion in fiscal 1981. These expenditures for hospitals, doctors, nursing facilities, laboratories, pharmacists, and others are not well regulated and vary considerably from state to state. For physicians, some variant of "usual, customary, and reasonable charges" is the phrase used to describe rates of reimbursement. In some states there is an explicit fee schedule for specific services. In general, the rate structure protects the income and profits of those in the medical industry. This is partly because of its political influence on reimbursement schedules and partly because those performing medical tasks also decide which services need to be offered (for example, what surgical procedures, how many laboratory tests, and what prescriptions are necessary). Thus, the cost of this program is not determined by either the recipients or the federal government, but by the medical practitioners—the same people who stand to profit. This arrangement is why the Medicaid program is so susceptible to waste, abuse, and fraud; for there is a tendency to perform unnecessary tasks, charge a little extra, and even to arrange kickbacks.

What should be emphasized in this context, however, is that most medical people have the interests of their patients at heart and are scrupulously honest in their dealings with the government. Nonetheless, the fact remains that the most serious forms of public assistance fraud are not committed by recipients but by white collar people, among them those in the medical industry. I will come back to this topic in the concluding section of this chapter.

The second fact to remember about Medicaid is that with some qualification, it has been a relatively successful program.[41] That is, along with the Food Stamps Program, nutrition programs of other sorts, Medicare, and additional measures undertaken to protect the health of the population, class-related differences in morbidity and mortality (disease and death) have declined significantly over the past 15 years. Similarly, the poor suffer less today from chronic conditions and have better access to hospital, physician, and dental care than they did prior to the implementation of Medicaid. It should be recognized, however, what these improvements do not mean: In nearly all cases, both the health of the poor and the care available to them are still much inferior to that which is characteristic of the rest of the population. Thus, underlying the success of Medicaid is a scandalous situation, especially when the United States is compared to other industrialized nations. I shall return to this topic in Chapter 5, when discussing the correlates of poverty.

The third fact to be remembered about Medicaid is that, like AFDC, there is incredible variation in both coverage and services.[42] Just being poor neither qualifies a family for health care nor guarantees what medical services are covered. This is why I referred to the scandal of health and health care in the preceding paragraph. It is a perverse fact of American life that medical treatment for poor people is dependent on where they live and their marital status.

Medicaid coverage varies sharply from one state to another. For example, the Medicaid program is optional to the states, and Arizona has never enrolled in it. Thus, poor people who happen to live in Arizona have no health insurance and obtain inferior (or no) care as a result. Further, while recipients of AFDC and SSI are covered in the other 49 states, many poverty-stricken individuals are still without basic health insurance. For this reason, the federal government allows the states to include people from intact families who are "medically needy" but not necessarily poor by any other measure. Only 29 states have chosen to do so. Similarly, the government lets states include the children of unemployed fathers, but only 27 states offer such coverage. Finally, the states also have the option of extending coverage to intact households that would be eligible for AFDC on a financial basis if the husband and wife had not chosen to stay together, but only 17 states extend this coverage. Overall, about 4% of the total population, or only about one-third of the poor were covered by Medicaid in 1980.[43] "Covered" in this context means that individuals were enrolled in the program, not that they received services.

Just as different groups are provided with health care in different states, so are various services offered in various states. The basic Medicaid program requires that the following services be offered: in-patient hospital treatment, outpatient hospital treatment, laboratory and X-ray services, physicians services, skilled nursing facilities, home health-care treatment, family planning services, and "early and periodic screening and diagnosis and treatment of children under twenty-one."

However, these features of Medicaid do not exhaust health problems. Here are just three examples of services that are sometimes offered and sometimes not. They are culled from a panoply of choices that the states have. Alaska and Wyoming do not include prescription drugs in their Medicaid programs. Thus, although poor people can be cared for when they are ill, in these states (plus Arizona) they cannot get antibiotics or other necessary drugs, at least under Medicaid. Similarly, even though cavities and other dental problems are clearly associated with illness, only 31 states provide dental services. Finally, despite the fact that not being able to see properly is a medical problem, only 32 states cover the cost of eyeglasses in their Medicaid program. Thus, poor children who cannot see the blackboard or read their textbooks because of eye problems are condemned in 18 states to fall further and further behind in school. This is because many poor families are forced to choose between purchasing food or medical care. Such households are not living adequately despite the in-kind value of Medicaid insurance.

The fourth fact to remember about Medicaid is that people must be destitute and stay that way in order to get it. This follows from the requirement that recipients of AFDC and SSI are automatically covered by Medicaid. It should be recalled, here, that nearly all AFDC recipients are from broken families; there is no federal law mandating medical care for poor intact households. Furthermore, to get health insurance, a family must meet the asset and income limits previously described for the two cash assistance programs. The median income of Medicaid households was $6,760 in 1981; 66% of them had incomes of less than $7,500. These are not families with a lot of spare cash around to use for medical expenses: Paupers who receive Medicaid are still poor, despite the illusion preferred by those researchers cited in Chapter 2.

As noted in Chapter 2, conservative analysts assert that when the "value" of Medicaid is added to the cash incomes of impoverished people, then significantly fewer of them are "really" poor. The ludicrousness of that claim should now be apparent. The Medicaid program is designed to provide income for medical personnel and care for poor people, and it has been reasonably successful at both tasks. What should be clear, however, is that the recipients of care do not become economically independent as a result. Rather, paupers who receive Medicaid benefits remain poor. Those who assert otherwise are dealing in illusion instead of reality.

SOME PROBLEMS WITH PUBLIC ASSISTANCE

In this chapter, I have shown that public assistance cannot eliminate poverty because it is not designed to do so and that public assistance does not cost very much in comparison with both the total federal budget and the economic benefits distributed to the nonpoor. Thus, the preceding analysis has been, in effect, a defense of the public assistance system, an orientation that is only possible under special circumstances. This is because public assistance is bedeviled with problems: It operates inefficiently; benefits are distributed inequitably and are often inadequate; there are work disincentives built into the programs; and there is pervasive fraud. The last argument I am going to make is that all these problems have become worse rather than better in the past few years.

The public assistance programs reviewed here are incredibly inefficient, primarily because administrative procedures are so complex, each state works autonomously, and financing is divided between the states and the federal government. The complexity of the public assistance sytem is nearly overwhelming, especially for the poor but also for academic observers and welfare bureaucrats. Readers should note that the foregoing descriptions were greatly simplified in order to present each program in a reasonably straightforward manner. Although some of the complexity inherent to public assistance cannot be eliminated because eligibility for these programs is based on need, which must be verified, the panoply of different programs with different requirements means that there is an elaborate process of filling our similar forms and churning over similar numbers, much of which is duplicatory and inefficient. All of this effort, which, it should be remembered, is designed to distribute relatively small amounts of money, results in a sort of administrative Alice-in-Wonderland world that no one is satisfied with and which wastes a great deal of money. Thus, the Inspector General of the United States has estimated (conservatively) that $5–6 billion a year is lost to inefficiency in public assistance programs.[44] About 40% of this amount is attributable to waste in the nation's health-care industry and involves the Medicaid and Medicare programs. In general, the states do not have the staff or the resources to run public assistance programs efficiently. In addition, billions of dollars more are lost simply due to the duplication inherent in having 50 autonomous state public assistance departments. In such circumstances, there is no hope for efficient use of public aid allocations.

With the exception of some minor changes in SSI, it is hard to find a recent initiative, either proposed or passed, that would increase the efficiency of public assistance. Rather, the general characteristic of the conservative proposals has been to make these programs more inefficient by adding new layers of decision-making criteria and by placing more responsibility on the states. Without regard to ideology, 50 programs must be more inefficient than one. In addition, it should be noted that most of the savings obtained because of program cutbacks can only be temporary. For example, the reductions in the Food Stamp Program and other nutrition programs will lead inevitably to increasing costs for health care in the future.

The public assistance system has always been inequitable because receipt of aid has depended on marital status and place of residence. Just being poor does not make one eligible for aid. Simply being malnourished does not make one eligible for aid. Only requiring health care does not make one eligible for aid. It is scandalous that an intact family cannot receive AFDC in most states. It is scandalous that in most states receipt of Medicaid is dependent on eligibility for AFDC. It is scandalous that different health problems are covered in some states but not in others. It is scandalous that many people still do not get enough to eat in America. Yet there is not one instance in which the Reagan administration proposed changing public assistance programs in order to make them less inequitable. Rather, in the name of an outmoded ideology, it chose to make the inequities worse. It is hard to see how this orientation is a step forward.

In addition, public assistance is also inequitable because, as shown in Table 3.4, there is considerable variation in benefit levels from one state to another. While aid allows poor people to live near the poverty line in some locations, it leaves them far below that threshold in others. Furthermore, public assistance has always been lowest in places where it is most needed: the poorest states and localities, and in those areas suffering from the most severe economic dislocation. This problem has been made worse, not better, in the past few years. For example, one study shows that the impact of the federal government's budget cuts will be greatest in those states which are least capable of absorbing them: 34% of the reductions will directly affect the 10 states with the slowest rates of economic growth in the 1970s.[45] Thus, it remains the case that the level of public aid paupers receive is dependent on where they happen to live.

Most Americans are concerned lest public assistance have built in work disincentives, for, as will be emphasized in the next chapter, work is a fundamental value in this society. Thus, one reason Congress enacted the income disregards already described was to alleviate this concern. And they have been very effective; many poor families have been able to live at or near the poverty line by combining low-wage work with public assistance. The SSI example is illustrative of such a possibility. This solution, however, was only partial, since it did not apply to some programs (for example, Medicaid). Thus, in the 17 states where poor intact families are eligible for Medicaid, such households have an incentive not to work, since to earn too much money would make them ineligible and force them to pay for health care out of pocket.

From this angle, then, one way to further alleviate the problem of work disincentives might be to establish a sliding scale of Medicaid payments based on ability to pay: The poorest people would pay nothing while fees would be established and increase as income rose. The Reagan administration, however, chose a different tactic: It has eliminated as many employed persons as possible from the public assistance rolls on the grounds that they are not "truly needy." Even though a simple calculation of family budgets at this income level would show that assertion to be puerile, and even though the participation of low-wage workers in the labor force is sound public policy, both practically and in terms of American values, the income disregards have been revoked. Excluding the possibility of civil disorder, the result of this perverse change will be an increase in pauperism and, most likely, a higher incidence of recipient fraud. As an aside, many people have wondered why the poor have not rebelled in the wake of the cutbacks in public assistance. I will explain why in Chapter 5.

Given the cost of public assistance, concern about fraud must be taken seriously. And it is natural that attention is directed mainly at recipients, because many nonpoor people view them in highly pejorative terms: as lazy, shiftless, unwilling to work, and as cheats. Yet there are at least two other sources of fraud built into the public aid system: third-party providers and public assistance employees. Third-party providers actually give service to the poor on behalf of the government, for which they are reimbursed directly.

Once it is recognized that recipients are nearly always individuals with low levels of education, it becomes clear that they are rarely capable of committing fraud on a large scale. For example, many potential beneficiaries need help in filling out the application forms properly. In addition, in the cash programs especially, it is usually very difficult to distinguish between fraud and error, since underpayments to recipients can (and do) occur as well as overpayments. In any year, less than 1% of all AFDC cases will involve suspected fraud and a much smaller proportion will be proven guilty.[46] Thus, the reasonable conclusion is that public assistance beneficiaries are not any more dishonest than the rest of the population and, because they are less skilled, they are also less able to cheat and get away with it. And even when they do, the amount of money involved is very low, as the payment levels specified in the preceding pages make clear.

In reality, fraud committed by third parties and employees is a much more serious problem for the public assistance system, since the amounts involved are often very high.[47] In contrast to paupers, these are highly educated people who not only have considerable opportunity but also have the skills with which to commit crime on a large scale. They can create "ghost" recipients and bill the government for services, charge for an excessive number of services, withhold services that are billed to the government, over-charge for services rendered, accept kickbacks, embezzle food coupons, generate false payments with the computer, and many other tricks. Now it should be made clear that most doctors and others in the health-care industry, most grocers and others providing nutritional aid, and most employees of public assistance departments are scrupulously honest. Nonetheless, the most serious forms of public aid fraud are white collar crimes committed by middle- and upper-class people. And such individuals receive thousands of dollars. For example, it has been estimated that $1 billion a year flows through what are called "Medicaid mills," organizations set up exclusively to handle Medicaid and Medicare patients, many of which provide substandard care in addition to bilking the government.

This is large-scale crime. The perpetrators often have high status and are seen as pillars of the community. As a result, juries generally do not perceive them as normal criminals and convictions are difficult to obtain. In general, combating public assistance fraud is a state responsibility. Yet the "states have complained to HEW of inadequate staff to detect and prosecute welfare fraud and of the relatively low priority assigned welfare cases by some prosecutors, sometimes because of budgetary problems."[48] For this reason, the House Committee on Government Operations recommended in 1979 that the federal role in this area should be expanded. Conservatives, however, have shown no interest in this idea.

It is unfortunate that America has stepped backward in time. Rather than more equality there is now less. And current public assistance policies will affect the working poor most of all. In the next chapter, I shall examine the relationship between work and public aid in more detail.

4

POVERTY, PUBLIC ASSISTANCE, AND WORK

This chapter answers a simple question: Do the poor want to work? This query is very controversial and not easily resolved, primarily because it is so tied to American cultural values, especially the work ethic, that it is difficult for many people to accept the facts. Rather, wedded to a value system that extols individual striving for economic success and individual responsibility for failure, people who are not poor (and this includes social scientists) often generalize from their own experiences in inappropriate and unrealistic ways. Thus, they frequently assume that impoverished persons have the same options and the same ability to solve problems — if they would just try hard enough. As will become clear, the problem with such a value orientation is not that it is good or bad in some evaluative sense, but rather that it is an inaccurate guide to reality because it embodies a dubious theory of personality and a naive view of the class structure. The ideological function of such attitudes, however, is to condemn the poor for being indigent while justifying one's own station in life.

I am going to begin this chapter with some examples of the importance of the work ethic and then examine the attitudes of poor people toward work, the extent of their employment, the relationship between work and public assistance, and the results of the work incentive program and the negative income tax experiments. In so doing, I shall suggest how the value placed on work can distort interpretation of the facts.

It will be recalled from Chapter 1 that conservatives assert that America's victory in the war against poverty has had a costly side effect: "the almost complete destruction of work incentives for the poor on welfare." In one form or another, the old canard that the poor do not want to work is an article of faith for many people. For example, in response to survey questions, four out of five Americans have agreed with the statement that "there are too many people receiving welfare money who should be working," while half of the population has accepted the assertion that "most people on welfare who can work do not try to find jobs so they can support themselves." These are typical results.[1]

Underlying such attitudes is a fundamental belief, most recently expressed by George Gilder, although it is hardly original with him: "The only dependable route from poverty is always hard work, family, and faith."[2] This confession of piety expresses a basic value that has characterized our nation since Puritan times. In its secular form, Robert K. Merton has summarized the dimensions of the work ethic in terms of three cultural axioms.[3] First, all individuals should strive for the same lofty goals, especially economic success. Second, a person's present failure is "but a way station to ultimate success," so one should keep on striving no matter what the odds against succeeding. And third, "genuine failure consists only in the lessening or withdrawal of ambition." In short, then, in American society people are enjoined to work.

The implications of the work ethic should be explicitly noted. Not only does it provide a straightforward explanation for impoverishment, one that places the blame for their life-style squarely on the poor themselves, it also allows middle-class people to see their own life-styles as a result of their hard work and an indicator of their good character. Phrased in this way, the ideological function of such beliefs is obvious: Those who have benefited from social arrangements are able to justify their social status and those who have been victimized by social processes are blamed for their oppression. The notion that the poor may be victims or that they may be exploited by the rest of society does not fit with American values and most people do not want to recognize such facts.

Thus, the survey results already cited are not only a popular manifestation of a dominant value system, they are also attempts at self-justification. It is extremely difficult for people to accept the notion that a great deal of luck underlies their achievements. The very word, achievement, especially when used in conjunction with one's occupation or class position, implies that neither luck of birth (sex, race, region) nor luck of circumstance (parents' socioeconomic status, schools attended, neighborhood residence) is very important. Rather, all that is necessary is for a person with ability to work hard. And this article of faith is seen as an accurate representation of reality despite the fact that everyone knows (including social scientists) that family background is one of the most important variables influencing occupational status attainment.[4] People do not always recognize such inconsistencies, either among their various attitudes or between their attitudes and realities.

The self-justifying nature of these values is often hidden by the sight of poor people, many of whom appear to be able-bodied, loitering in the streets and apparently refusing to work. We have all either seen this sort of thing or heard stories of it. And individuals who are active, who are working, who are (more or less) successful, find it extremely disquieting to observe such "freedom," such "leisure," such "laziness," especially when they believe that people "like that" are being taken care of by the public assistance system. These are the descriptive terms that are used, both popularly and, somewhat surprisingly, in the social science literature. This terminology immediately indicates the value judgments being made. Yet such judgments are completely inaccurate, as the following pages will show.

THE ATTITUDES OF THE POOR TOWARD WORK

Studies of the attitudes of impoverished people toward work are now abundant, and the findings all point in the same direction: There are no differences between the poor and nonpoor in the desire to work, the desire to get ahead, the desire to be occupationally successful, or any other measure — direct or indirect — of work values. The best recent quantitative study is by Leonard Goodwin, whose analysis will be briefly summarized here.[5]

Goodwin compared the attitudes of long- and short-term public aid recipients, black and white suburban mothers and fathers, black teenagers, and trainees and staff members in the work incentive (WIN) program, in terms of two variables: *adherence to the work ethic* and *confidence in ability to succeed in the work world*. The variable, work ethic, was an index compiled from the responses to such assertions as "If I don't have a regular job, I don't feel right," or, "A man can't really think well of himself unless he has a job," and the like. Similarly, the variable, lack of confidence in ability to succeed in the work world, was an index compiled from responses to such assertions as "In order to get ahead in a job you need to have some lucky breaks." The practice of measuring a variable by means of response to a series of specific indicators is a well established methodological technique.

The findings are clear: There are no differences in adherence to the work ethic between the poor and the nonpoor people who participated in this study. For example, suburban parents and paupers have essentially the same scores on the measure of work ethic. Further, there are no differences in adherence to the work ethic between long- and short-term public aid recipients. What distinguishes the poor and the nonpoor, what differentiates those who have failed and those who have somewhat higher status, is their level of self-confidence rather than acceptance of the work ethic. Among the poor there is a consistent inverse relationship between adherence to the work ethic and confidence in ability to succeed in the work world. Phrased as a statement of covariance, Goodwin's finding can be summarized as follows: the lower the social class and the higher the work ethic, *then* the lower the confidence in ability to succeed. Thus, poor people want to work; the significance of impoverishment lies in its effect on confidence rather than salience of the work ethic.

As the literature cited in note 5 indicates, Goodwin's findings are not unique. They are, however, based on quantitative analyses of work orientations and it should be recognized that such studies are always prone to the "garbage in, garbage out" syndrome; that is, it makes a great deal of difference how the data are manipulated in the process of machine analysis. Hence, it is worth noting that the findings in the quantitative literature are replicated in ethnographic studies of poor whites and blacks conducted by urban anthropologists.[6]

They describe people, especially men, whose most desperate yearning is for a secure job that pays a livable wage and allows for a stable family life. They portray people who work at the only jobs available, when they are available: low wage, low skill, short term, boring, and dead-end jobs. In reality, Elliot Liebow says, these human beings live in an endless sea of want from which there is often no hope for escape: "The busboy or dishwasher who works hard becomes, simply, a hard-working busboy or dishwasher." Furthermore, he shows that such individuals are surrounded by failure, both their own and others', and that they come to each new job flat and stale, weary, convinced of their own incompetence, and terrified of responsibility (since the pain of being tested and failing again is overwhelming). For many poor people, the work ethic is truly an affliction; they keep trying, but they often do so in ways that guarantee failure. The salience of the work ethic is why poor persons who are lucky enough to have stable jobs, even if they are low paying, often remain in them rather than take a chance on failure elsewhere. For they enjoy status in the community based on their employment. In general, it is shortsighted to underestimate the importance of prestige in American society, perhaps especially among the poor. In a perverse sense, the salience of the work ethic is also why some impoverished people react in nonadaptive ways to continued failure and are sometimes unable to take advantage of opportunity. I will return to this topic in Chapter 6.

Although it is easy to suggest that ethnographers are just bleeding hearts, the best studies in this research tradition are useful because their authors succeed in "taking the role of the other" and thereby depicting the world view and experience of people who are much different from themselves. Such studies require enormous sensitivity and talent. When their portrayals are used in conjunction with quantitative analyses, as in this case, they are very persuasive.

These quantitative and ethnographic findings directly challenge the beliefs of the nonpoor presented at the beginning of the chapter, for the empirical literature plainly shows that the poor want to work, that they share dominant values. However, these data are often disregarded by conservatives (some of whom are social scientists and should know better) because, as noted, their world view provides a simple means of explaining away such findings. What apparently happens is that people for whom hard work has led to occupational success extrapolate their personal experiences to others. Thus, they think that if individuals want to work then they can sacrifice, find a job, and eventually achieve success. The average professional, managerial, and sales worker has had just this kind of experience: sacrifice while obtaining training, finding a job as a result, and ultimately achieving some degree of success and security.

It should be recognized, however, that such experiences are class related; other things being equal, persons from middle-class backgrounds have more options and these options are often more effective problem-solving strategies. This means that their experiences are more likely to teach them that hard work will produce success and this is why middle-class people usually have a more positive self-concept than do lower class persons.[7] What happens when middle-class individuals generalize from such experiences is that the complexity of human motivation is reduced to mere desire: One can achieve whatever one wants to achieve. This very simplistic and dubious theory of personality underlies the harsh judgments such people make. It is useful in this context to recall from Chapter 1 the pejorative question posed by many conservatives. "Why should someone work," it is asked, "40 hours a week, 50 weeks a year, for, say, $8,000 when it would be possible not to work at all for, say $6,000?" Orthodox economists, of course, answer this question by asserting that people's choices reflect their values. From this point of view, it makes sense to assert that if indigent people really wanted to work they would obtain jobs, they would try to get ahead. And because it appears to many observers that poor persons do not want to be employed, it also makes sense to conclude that they prefer the dole to making their own way, they are somehow contented in their poverty. One result of this line of reasoning is that the data reviewed here are simply disregarded.

However, when these data are taken seriously, they suggest that impoverished persons are like the members of other social classes in that they have internalized the desire to work, not just for the money but because each individual's sense of self is, in part, justified and made whole through productive labor. This is what the work ethic means. But unlike the members of other social classes, the poor have learned that their chances of success in this world are not very great, and they lack self-confidence as a result. As will be seen later in this chapter, most continue to try. Others give up; their objective situation combines with their uncertainty to become a self-fulfilling prophecy. Despite facile notions of unemployment as leisure time, the human suffering involved here is very great, for people have to come to grips with their feelings of inadequacy and with the fact that they are not wanted by the society. This is one reason why, like the rest of the population, poor people blame themselves for their situation in life; they think they are responsible for their own failure. Partly as a result, they do not protest very often or rebel against the system into which they are locked. Rather, they develop behavioral and psychological characteristics that serve as a means of coping with stress rather than solving problems. I shall return to this topic in Chapter 6.

EMPLOYMENT AND POVERTY

Another way of assessing whether the poor want to work is to look at employment data. Table 4.1 depicts the work experience of poverty-stricken families headed by men and women in 1981.[8] As can be seen in the table, half of all poor household heads were employed at least part of the year. The figures vary dramatically by sex, however, since 60% of all poor male householders were employed for some portion of the year, compared to only about 40% of all female heads of household. These differences make sense in light of the fact that many women householders have small children who need to be watched over. Thus, the AFDC program allows impoverished mothers to care for their children. It should be recognized, however, that that data reviewed in Chapter 3 showed clearly that most AFDC children are on the rolls for relatively short periods, mainly while their mothers are young. So there is considerable turnover in the figures reported in Table 4.1.

TABLE 4.1: Work Experience of Householders Living Below the Poverty Line, 1981, by Sex

	All families		Female Householder, No Husband Present		Two Adult Families	
	Millions	%	Millions	%	Millions	%
Did not work	3.4	49	2.0	61	1.4	39
Worked 50-52 weeks	1.5	22	.4	12	1.1	30
Worked part of year	2.0	29	.9	27	1.1	31
	6.9	100%	3.3	100%	3.6	100%

As indicated, the data in the table are for heads of households in poverty-stricken families. Unfortunately, the Census Bureau does not report why these particular people were unemployed. What it does record is why all poor persons 15 years of age and over did not work at all in 1981.[9] In this group, 25% said they were disabled, 15% indicated they were retired, and 33% declared they were keeping house. These figures add up to 73% of those impoverished individuals who were not employed in 1981. In general, even allowing for some exaggeration, most people who did not work could not work, regardless of the availability of jobs. Another 25% of those poor persons who were not employed reported that they either could not find jobs or were attending school. These individuals plainly could have been employed if work had been available.

Unfortunately, there are typically few jobs for impoverished people. This is so even though many well-meaning observers see pages of "help-wanted" advertisements in newspapers and conclude that there is plenty of work available, plenty of opportunity out there waiting. It is true that there are jobs, but not for individuals without education or skills. For when the help-wanted section is systematically examined, it becomes clear that few advertisements—less than 20%, often much less—offer work for unskilled people.[10] And it is frequently the case that the jobs that are accessible to the poor require individuals who are both healthy and physically robust. For example, the average person who is used to working indoors, say, as a dishwasher or as an accountant, usually cannot do the tasks required on construction jobs; not only are complex skills required but the work is extremely strenuous. Furthermore, the number of jobs advertised bears no relationship to the number of people who are officially unemployed, without even counting those who are underemployed, or discouraged.

For example, in one study of a small town, the ratio of unskilled jobs advertised in the newspaper to the official unemployment rate was 1:185. Similarly, in an analysis of the Washington, D.C. area, the ratio of unskilled jobs in the help-wanted section to the adult public assistance population was 1:310. These ratios, of course, grossly understate the number of potential job applicants, since they do not take discouraged and underemployed people into account. The differences between the quantity of potential job seekers and the number of actual jobs is why openings for work are filled extremely fast, within two days, and why employers are inevitably left with stacks of applications and requests to be trained. The press of people looking for work is so great, in fact, that many firms do not even bother to advertise. They simply let their employees know that jobs are opening up and applicants learn of this fact through word of mouth. There is evidence that many jobs are filled in this way.[11]

The data on employment rates as well as the reaction of poor people to job advertisements or to news that work is available show clearly that indigent persons who are able are also active members of the labor force. In other words, the poor not only want to work, they do work. Yet many people disregard these findings, mainly because they have a view of the class structure which is sociologically naive. That is, it is often asserted that American society has an open-class system of stratification in which there is plenty of opportunity. Given such a world view, it makes sense to assert that there are plenty of jobs, that the chance to get ahead is there, and that those who are not successful have no one to blame but themselves. This is not, however, the experience poor people have. In general, no matter how hard they work, indigent people do not get ahead. While the job advertisement data previously cited give a clear view of the limitations with which impoverished persons must deal, the more general analysis of the reproduction of the class system and the organization of the economy in Chapter 7 will show that Horatio Alger is a myth, fostered by the nonpoor for their own benefit. The myth persists, in part, because it is congruent with a view of the class system that is wishful and, in part, because visions of able-bodied men who seem to prefer standing on street corners are hard to erase from one's mind.

PUBLIC ASSISTANCE AND WORK

It is easy to indict the public assistance system for discouraging work, partly because such an accusation fits the stereotypes people have and partly because there is some truth to the charge. The cumbersome nature of the public aid system, with its complex rules, their arbitrary enforcement, and frequent changes, has always had an inhibiting effect on work activity. Nonetheless, it can be argued persuasively that, until very recently, pauperism has encouraged employment among the poor.

First, benefits are so low and the conditions under which they are obtained are so demeaning that most people struggle mightily to avoid publicly acknowledging their dependence and strive to become independent as soon as possible. Benefits are kept low because one of the most important functions of public assistance has always been to buttress the wage system.[12] It is important to ignore the rhetoric of both conservatives and liberals in considering this issue, for no one has ever seriously argued that "welfare" (despite the connotations of the word) can or should substitute for work. Just a glance at the poverty-line budget constructed in Chapter 2 and the benefit levels outlined in Chapter 3 shows clearly that the "choice" of pauperism nearly always reflects desperation or acceptance of failure (with all that state of mind implies) or both, for the "choice" requires a public declaration of destitution. In short, the assistance component of public assistance is really secondary to the interest of the general public, and this interest is perceived to be in keeping the poor employed at low wages. This is why benefits are so minuscule and why they will continue to be so small, under both Democratic and Republican aegis.

Second, the income disregards enacted during the 1960s and 1970s were designed, in part, to avoid the problem of high marginal tax rates that accompany public assistance benefits and thereby seem to encourage a choice of pauperism over employment. The result, as seen in Chapters 2 and 3, has been an increase in public aid costs over the past 20 years due to the fact that poor people have taken full advantage of the opportunity to combine work and public assistance. This is *prima facie* evidence, of course, that impoverished persons, even paupers want to be employed. Although they are very shortsighted, the recent changes in public assistance policy have restricted the opportunity of paupers to receive benefits and be employed at the same time. One indicator of the salience of the work ethic is the fact that there is no evidence that employed persons have given up jobs in order to obtain aid. However, it can be safely predicted that recipients will continue to try to combine work and public assistance, even if it means committing fraud. It may seem perverse, but evidence of illicit economic activity among paupers is not only a good indicator of the pervasiveness of the work ethic, it also suggests a solution to the problem of recipient fraud: more jobs coupled with changes in public assistance rules such that low-wage workers can legally combine employment and aid. Understanding poverty and pauperism depends a lot on one's angle of vision.

The most direct way of assessing the relationship between public assistance and work is to look at patterns of recipiency over time. For in this way it is possible to assess whether relief creates a permanently dependent population. Although these worries are occasionally expressed too stridently and even irrationally, as seen in Chapter 1, they are nonetheless pervasive and reasonable, simply because dependence is so anathema to American values.

As with other problems, the best way to deal with this one is to ask the right questions. In this case, there are two inquiries of importance. (a) How long do most people receive public assistance? (b) How dependent are they? The second query refers to the mix of wage income and public aid benefits; some persons need public assistance as a supplement to income while others use it as a substitute. In dealing with these two questions, it is useful to divide paupers into four groups. Surprisingly, the simple act of specifying the objects of concern provides some answers to the two questions and thereby aids in addressing the main issue dealt with in this section.

The first group is comprised of those individuals and families who use AFDC and other forms of assistance as an income supplement for short periods. The second group is made up of people who use relief as an income substitute for short periods. By definition, then, families in these first two groups are composed of low-wage workers who are suffering from a temporary drop in income, whether due to loss of job, family breakup, or some other catastrophe. Furthermore, also by definition, these families recover fairly swiftly, say, in a year or so, and leave the public assistance system. Finally, and this is implied in the identification of these two groups, such households may periodically return to pauperism, mainly because their skills and social circumstances make them especially vulnerable to economic fluctuations and changes in public policy. The important point to remember, however, is that over the long run wages constitute the most significant component of the total income package obtained by families in categories one and two.

The third group of individuals and families is comprised of those who use the public assistance system as an income supplement for long periods of time, for several years. By definition, then, these households are headed by workers who are steadily employed but whose wages are so low that they need help in order to meet all their expenses. So despite the fact that they are dependent on aid for subsistence, wages also constitute a vital element in the total income package of families in category three. It should be recalled, here, that the recent changes in public assistance have eliminated many people in this category from the rolls.

Now the fact is that most paupers, between 75% and 90%, are in these three groups, primarily because their incomes fluctuate widely over time. Studies of "welfare dependency" indisputably verify this assertion.[13] Most people would agree that this pattern of pubic assistance utilization is proper; to use Ronald Reagan's phrase, until recently, relief has functioned as a social safety net for the vast majority of recipients. It will be recalled from Chapter 3 that most AFDC beneficiaries are young children of young mothers who are on the rolls for 3 years or less. The analysis presented here suggests that these families usually become economically self-supporting over the long term. From this angle, then, concern about a permanently dependent population is misplaced. Nearly all recipients are people with few skills, the victims of economic dislocation, or suffering from some other calamity. In general, they become paupers when necessary and work when they can. Thus, for most poor people, the solution to the problems of poverty and pauperism is simple: jobs that pay livable wages.

Nonetheless, the fact is that there is a fourth group, made up of between one-fourth and one-tenth of all paupers, which uses public assistance as an income substitute for very long periods, 4 years or more.

The difference in estimates of the proportion of long-term recipients is a result of the data used and the way they are manipulated. For example, cross-sectional data will yield a larger proportion of people who are highly dependent for an extended duration than will longitudinal data. This is because the former constitute a picture at one point in time while the latter trace the dynamics of movement on and off the rolls.[14] Thus, when longitudinal data are used (as they should be) it is clear that, at most, only about 10% of all AFDC recipients comprise a "welfare class;" that is, they are paupers for more than 4 years and depend on government aid for most of their income. These individuals and families receive more benefits, take up more time, and are more visible to the public than any other category of recipients. This is one reason why many people and some policymakers misperceive the nature of poverty and pauperism in America.

The characteristics predictive of long-term public assistance use are well known: education, family size, sex of household head, race, age, social isolation, work experience, and previous public assistance recipiency. For example, a 25-year-old woman with five children, an eighth-grade education, little work experience, and few friends or family ties, is especially likely to get locked into long-term pauperism. And the chance of this occurring is even greater if the woman is black or Hispanic.

Given the importance of individual responsibility in our society, it is necessary to realistically assess what a woman like this can do to help herself. It is easy to assert that this woman should not be a baby machine. But the reality is that birth control information, contraceptive devices, abortions, and counseling or therapy all must be available, or this is an empty argument. Yet many of the same middle-class persons who make pejorative statements about welfare mothers being baby machines often deny the poor the opportunity to control births. Further, assertions like this assume that the decision to have and keep children is rational in some sense; that is, they assume a simplified theory of personality similar to that described earlier. Actually, of course, such choices have an emotional and sexual basis and, although it is tragic, psychological analyses show that for some women (and girls) procreation is the only evidence they have of their humanity.[15] It should be clearly noted here that I am not arguing that it is good to have an excessive number of children when one lives in impoverished circumstances. Rather, my purpose is merely to point out some of the social and emotional parameters within which such events take place.

Similarly, it is easy to assert that a woman like the one described here should get a job, go back to school, get trained in an occupation, get married, or do any number of other things to improve her situation.

Most long-term paupers have tried all these strategies. It is also easy to depict her inability to succeed at any of these options as simple laziness and to condemn her on this basis. Perhaps reflecting this facile judgment, the literature on "welfare dependency" (see note 13) describes this process as the "settling in effect"; that is, one "settles into" long-term pauperism. But this phrase is misbegotten because it connotes settling into an easy chair, an easy life. In reality, the process of becoming a long-term pauper is best described as the "beaten-down effect," a phrase that connotes the pathos that accompanies acceptance of dependency, and all that is implied about one's sense of self-worth, economic situation, and status in the community. Such persons are truly at the bottom of society and they are perfectly aware of that fact. This is why they sometimes react by criminal behavior, political unruliness, or display some form of deviance (see Chapters 5 and 6). Hence, one of the most important issues of our time is how these human beings are to be protected and, if possible, helped. Although use of the word "protected," many strike some readers as odd, it is entirely appropriate; for families headed by people like the woman described here have a "right to life," although such a right is not usually recognized by those who use this slogan. From this angle of vision, the problem of how work combines with poverty and pauperism has a rather different hue, one that is somewhat less moralistic than that propounded by people who write books titled *Wealth and Poverty*.

In evaluating the relationship between public assistance and work, however, it is important to emphasize that this fourth group of paupers constitutes only a small minority of recipients, about 10%. Rather, given that poor people want to work and that a very high percentage of them do have jobs, and given that wages make up a large proportion of the long-term income package of most paupers, it is essential to understand why it is they remain poor. Although George Gilder and others of his ilk glibly argue that the only sure route from poverty is hard work, family, and faith, it is clear that many people possess all these traits and remain poor or close to it. The fact is that impoverished people do not just need jobs, they need better jobs. This necessity is clearly shown in Table 4.1: nearly one poor family in four is headed by a person who works all year long, while half of all indigent households are headed by an individual who works part of the year. These are fairly stable figures and they imply that hard work is not the main solution to the problems of poverty and pauperism. Rather, these data suggest that one reason why so many people are poor is that there are not a sufficient number of jobs available that pay high enough wages for workers to support themselves and their families. Put differently, the organization of the economy both causes and perpetuates poverty. I shall return to this topic in Chapter 7.

THE WIN PROGRAM AND NEGATIVE
INCOME TAX EXPERIMENTS

What should be apparent here is that the various work incentive programs, which have formed an important part of the federal government's attempts at reforming public assistance and eliminating poverty, are misbegotten, even ludicrous. This fact can be seen by looking at one such effort: the WIN program.

The WIN program began in 1968 and continues to the present. Its main purpose has been to reduce the size of the AFDC rolls by making recipients more employable and requiring them to register for work.[16] Persons who refuse to work can be denied benefits. In other words, having expanded the relief rolls by legislation designed to alleviate some of the worst aspects of poverty (see Chapter 3), the Congress then chose to rely on WIN and other person-power programs to eliminate pauperism or at least reduce it. Underlying this procedure is the simplified view of personality already described, the assumption that America has an open system of stratification, and the belief that increasing poor people's skills (their human capital, as the economists would say) offers a long-term solution to the nation's public assistance problem.

The shortsightedness of this approach should be apparent, and the results of WIN reflect its lack of soundness. The first fact to be remembered is that most adult AFDC recipients cannot be referred to WIN, mainly because they are needed in the home, they are too old or in ill health, they are attending school full time, or they are already enrolled in vocational programs. As a result, and this is the second fact, the WIN program has been "successful" in placing only about 2% of the total eligible population of AFDC recipients in jobs. Third, those who obtain work as a result of WIN are nearly always paid at the minimum wage, a figure that is well below the poverty level (recall the example in Chapter 2). Hence, while their employment may reduce their dependence, it cannot eliminate it.

Fourth, it appears that those AFDC recipients who registered for WIN and were able to achieve some measure of economic independence did so because they had special characteristics: for example, a stable work history and higher levels of education (especially a high school diploma). In this same vein, it also appears that some registrants who obtain work through WIN are individuals who have suffered an unexpected job loss, which precipitates their entry onto the AFDC rolls, and that their subsequent "success" merely signifies a return to their previously stable, if low-income, employment. Hence, virtually all observers conclude that, while the WIN program may serve political and ideological functions for legislators who wish to placate constituents, and while it provides jobs for middle-class people, it cannot be a solution to the AFDC problem. This is mainly because the assumptions underlying the establishment of this program are unrealistic.

A fifth point should be made here. Not only is the WIN program not very useful to participants, it may be quite dysfunctional. Goodwin, for example, has emphasized the discouragement effect WIN has on many participants.[17] These are people who are motivated to work, who are told that they are either going to be trained or placed directly in jobs, and the reality of the situation is that the job market has little room for persons with their education and skills and that, even after employment, they usually cannot earn enough to support themselves and their families. The WIN program, then, becomes one more failure for people who have experienced little else in their lives, and the result is often to make them more discouraged than they were before and less likely to try again. Yet many of the people who established this program in the first place will campaign for public office by denouncing welfare recipients as lazy.

The last topic I want to discuss in this chapter is the negative income tax experiments, for they were undertaken in order to understand whether poor people would work less if a guaranteed income plan were adopted. There has been a great deal of public and academic controversy over the results.[18] The issue is important because the very name, guaranteed income, evokes fears on the part of many people that the work ethic would no longer be salient for poor persons and that they would labor less as a result. As noted earlier, the fantasy that poverty and leisure are somehow connected is widespread.

The fear people have is sometimes expressed hysterically. For example, as will be recalled from Chapter 1, Martin Anderson asserts that "a small group of committed ideologues...want to institute a guaranteed income under the guise of welfare reform" and such a policy "will cause a substantial reduction—perhaps as much as 50%—in the work effort of low income workers."[19] Sometimes, however, similar fears are expressed by more moderate observers.[20] In either case, such misgivings must be taken seriously, partly because they express the importance of work as a fundamental American value and partly because they have an impact on the formation of public policy.

A negative income tax is a guaranteed minimum income coupled with an incentive to work. It is called a negative income tax because it is a reversal of the positive, or progressive, income tax. That is, a minimum income guarantee is established, which is linked with a reduction, or tax, rate that is dependent on earnings. How these two factors combine is illustrated in Table 4.2, which assumes that the income guarantee is set at $4,000 for a family of four and that the reduction rate is 50%.

As can be seen in the table, the income guarantee received by a household is reduced by 50% of earnings as they increase. Thus, in this example, families with earnings of $4,000 would still live below the poverty line when their benefit, the income guarantee, is added to their wages. Such households would still not have an easy time, of course, but the adults would have an incentive to work.

The attractiveness of a negative income tax should be apparent. In principle, it would be simpler (and, hence, cheaper) to administer than AFDC, even if it were combined with food stamps and Medicaid, and it would allow for the application of uniform standards nationwide. In addition, a negative income tax would avoid the antifamily bias inherent in the current AFDC program.[21] Finally, an income guarantee that is combined with a reduction (or tax) rate that is straightforward and easy to understand would not only eliminate the perception of subjectivity and bias that many AFDC recipients have, it would also function as an incentive to work. These advantages are one reason why the President's Commission for a National Agenda for the Eighties recently recommended the creation of a "minimum security income" program.[22] One need not be either a conspirator or a committed idealogue to make such a proposal.

A negative income tax was first proposed in 1962 by Milton Friedman and subsequently taken up by a number of politicians, liberal and conservative.[23] In this climate, the Office of Economic Opportunity decided to sponsor a series of experiments in order to discover whether the work effort of the poor would decline if a negative income tax were instituted.

TABLE 4.2: Relationship between the Income Guarantee and Earned Income under a Hypothetical Negative Income Tax Plan[a]

Earnings	Income guarantee	Total income
$ 0	$4,000	$4,000
1,000	3,500	4,500
2,000	3,000	5,000
3,000	2,500	5,500
4,000	2,000	6,000
5,000	1,500	6,500
6,000	1,000	7,000
7,000	500	7,500
8,000	0	8,000

[a] Assumptions: Intact family of four;
Income guarantee = $4,000;
Rate reduction = 50% of earnings

However, and this was a fateful decision, rather than obtaining a random sample of all poor households, the experiments were conducted at five different locations around the country between 1968 and 1975. In three cases, only intact families participated, while female householders (with no husbands present) also took part in two instances. All five experiments involved a comparison group whose members did not receive a guaranteed income and an experimental group whose members did receive such a benefit. The level of the income guarantee varied between 50% and 125% of the poverty line, while the reduction rate varied between 30% and 70% of the benefit. The issue, then, is whether those in the experimental groups worked less than did those in the control groups, given different guarantees and reduction rates.

Virtually all the experiments are deeply flawed, mainly because of sampling and other design problems.[24] Nonetheless, one of the main benefits of the experiments has been administrative: It is now clear how to run large-scale income guarantee projects efficiently. This experience is probably generalizable to the national scene.

Unfortunately, the findings cannot be extrapolated to the poor population as a whole or even to significant segments of it, primarily because of the use of accidental rather than random samples.[25] Thus, it is not clear whether the behavior of the participants in the experiments reflects that of the poor population. Regardless of this fact, there has been considerable controversy about the findings, which have been treated as though the data were generalizable. Hence, a brief comment on the experiments' results is necessary here.

Some observers have interpreted the data as showing no differences between the experimental and control groups (that is, as indicating no decline in work activity among recipients), while others have found "alarming evidence" that members of the experimental groups worked less. My own view is that the latter investigators are probably wrong, for two reasons:

1. Their interpretations usually specificy unrealistically high-guarantee levels (at the poverty line or above)
2. Their reasoning is often awkward.

Here is an example that illustrates both problems.

Robert Moffit examined the results of the experiments by statistically converting all the data in such a way that the income guarantee was set at the poverty line and the reduction rate was 50%.[26] Apart from the heroic assumptions necessary when constructing statistical models such as these, when the guarantee level is set at the poverty line people can earn up to two times the threshold and still receive benefits. The arithmetic is very simple: 50% of earnings are subtracted from the guarantee with the remainder (if any) going to the recipient. Thus, if the income guarantee is at the poverty line, as Moffit's model assumes, then a family of four with no earnings in 1981 would have received $9,287; if it had earnings of $9,000, it would have received an additional $4,787 for a total income of $13,787; and if it had earnings of $18,000 it would have received an additional $287 for a total income of $18,287. The likelihood of the public supporting or Congress passing a plan such as this is exactly zero. However, even though the example is unrealistic, this statistical model is useful because it increases the likelihood of showing that work disincentives accompany a negative income tax.

Moffit, in fact, begins his exposition by claiming that his data show "unequivocal evidence that the hours of work are reduced by the negative income tax." Actually, the figures show no such thing, even though the income guarantee is set at such a high level, for very few of the results are of either statistical or substantive significance. Thus, for both married men and women in intact families, only three of nine comparisons are statistically significant, and then only at the .10 rather than the usual .05 level. While .05 is not sacred, of course, using it decreases the possibility of attributing differences to the two groups that may be there only by chance. Further, there is little substantive significance that can be gleaned from the findings, as Moffit goes on to admit that "the ranges of responses are rather disconcerting" and he is forced to engage in a lot of guesswork. His conclusion, then, is rather different from the initial strong statement: "The policy implications of this finding are ambiguous,...The negative income tax does not appear to have a pervasive effect on the work ethic of the low-income population; in fact most of the men do not respond at all" to the experimental treatment. That is to say, they do not work less as a result of receiving a guaranteed income set at the poverty line. Nearly all observers agree that when income guarantees are set significantly below the poverty line, as illustrated in Table 4.2 they produce no decline in hours worked.[27]

This chapter opened with a simple question: Do the poor want to work? The answer is clearly yes. All the available data show that the vast majority of impoverished persons want to work and do work when opportunity is available. In general, the labor force participation of the poor is determined by factors over which they have little control. Some of these issues will be dealt with in the next chapter, which examines the correlates of poverty. In addition, it was seen that one way of "explaining" the stereotype that indigent persons do not want to work is to assume they have different values. This chapter has shown that, at least in terms of the work ethic, the poor share dominant evaluative beliefs. However, I shall return to the general topic of the relationship between cultural values and poverty in Chapter 6 in order to suggest a more sociological way of understanding the behavior of the poor. In that context, the implications of Goodwin's finding that the poor are distinguished from the nonpoor in terms of their lack of confidence in their ability to succeed will be explored. Finally, implicit in the stereotype that the poor do not want to work is an individualistic explanation of the causes of poverty. In Chapter 7, I shall show that the causes of poverty can be better understood by ignoring how individuals act (or do not act) and focus instead on the way social processes in the United States produce a class of poor persons.

5

SOME CORRELATES
OF POVERTY

This chapter analyzes some of the correlates of poverty. In so doing, I shall employ a common sociological point of view, one that cuts across the Marxist and Functionalist perspectives that so often seem to divide sociology: people choose among socially structured alternatives.[1] Most empirical studies of the correlates of poverty are atomistic in the sense that they are not imbued with a sociological vision. Yet the benefits of such an insight are plain. It is not possible to understand why people choose to vote or riot (both are political expressions), why they commit crimes or are victims of crimes, or why they choose to seek health care or not without knowing the options that are available to them. It does little good to assume that those living poorly have the same alternatives or operate under the same constraints that middle- or upper-class people do. Yet this assumption underlies many academic commentaries, which is why impoverished persons are so often portrayed as irrational or possessing different values than the nonpoor. As will be seen in the following chapter, both the psychological and many of the behavioral characteristics of the poor follow directly from their limited choices and the experiences that result.

An examination of the correlates of poverty is facilitated by asking provocative questions, such as the following: Who benefits? Answering this query will nearly always improve an analysis of American society (or any social organization, for that matter) and make the result more interesting. For example, much more is known about what it is like to live poorly in the United States when it is clear who benefits from low levels of political participation by impoverished people, from the failure of the criminal justice system to control street crime, and from the relative inability of indigent people to obtain health care. As will be seen, it is possible on this basis to understand the social and psychological characteristics of the poor without imputing deviant values to them. The important point to note here, however, is that one does not need to be a Marxist in order to ascertain who benefits from ongoing social arrangements. Rather, by paying attention to this issue, the vulnerability and limited choices available to people without money are highlighted.

Similarly, there is an ironic aspect to nearly all facets of social life in the sense that it is filled with incongruities between expected and unexpected results.[2] Irony is often exposed when attention focuses on the functions or consequences of social phenomena, as with the functions of poverty reviewed in Chapter 1. The same kind of point can be made when examining the correlates of poverty. Thus, much more is known about what it is like to live poorly in the United States when it is clear that one of the functions of pluralist dogma is to ensure that impoverished people find it difficult to participate in the legitimate political arena. This is surely unintended, since the American political system is designed to allow maximum levels of participation on the part of all those who are interested. My point here is that, as mentioned, the extent to which destitute people are vulnerable and have limited choices can also be demonstrated by looking for the unexpected, ironic consequences inherent in social structures. One does not have to be a Functionalist, in the doctrinaire sense that word is often used in sociology, in order to note the usefulness of such observations. For they are another way of getting at the significance of structural effects.

By systematically emphasizing the empirical importance of the fact that people's choices are socially structured, it is possible to produce a synthetic analysis of the sort that is not ordinarily characteristic of academic sociology. In describing the correlates of poverty I shall portray the options the poor have in three social contexts: politics, crime, and health. In each case, I shall emphasize the inherent connections among all these elements of life, who benefits from current social arrangements, and the unintended consequences such arrangements have for both the poor and the nonpoor.

As the title of this chapter makes clear, the topics considered here do not constitute a complete list of the correlates of poverty. Pauperism is obviously related to impoverishment. In addition, I shall show in Chapter 6 that analgesic behavior (rather than deviant values) is also related to poverty. Finally, the constraints engendered by family organization, educational experiences, and racial and sexual discrimination will be considered in Chapter 7. The argument I shall make there is that the correlates of poverty redound to perpetuate it.

POLITICS AND POVERTY

The first correlate of poverty dealt with here is political disenfranchisement, and, hence, apathy; the two go together, for they reflect both the vulnerability and the limited options available to people who live poorly in America. It was shown in Chapter 3 that the poor receive fewer monetary benefits from the federal government than do other classes and that public assistance actually functions to preserve the economic status quo rather than to redistribute wealth. Here is an empirical generalization that explains why this is so, at least in the United States: the lower the social class, *then* the lower the rate of political participation.[3] Put differently, the poor are less active politically than any other stratum in American society and they benefit less as a result. It does not matter what form of political participation one looks at: The poor are less likely to belong to political parties; they are less likely to belong to interest groups that might stimulate or direct political activity; they are less aware of the issues facing the nation and the decisions that have to be made; they vote at a lower rate; and, surprisingly, they usually do not protest when their interests are harmed. As a result, they are disenfranchised: Except during periods of unruliness (which will be commented on later), poverty policy is made by the nonpoor without input from the poor, and this is true whether the programs that result are compassionate or heartless, wise or foolish. This is why poor people do not benefit very much and nonpoor people do.

In order to understand the political apathy of the poor, which is, after all, contrary to their self-interest, it is useful to reflect for a moment on the nature of the American political system. Most of us view the political arena, with varying degrees of cynicism, as governed by law and as relatively open and responsive to the needs and desires of citizens. This perception is reflected, indeed reified, in the political science literature by the notion of pluralism.[4]

From a pluralist point of view, the American political system has two characteristics. First, people act within the rules to influence public policy. These rules stipulate that disruption, violence, and other extralegal forms of protest or constraint are inappropriate. Rather, laws are legitimate because people are expected to follow correct procedures and generally do; for example, citizens vote, representatives decide, judges interpret, and so on. Second, there is open access to the political arena: Anyone can compete. The idea here is that because everyone can vote and participate in other ways, and because people have multiple ties—as indicated by their religious, ethnic, occupational, regional, community, and other group memberships—there is always a certain balance of power. No one group can dominate because new coalitions are always forming. Robert Dahl, among many others, has argued that there is overwhelming agreement on these points and that they are what makes the United States different from so many other nations.

Now this picture of the American political system is not a very accurate description of how it really operates. Nonetheless, this portrayal is significant here precisely because so many of us agree with it, for it depicts how the political system should work. That is, people ought to participate in procedurally correct ways (by voting, for example, rather than rioting) and the system should be open to pressure from all sectors of the society. Hence, this is the normative context within which poor people are forced to act, which constrains their options.

This normative milieu suggests an obvious explanation for the political apathy of the poor: First, they do not have the resources, economic and social, or the personal characteristics that normally stimulate participation in a pluralist system; second, the system itself, as embodied in the major parties, neither mobilizes the poor nor appeals to their political interests. This is why they are disenfranchised. I shall review each of these factors in the following paragraphs.

The most important resource is clearly money, for politicians and policymakers pay attention to those persons who contribute to campaigns and to voters, in about that order. Thus, the poor are shut out from one of the most important means of political participation in a pluralist system; the budget described in Chapter 2 does not include money for campaign contributions.

Another very important factor stimulating participation is membership in voluntary associations, whether they be for leisure (sports or hobby groups), community services, religion, or some other purpose.[5] Membership is important as a stimulus for political activity even when groups have nonpolitical purposes, partly because people talk about politics in such contexts and partly because organizations can be transformed into activist groups when their interests are affected. Thus, group membership is a social resource that is vital to political participation in a pluralist system.

But belonging to organizations requires social and economic characteristics that the poor often do not have: transportation, literacy, decent clothing, child care, time, money to pay dues, freedom from fear, and many other characteristics. For most people, these problems are not serious, but for those without money they frequently become insurmountable obstacles to group membership. For example, the effects of inferior schools and lack of education are pervasive, since individuals who do not read very well or speak correctly feel out of place and so withdraw from situations, such as formal organizations, in which these deficiencies are obvious. In addition, the effect of crime is also pervasive, since in many poor neighborhoods people are afraid to go out at night. As a result, poor persons do not belong or attend: the lower the social class, *then* the lower the rate of voluntary association membership. This is true, by the way, even for religious participation, especially among whites, despite the stereotype that religion is a haven for the oppressed.[6] Thus, the poor do not have the social resources which promote institutional ties that, in turn, can galvanize them to act politically within a pluralist system. As a result, public policy is made without input from the poor. This means that they are disenfranchised, regardless of their formal right to vote.

In addition, political participation is affected by a variety of social–psychological characteristics, most of which the poor do not possess: interest in and information about politics, feelings of competence, beliefs that political decisions can be made in one's own interests, and a generalized sense that political issues are of importance. Political scientists call these characteristics civic orientations. As mentioned earlier, the effects of lack of education and low income are ubiquitous: Those who do not get newspapers or magazines either because they cannot afford them or because they do not read very well find it very difficult to have adequate information. Further, education is most people's introduction to bureaucracies; one of the functions of education is to provide students with the interpersonal skills and confidence to participate effectively in bureaucratic settings. Those individuals who have not excelled in dealing with teachers and principals are likely to have trouble in other contexts as well. For example, voting requires that one read and write, fairly swiftly, in order to register and then vote. It also requires interacting with middle-class bureaucrats who are often condescending or rude. Virtually all other political activities, at least in a pluralist arena, require even more skills than does voting. Like most adults, poor people do not relish being treated like children or being abused and, given a choice, will avoid such contexts. Again, this means that the poor are disenfranchised.

It should be noted here that these personal characteristics reflect poor people's life experiences: It is the typical experience of impoverished persons that they do not control their own destiny. For example, they do not have job protection if they are fired unjustly or legal aid if they are denied unemployment compensation. They do not have legal resources if they are evicted from their homes illegally or if landlords do not maintain their dwellings properly. If they are female, they often do not have access to contraception or to abortions and, hence, cannot even control what happens to their own bodies. There is, then, little in the everyday experiences of poor people to indicate to them that they have control over their own lives. They learn, as a consequence, that the best thing to do is not to have very high expectations for themselves or for others, not to question authority, and not to persevere; such behavior will only bring trouble. Hence, the political apathy of poor persons is, in many cases, a specific example of a more general personality orientation: passivity coupled with a sort of learned helplessness that makes it difficult to take advantage of opportunities. As will be seen in the next chapter, such characteristics are one way of coping with vulnerability even though they help to perpetuate political disenfranchisement.

Thus, for those who live poorly, a pluralist system may be open in principle but it is closed in fact. In the United States, the rate of political participation and the degree of political influence depend on location in the social structure. Individuals with high income and occupational prestige, especially those with wealth, have the economic and social resources along with the personality characteristics necessary to participate and have influence.

Those who benefit from the political apathy of the poor are, of course, middle- and upper-class people, who not only participate by voting or contributing money, or both, but also define and enforce rules regarding the correct (or legal) modes of political activity. The nonpoor benefit in very material ways. As noted in Chapter 1, the existence of an impoverished class keeps prices down, provides low-wage workers for the economy, and creates jobs for the nonpoor. In addition, as shown in Chapter 3, the nonpoor receive more economic assistance from the government than do the poor. Hence, it can be concluded that the higher the social class, *then* the greater the benefit resulting from poor people's political disenfranchisement and apathy. The unintended, or at least unrecognized, consequence of the extraordinary value placed on certain modes of political participation is to make it extremely unlikely that this situation will change much in the future. This is one reason, a structural reason, why the war on poverty never had much of a chance, despite the good intentions of many participants. Truly effective programs for nonvoting segments of the population are extremely difficult to enact or maintain, especially during periods when there is little unrest. This is why public assistance can, at best, merely sustain the economic status quo rather than redistribute wealth. It is also why these programs have been emasculated in the last few years.

The second reason the poor are politically disenfranchised and apathetic follows from recognizing who benefits: The major parties do not attempt to mobilize impoverished persons or appeal to their political interests. It is important to understand that the effects of limited resources are not immutable and that the relationship between class and participation previously cited does not occur in every country. In most of Western Europe, for example, working-class levels of voting are as high or even higher than those of the middle class.[7] In the United States, it is known that contacting voters increases participation and there is some evidence that this is true across all social classes.[8] Yet, by and large, poor persons are not actively contacted and, hence, are not aware of the issues, do not believe they can have influence over policies affecting them, and do not vote. This is why public assistance programs so often seem like charity bestowed on destitute people. If such citizens were active voters on whom political parties depended for success, as is the case in Western Europe, these programs would seem altogether different. For example, since income support programs can prevent recidivism among ex-felons, and since the poor are harmed most by street crime, they could force the development of effective programs to deal with the problem. This does not occur because the poor are actively excluded by the major political parties, both of which are mainly oriented to the needs of other segments of the population.

The irony inherent in this situation is clear: Poor persons are told, and for the most part believe, that the only legitimate means of influencing public policy is by organizing, lobbying, voting, contributing money, and the like, yet these modes of participation are effectively closed to them. This contradiction leads to some interesting conclusions. First, as might be expected, any form of disruptive protest will nearly always be condemned as illegal and immoral by the majority, mainly because most people believe that America ought to be and is a pluralist society in which the opportunity for political expression is open to all. Second, unexpectedly, since the ability to use legitimate means to participate effectively in the political arena is limited for impoverished persons, the only alternative is some type of political unruliness, whether violent or not. Finally, even though it is sometimes the only way to influence public policy, protest behavior is not a matter of free choice and, hence, usually cannot be planned or selected in a rational way. This is because there are structural limits on this mode of participation.

It is easy to discredit unruliness, especially if it is violent, because it seems so irrational and so inherently wrong. Yet this is a very easy judgment to make, especially by those who have other options. It is also a very common judgment. For example, many people—including many sociologists—would endorse the following statement. "The course of violence would be terribly, awfully wrong: not just because hatred and violence are self-defeating, [but also because] they strike at the heart of obedience to law, peaceful progress, and political cooperation which are man's last, best hope for a decent world."[9] It would be hard to find a better assertion of pluralist doctrine. From another angle, however, Piven and Cloward argue that the labels used to describe defiance by the lower classes—the pejorative labels of illegality and violence—testify to the vulnerability of poor persons, justify severe reprisals (jail, beatings) against them, and indicate the extent to which political coercion is inherent in their everyday lives.[10] In this juxtaposition the ironic aspect of pluralist doctrine becomes clear: On the one hand, it is a means of making decisions and resolving conflict without violence, which is good, while on the other hand, it is a system of social control that operates to keep members of the lower class in their place, which is contrary to American values as expressed in pluralism.

Thus, the grim fact is that despite the laudable sentiments expressed in the preceding quotation, some form of political unruliness is often the last, best, indeed the only hope poor people have. For it plainly does little good to tell individuals who have been denied AFDC benefits because the law has been changed to lobby members of Congress. Members of Congress, Democrat as well as Republican, are usually not interested in hearing from poor people. As a result, their voices are more likely to be heard if they disrupt public assistance offices in some way, even though the immediate response from the police may be violent and will certainly be repressive. This is, however, a fairly mild form of unruliness. Sometimes, as indicated when discussing voluntary organization membership and the personality characteristics of the poor, people without money are so isolated from the political system that the only form of protest available to them is to rebel against participating in ordinary life altogether: They can riot.[11] Whatever form unruliness takes, it is important to pay attention, for such actions are a form of political behavior and one of their functions is to call attention to serious social problems that have not been resolved through normal channels. As Lewis Coser has noted, violence and other forms of disruption are not merely protests, they are claims to be considered.[12] And there is evidence that, under certain conditions, claims made in this way are very effective.[13]

From this point of view, the best response (that is, the best political strategy) for disenfranchised people to pursue is to become unruly, even though it may seem irrational. But such actions do not occur very often and rarely become an overt or planned political tactic. This is because, in addition to the psychological inhibitions resulting from a constant exposure to their own powerlessness, there are built in limits on the possibility for protest.The most important of these limits is the pattern of everyday living: The predictable regularities of daily life so enmesh people that they are acquiescent nearly all of the time. This is, of course, especially true for the poor because the struggle to survive—to put food on the table, to pay the electric bill and the rent, to preserve some self-respect in a context where little is possible—leads to acquiescence. In addition to the problems of everyday life, the poor have been taught to believe that the prestige, wealth, and power that others possess is deserved by them, with the result that the existing scheme of life seems just. In this context, then, protest appears to be both unwise and unreasonable most of the time. It seems unwise because the poor have little defense against penalties that can be imposed: jail, loss of job, termination of public aid, eviction from one's home, etc. It seems unreasonable because the moral order, epitomized by pluralist doctrine, appears to be so inherently right. In general, victims usually do not recognize the structural sources of their oppression. Thus, as Piven and Cloward, Coser, and others have recognized, protest comes to seem possible, even reasonable, only when large masses of people are jerked out of established ways of doing things in such a fashion that the system loses its legitimacy; violations of their rights become salient; and they feel a sense of personal efficacy. This process usually requires an ideology that activates people and legitimates their rebellion. But moments such as this are rare and usually not predictable in advance. This is why mass protests do not occur very often. It is also why they should be heeded.

In summary, the political disenfranchisement of the poor and their apathy occur because destitute people have neither the social nor the personal resources necessary to participate in a pluralist system and because the major parties—which are run by and for the nonpoor—make no effort to mobilize the poor. The economic vulnerability of impoverished persons is thus reinforced by their political helplessness. I will argue in Chapter 7 that poverty and political disenfranchisement are part of a vicious circle that enmeshes people and makes change extremely difficult. I want to turn now to a consideration of crime, justice, and poverty.

CRIME AND POVERTY

The second correlate of poverty dealt with here is crime. As both victims and perpetrators, criminal behavior reflects the vulnerability and limited choices available to impoverished persons. I am going to begin this section by asking a series of questions designed to place the problem of crime into the context of poor people's lives. What kinds of crimes do poor people commit? Why do they commit these sorts of crimes rather than some others? What are the consequences of such crimes, both for poor neighborhoods and for the perpetrators? And are there ways of reducing the rate of street crime?

The answer to the last question leads to a more provocative query: Who benefits from the fact that the criminal justice system perpetuates rather than reduces street crime? That is, since ways of reducing street crime are not only known but could be implemented, then its perpetuation must serve the interests of a powerful segment of society. I shall argue that the relationship between poverty and crime benefits the rich and that this class has an important stake in its perpetuation. This is why the reciprocal relationship between crime and poverty is allowed to continue.

What kinds of crimes do poor people commit? Although most impoverished persons do not come to the attention of the police or serve time in jail, a fact that should be remembered, when the poor do commit illegal acts they usually engage in what is popularly called street crime. These are crimes that involve one-on-one harm; that is, they inflict personal injury on victims or rob them of something valuable, or both. These crimes are particularly scary. They may involve the use of guns to rob grocery or liquor stores, or to mug individuals. Or they may involve the use of drugs, as when heroin addicts burglarize homes to finance their habits. I shall come back to these examples subsequently.

Partly because of the frightening quality inherent in such crimes—after all, nobody wants to be mugged and nobody wants to have one's home violated—people who commit such acts seem to represent particularly dangerous threats to society. Hence, the criminal justice system pays special attention to these types of crimes. As a result, the following empirical generalization can be made: the lower the social class, *then* the higher the arrest rate, the longer the time spent in jail prior to trial or adjudication, the higher the conviction rate, and the longer the prison sentence.[14] Phrased differently, these findings mean that poor people are more likely to be arrested, less likely to post bail, more likely to be found guilty (whether by trial or, more often, through plea bargains), and likely to get longer prison sentences. For the most part, these facts are true regardless of an individual's actual guilt or innocence.

These findings do not constitute a very accurate picture of the nature or extent of crime in American society, since, as will be shown, there is really no relationship between class and actual crime rates (as opposed to arrest rates, see note 14). Nonetheless, these findings are of considerable interest because they reflect the types of crimes poor people commit and they suggest the extent to which the legal system is designed to control the behavior of impoverished persons. I will postpone a consideration of the latter topic until later, as it has to do with the prolem of who benefits.

Why do poor people commit street crimes rather than some others? The association between street crime and poverty results from the opportunities that are and are not available to persons living in such circumstances. Indigent people cannot embezzle money, construct unsafe automobiles, fix prices, or use computers to abscond with bank deposits or public assistance money. Such opportunities are not present because lower-class individuals lack education and, all too often, lack jobs. These facts restrict their choices. Hence, what poor persons can do is get a gun.

And that is sometimes what they in fact do, with serious consequences for public safety.

In addition to opportunity, perhaps the most famous overall explanation of why poor people engage in these forms of crime has been advanced by Robert K. Merton.[15] He argues that American society is characterized by a disjunction between approved goals and legitimate means. That is, as noted in Chapter 4, there is overwhelming value placed on occupational and economic success in the United States while, at the same time, access to legal means for attaining success is class related: the lower the social class, *then* the more limited the legitimate means for achieving success. This combination of characteristics, which is inherent to American society, requires most individuals to adapt in some way to the fact that they cannot rise to the top; most of us stop far short of ultimate success. Thus, one mode of adaptation is ritualistic, scaling one's goals down to the point where they can be satisfied while still adhering to dominant values. Among the poor, for example, garbage collectors may perceive themselves as having status in their community, not because they have high incomes or prestigious jobs, but because they are regularly employed and able to provide for their families. They are, in effect, adapting by defining "success" in more prosaic terms, even as they accept dominant values.[16] Sometimes survival is success in America. Similar processes go on among members of all social classes.

Another way of dealing with the disjunction, however, is to become successful through illegitimate means. From this point of view, vice and crime appear as normal, indeed reasonable responses to lack of opportunity in other spheres. Merton refers to this tactic as a form of innovation, observing that "despite our persisting open class ideology, advance toward the success goal is relatively rare and notably difficult for those armed with little formal education and few economic resources. The dominant pressure leads toward the gradual attenuation of legitimate, but by and large ineffectual, strivings and the increasing use of illegitimate, but more or less effective, expedients."[17] Hence, a fundamental irony is built into American society: Many people who engage in street crime are trying to achieve a thoroughly respectable goal—economic success—in a context where the legal means to attain such a goal are not available. Thus, here is a case where ambition, clearly a virtue, produces a vice. As an aside, although Merton believes that crime is primarily a lower-class response to the goals–means disjunction, I shall argue that this is not the case.

However, street crime requires more than opportunity and ambition without means. Like all forms of social action, street crime cannot flourish without role models who can serve as examples of successful people and who can socialize others, especially young persons, by providing them with the knowledge, skills, and motivation to succeed via criminality.[18] Put differently, people must be educated to crime, which means that patterns of social organization must exist to fulfill this task. For example, individuals must learn how to pick locks, obtain weapons, sell stolen goods to fences, and the like. They must also learn to have cynicism about the police and about the sanctity of other people's property. There is abundant evidence from both ethnographic and autobiographical sources that such learning processes go on routinely in poor neighborhoods, where examples of successful criminals are widespread.[19]

Before leaving the topic of why poor people commit the crimes they do, it should be noted that Merton identifies two other modes of adaptation to the disjunction between approved goals and legitimate means: retreatism and rebellion. Although he does not say so, each of these reactions often leads to street crime.

Some people resign from the struggle altogether, for they are unable to either achieve occupational success or adopt illegitimate means, often because they have internalized prohibitions against criminal behavior. Hence, they retreat into themselves, into their own world where the conflict does not exist. Examples of such persons are psychotics, "street people," and drug addicts (whether alcohol, heroin, or something else). These social types are often self-destructive in ways that seem incomprehensible to most middle-class people, including social scientists, who have not thought through the social consequences of pervasive frustration. I shall return to this topic in the next chapter. Here I merely want to point out that one of the unintended consequences of our society's emphasis on success through legitimate means is to sacrifice certain persons, to destroy them for the sake of our values. Yet, ironically, some of these individuals end up posing grave threats to public safety, since after we sacrifice them we also force them to survive (and suffer) without help. Thus, paradoxically, and despite whatever inhibitions they may once have had, they often turn to crime. For example, it has been estimated that heroin addicts account for 20–25% of all burglaries, robberies, and larcenies in New York City each year, and this figure can probably be extrapolated to most urban areas.[20] What to do to or for such persons is a question of great importance for public policy. I shall make a suggestion later on.

Finally, Merton observes that some people rebel. While this option rarely occurs on an organized basis, as seen previously, much of what appears to be "senseless" vandalism and violence on the part of poverty-stricken individuals, especially youths, is simply an anomic alternative to mass unruliness. There are a lot of thugs on the street. Nonetheless, such responses are political protests, even if they are inchoate and violent. Given the difficulty of political participation in the legitimate arena as well as the lack of opportunity for large-scale disruption, this option (which is probably not consciously chosen most of the time) is often the only one available to people who are frustrated and refuse to become docile. While this fact does not excuse brutality or terror inflicted on innocent persons, and although it must be controlled, it makes such behavior more understandable.

The consequences of street crime attest again to the vulnerability of impoverished individuals, for they are the victims. One consequence is that poor neighborhoods are disrupted and disorganized, primarily because indigent persons are more likely to be victimized by street crimes than are the nonpoor.[21] As a result, corporations do not want to locate in such areas and job opportunities are reduced. This is one reason why teenage unemployment is so high, especially among blacks. And the significance of this fact is that many young people enter adulthood without ever having had an opportunity to obtain work experience and skills, and hence, without being socialized into legal means of attaining success. Many poor youths have given up hope before reaching adulthood, which often means that—from their point of view—the only realistic alternative is crime.[22] This situation is compounded by disorganization in the schools, for the educational process (which includes getting to and from school) is often disrupted by drugs, violence, and theft. In such environments, people live with the constant knowledge that they can be accosted at any time and that neither they nor their belongings are ever safe. In addition, parents who work long hours at low wages far away from home often find it difficult to regulate their children's associates or control their behavior, even though these socializing experiences fundamentally influence which mode of adaptation they choose. Finally, as previously observed, poor people are often afraid to go out at night, especially if it involves going into unfamiliar sections of the city. This means that joining or forming voluntary organizations is very difficult. In such a social context, individuals do not believe they can control their own destiny. This is because their everyday lives are marred by disorganization and unpredictability.

Another consequence of street crime is recidivism on the part of those convicted, primarily because of the way the criminal justice system works. The empirical generalization is as follows: "the higher the employment rate of former offenders, [*then*] the lower the rate of criminal recidivism." And this fact has been known for many years.[23] Despite this knowledge, it is clear that prisons create crime by housing people in overcrowded conditions, demeaning them by taking away their privacy, and threatening them constantly with homosexual rape and assault. Human beings forced to live in environments like this become frustrated and enraged and, hence, less capable of blending into the law-abiding population after their incarceration ends. In addition, even though such persons typically had little work experience, little education, and few skills prior to entering prison, they receive little job training while there. What they do receive is experience, education, skills, and psychological orientations that are extremely dangerous to society.

This milieu is the background influencing ex-offenders as they look for jobs. Yet they are often denied access to stable employment, even though it may be the only "antidote" for their prison experiences. Not only do corporations and other employers often refuse to hire "ex-cons," but licensing laws and other regulations severely restrict their options.[24] For example, the state of New York prohibits ex-felons from taking civil service exams and from being licensed as auctioneers, junk dealers, gunsmiths, waterfront workers, barbers, watchguards, insurance adjusters, real estate brokers, bingo operators, and many other occupations. Although the number of restricted jobs varies from one state to another, a similar pattern occurs everywhere. For example 46 states prohibit ex-offenders from becoming barbers. Hence, the criminal justice system functions to provide an active impetus back into a life of crime.

The irony inherent in the criminal justice system is that it defeats itself. And it does so even though we know how to reduce the rate of street crime. "The solutions are so obvious," observed Norval Morris, dean of the University of Chicago Law School, that "it's almost as if America wished for a high crime rate."[25] Perhaps it does.

We know, for example, that poverty is associated with street crime. As the President's Crime Commission concluded in 1967, "The most significant action that can be taken against [street] crime is action designed to eliminate slums and ghettos, to improve education, to provide jobs, to make sure every American is given the opportunity that will enable him to assume his responsibilities."[26] Yet we persist in believing that more police and more prisons will solve the problem. The result is predictable: More criminals are created and more social control is needed, in an endless spiral.

In addition, we know that the prison system is a source of crime. Put dramatically, the state—meaning all citizens—has an interest in treating prisoners humanely and providing realistic job training so that, having paid their penalty, offenders might emerge as law-abiding members of society. Instead, prisons strip human beings of all self-respect and respect for society (the two go together) and deny them all opportunity. The result is predictable: More victims are created, nearly all of them impoverished.

Furthermore, we know that handguns are involved in most murders, assaults, and robberies. It has been estimated that the fatalities associated with such crimes could be reduced by 80% if the perpetrators switched to the next deadliest weapon, a knife. Yet, unlike the public, our national leaders are opposed to handgun control. The result is predictable: more victims.

Finally, we know that treating the possession of heroin as a crime creates much more illegality than it prevents. Heroin is a tranquilizing drug; it does not cause crime. Although many persons would be opposed to such a policy on moral grounds, the blunt fact is that dispensing drugs directly to addicts, as has been done in Great Britain for many years, would be a simple and cheap way of reducing their crime rate. It would also make the streets safer. What must be recognized is that, precisely because possession is illegal, those who supply it charge wildly high prices and those who need it must pay the premiums. The result is predictable: more victims.

It is important to understand the implications of this analysis. As it is currently organized, the criminal justice system not only fails to reduce crime, even though methods of so doing are available, it also perpetuates the relationship between crime and poverty. Why? When patterns of social organization endure over time and choice is clearly involved, as is true here, then some segment of society usually has an interest in maintaining the status quo. In this case, as Jeffrey Reiman has argued, the failure of the criminal justice system benefits the rich.

The rich benefit to the extent that middle-class Americans believe they have more to fear from the crimes committed by the poor than the rich. Ironically, this belief is made to seem realistic because of the failure of the criminal justice system. Despite the generalization just cited, there is no relationship between class and crime—everyone does it. This fact is seen clearly in the pervasiveness of white-collar crime as well as in self-report studies. For example, 90% of all respondents will admit to survey researchers that they have committed acts which, if they had been caught and prosecuted, would have resulted in jail sentences. The other 10% are dissembling.[27] Furthermore, a good case can be made that the crimes committed by white-collar people and corporate leaders are both more dangerous and more costly than street crimes. Nonetheless, the failure of the criminal justice system to reduce street crime, along with its inherently frightening quality, means that many people are hostile to and fearful of impoverished persons, and supportive of stronger doses of "law and order" aimed at lower-class individuals. Such policies will not work, of course, but perhaps that is not the point, they will serve to confirm the public's view of who is most to be feared and thus perpetuate the criminal justice system as it is currently organized. As a result, the crimes committed by white-collar people are less salient to the public.

The rich also benefit because they are systematically weeded out of the legal system and because many of the crimes they commit are either treated lightly or ignored altogether. And as noted, this occurs despite the fact that their crimes are both more costly and more dangerous than those committed by the poor.

The weeding-out process begins with the decision to arrest and continues through every stage of the system. It occurs not only because citizens, police, prosecutors, judges, and juries have an enduring image of the "normal criminal," who is invariably poor and often black, but also because white-collar persons are able to use the law to their advantage.[28] There is nothing particularly wrong with this latter process, as everyone ought to have their rights protected, but it reflects the political power of the nonpoor and ensures that our prisons function as national poorhouses. And this result, in turn, confirms the image most people have that crime is mainly committed by poor persons and thus perpetuates the criminal justice system as it is currently organized.

Even when they proceed through the system, most crimes committed by white-collar people are treated lightly. This is partly because their illegal acts often do not involve one-on-one harm; rather, they are accomplished in indirect but more dangerous and costly ways. For example, while the typical robbery nets about $250 and the perpetrator receives a sentence of about 133 months (more than 11 years), the average case of embezzlement nets tens of thousands of dollars and the perpetrator receives a sentence of about 21 months (less than 2 years). In 1974, the U.S. Chamber of Commerce estimated that white-collar crime cost "not less than" $40 billion. This figure, which was undoubtedly low even then, was more than ten times the cost of all property crimes in that year.[29] Thus, white-collar crimes are not only more costly than street crimes, their long-term effects are more serious. For example, while the robber may take the contents of a victim's wallet, the embezzler can destroy the equity of a family, ruin a firm, or render corporate stock valueless. The Chamber of Commerce estimates that one-third of all business failures are due to white-collar crime. Yet most such criminals do not go to jail, even for one day. This fact also reflects the political power of the nonpoor and, as cited, confirms the image people have that street crimes committed by poor persons are what law-abiding citizens have to fear most.

Finally, many acts committed by corporations, which result in death, injury, and sickness for thousands of innocent victims, are ignored in the sense that they are not treated as criminal behavior. Yet a good case can be made for the argument that white-collar acts which are harmful to public safety are more dangerous than street crime. For example, when a mine company is cited for safety violations, fails to correct them, and miners die in a subsequent disaster, the corporate leaders who failed to protect the victims are not arrested for murder. Rather, the company pays a fine, usually a small one. Or when a corporation illegally pollutes the environment, causing sickness and death for untold millions of people, its executives are not arrested for assault or murder. Rather, the company signs a consent decree, promising never to do it again. These are additional examples of the way ambition for success, a virtue in our society, produces a vice. Despite Merton's argument, crime is not primarily a lower-class phenomenon. What is significant about white-collar and corporate crime is that the perpetrators are often not held responsible. Burglars are rarely offered consent decrees. Rather, the criminal justice system puts them in jail and keeps industrial leaders out of it. This fact also reflects the political power of the nonpoor and perpetuates an image of who is the most dangerous to public safety, of who commits crime.

Before leaving this topic, I want to make one last point: The reciprocal relationship between poverty and crime also implies that the legal system is used by the nonpoor to exploit the poor and that they cannot obtain adequate legal services to prevent such exploitation. Here is an empirical generalization: the lower a person's social class, *then* the more the legal system is used to one's disadvantage.[30] What this assertion means is that, even though the poor often buy in market situations where illegal practices are pervasive and even though they often need government agencies to protect them, they find it difficult to use the law to obtain redress and they are more vulnerable to exploitation as a result.

Here are some examples of the way the legal system is used to exploit indigent people. Consumer frauds, such as misrepresenting the price of goods or the cost of credit, are more commonly inflicted on the poor than on other social classes. Similarly, impoverished persons are more often subjected to illegal collection practices. Indigents are often forced to pay for services they do not get, as when leases obligate a tenant to pay rent but owners do not keep up the property. Typically, appeals to government agencies for housing code enforcement, street repairs, or other services are not very effective without the help of a lawyer.

But the poor have less access to legal aid than any other segment of the population. The 1982 budget for the Legal Services Corporation, which is the main provider of lawyers for the poor, was cut two-thirds by the Reagan administration. This has resulted in one-third fewer lawyers being available to aid destitute people.[31] As noted previously, effective programs for nonvoting segments of the population are extremely difficult to maintain, especially when such programs are adversarial by definition. Politicians, not all of whom are conservative, do not want poverty lawyers paid for by the government suing private industry or the government itself. So their opportunity to do that has been restricted.

HEALTH AND POVERTY

The third correlate of poverty dealt with here is ill health and lack of access to medical care. It was noted in Chapter 3 that Medicaid has been a relatively successful program: Along with nutrition programs and other measures designed to improve the health of the population, both health levels of the poor and their access to medical care have improved over the past 10 to 15 years. Despite this fact, the health gap separating the poor from the nonpoor remains very wide. What I intend to do in this section is begin by summarizing the available data on class and health. Once the dimensions of the health gap are clear, I shall suggest why it occurs, who benefits from it, and how it is related to other aspects of poor living. In the process of this analysis, both the vulnerability and the limited choices available to impoverished persons will become obvious once again.

Such vital statistics as death rates, life expectancy, infant mortality, and maternal mortality are commonly used as indicators of the overall health of the population. This is partly because such data are easy to collect in quantified form and partly because they represent such intrinsically important issues. The empirical generalization is as follows: the lower the social class, *then* the higher the death rate, the shorter the life expectancy, the higher the infant mortality rate, and the higher the maternal mortality rate.[32]

What this finding means in terms of real lives can be seen by using race as a proxy for class. This is often done when analyzing vital statistics because the data are readily available and because blacks are three times more likely to be poor than whites (see Chapters 2 and 7). White males born in 1978 could expect to live 70 years on the average, whereas black males could expect to live only 65 years. The ratio is similar for females, although women of both races live longer than do men. Further, the infant mortality rate among white children was 12 per thousand in 1978, while it was 21 per thousand for black newborns; in other words, black infants were 75% more likely to die than white infants. Finally, the maternal death rate for whites was 6 per thousand in 1978, compared to 23 per thousand for blacks; in other words, black women were 283% more likely to die while giving birth than white women.[33] It should be emphasized that these figures represent a significant narrowing of racial differences in vital statistics.

Although data on class and vital statistics are often more difficult to obtain, infant mortality is an exception. The literature clearly shows that socioeconomic status and infant mortality are inversely related; that is, the lower the social class, *then* the higher the infant mortality rate. For example, in the most recent study, it was found that while the infant mortality rate in San Antonio, Texas, was 11 per thousand among high-income families in 1979, it rose to 17 per thousand among low-income households. Put differently, children from poor families are 55% more likely to die within a year of their birth. It should be noted that these findings replicate previous work using both states and counties as the unit of analysis.[34]

Infant mortality rates are a particularly useful indicator of the health of the population because newborn children's health is not only influenced by their immediate environment but also by the health of their mothers. The latter, of course, reflects the long-term consequences of the environment in which women live. The factors contributing to infant mortality are well known: low socioeconomic status, low birth weight, youth of mother, number of live births (parity), and out of wedlock births. The point to remember here is that social class not only affects infant mortality directly but also indirectly because it influences all the other factors affecting infant mortality.[35]

Acute conditions are those of less than 3-months duration for which medical attention is sought or which result in restricted activity. For example, the flu, the common cold, and assorted viruses are acute diseases. In covariance form, the finding is: the lower the social class, *then* the higher the rate of acute conditions. Thus, in 1975, adults in families with incomes of less than $10,000 had a 19% higher incidence of acute diseases than did adults in families with incomes above that level.[36] It is likely, however, that the gap between the poor and nonpoor is considerably greater than 19%, as the data in this case are only applicable to people who are in the labor force; they exclude both children and those not employed or looking for work. Hence, persons who live poorly are especially vulnerable to short-term diseases of all sorts. This is because impoverished persons are less able to be immunized against disease, less able to engage in other forms of preventive health care, and less able to visit a physician when illness strikes. The phrasing used here—less able to take health action—is deliberate; I shall come back to these topics.

Chronic conditions are long-term health problems. The conclusion is straightforward: the lower the social class, *then* the higher the rate of chronic conditions. What this means is that people with low incomes are afflicted with chronic conditions at a two to three times higher rate than those with high incomes, and in this case high income means above $15,000.[37] This finding is true not only for the leading causes of death—heart disease, cancer, stroke, and diabetes—but also for such diverse conditions as asthma, arthritis, hernia, ulcers, hearing impairments, vision impairments, back or spine impairments, and many other problems. For example, in 1973, the diabetes rate for adults in families with incomes of less than $5,000 was 74 per thousand, while it was only 31 per thousand in households with incomes above $15,000. Similarly, in 1971, people in families with incomes of less than $5,000 had a visual impairment rate (i.e., difficulty seeing) of 96 per thousand, while households with incomes above $15,000 had a rate of 35 per thousand.[38] These figures have probably not changed very much over the past decade. The point to remember here is that many of these conditions are both preventable and correctable. Yet poor persons are much less likely to be able to do either. For example, although Medicaid is supposed to provide early screening of children in order to detect vision and other health problems before they become chronic, such examinations often do not occur. Furthermore, as shown in Chapter 3, Medicaid often does not cover the cost of eyeglasses and other types of care. It should be noted that the data used here are older than I would like, although (despite what many think) more recent numbers would produce the same conclusions. It is very difficult to obtain current data on social class and vital statistics.

It is probable that various forms of preventive health practices—including obtaining periodic physical examinations, increasing immunization rates, obtaining adequate nutrition, and other actions—would do more to decrease the health gap than additional medical care. Yet in all these cases, the poor are less well off than other segments of the population. The summary statement is: the lower the social class, *then* the less preventive health care obtained. For example, in 1973, 71% of women with family incomes above $15,000 saw a doctor in the first trimester of their pregnancy, compared to only 47% of women with family incomes of less than $5,000 and 54% of women with family incomes between $5,000 and $10,000.[39] It is doubtful if these figures have changed very much. Thus, despite the Medicaid program, only about half of all poor women are able to obtain preventive care that can ensure their own and their baby's health. This is one reason why maternal and infant mortality rates vary by social class.

Similarly, immunization rates for all persons, and especially children, are much lower than they should be. Thus, in 1980, among children between the ages of one and four, 63% of whites were vaccinated against polio compared to 38% of nonwhites. Similarly, 70% of whites were vaccinated against diphtheria–typhoid–pertusis compared to 47% of nonwhites.[40] Like the chronic conditions cited earlier, these racial differences (which reflect class differences, of course) occur despite the early and periodic screening, diagnosis, and treatment component of the Medicaid program. The intent of the Congress in adding this element to Medicaid was to ensure the health of poor children and thereby keep long-term welfare costs down by requiring that the states actively engage in preventive health care. Nonetheless, federal enforcement and leadership (mainly by the executive branch) has always been minimal.[41] As might be expected, this problem has become even more pronounced in recent years, since funding for immunization and other programs designed to prevent the development of chronic conditions has been radically reduced. What this means is that the proportion of poor children immunized against disease will decline and that impoverished kids will get polio, diphtheria, and other diseases while nonpoor children will not.

The findings reviewed here show conclusively that a health gap exists such that the poor suffer from ill health a great deal more than do the nonpoor. The real question is why. I shall argue that the best explanation is structural; that is, the organization of the health-care delivery system produces the health gap because it is designed to benefit the providers of health rather than the recipients. Some observers have taken a rather different view, one that focuses on the attitudes of the poor toward health and medical care. For example, it has been asserted that the poor have different health priorities and diverse values with regard to health care and that these factors help to explain the findings already cited. This argument is a variant of the culture of poverty interpretation, an orientation that—put most simply—blames the victims for having health (or other) problems.[42] In the paragraphs to follow I shall suggest that, although poor people's attitudes and behaviors are often not conducive to good health, they are a product of vulnerability and limited choices. As such, they constitute a predictable and even a realistic response to the situation in which such persons find themselves. The culture of poverty thesis will be discussed in the next chapter.

The cost of obtaining health care is still enormous, and much of it must be borne by the poor. This is the first factor that inhibits impoverished people from getting treatment. It will be recalled from Chapter 3 that one-third of all poor families are not covered by Medicaid. This includes most two-parent families, single women pregnant with their first child in the 20 states that do not provide coverage for unborn children, and many others. This is why government data show that a family of four earning less than $10,000 spent an average of $640 per year on health expenses in 1975.[43] This figure excludes insurance premiums, but includes expenses for doctors, hospitals, dentists, prescriptions, glasses, and other health-related items. Many of these expenses are not covered by Medicaid. In Chapter 2, it should be remembered, it was shown that a family of four living at the poverty line has very little money left each month after meeting its basic expenses. And this amount must cover clothing, entertainment, and all other incidental costs, in addition to health care. This financial situation is why poor families have a difficult time making do. It is also one reason why they have a tendency not to recognize symptoms of ill health and to postpone visits to the doctor.

Furthermore, apart from the direct expense of health care, there are indirect (but no less real) financial costs for the poor that middle- and working-class people usually do not bear. This is because the nonpoor nearly always have sick leave built into their jobs—which is a form of in-kind income, by the way. Poor people rarely have such benefits, even when they are employed. When they take off from work, they do not get paid. Thus, like the business executive, people working by the hour know perfectly well that time is money. For impoverished persons who are employed know that even a simple doctor or dental appointment can mean a full day's pay lost. Thus, when a family is living on the edge of financial disaster, there is a strong impetus not to define oneself as sick and not to seek health care unless it is absolutely necessary.

In addition to financial costs, obtaining health care is incredibly time consuming because of both the distance that must be traveled and the waiting time involved. This is the second factor inhibiting impoverished persons from getting treatment. Essentially, very few physicians want to locate their offices in poor areas and very few hospitals are available either. As a result, the sheer distance that must be traveled represents a great problem for poor people who want medical care. In rural areas, as might be expected, it is common for people to travel hundreds of miles to see a doctor. But a similar pattern occurs in some urban environments as well because medical facilities are increasingly located far away from poor neighborhoods. For example, the Ehrenreichs' report that Milwaukee County Hospital, the major source of health care for thousands of people in that area, is 16 miles outside the city. This is a 1½-hour ride by bus.[44] After arriving at a hospital or clinic, however, poor people usually wait considerably longer in order to see a physician than do nonpoor persons.[45] Thus, the inconvenience intrinsic to obtaining health also makes indigent people hesitate before seeking treatment.

Assuming, however, that poverty-striken individuals can bear the costs and have the time to obtain medical care, they must then confront the confusing fragmentation that is characteristic of the health system. This is the third factor inhibiting impoverished persons from getting treatment. Unlike middle-class patients, who often have a family physician to guide them among the various medical specialties, poor people nearly always end up in hospital emergency rooms or clinics (often more than one) where no one person is responsible for seeing to it that their particular problems are correctly diagnosed and treated. Most public clinics and hospitals are confusing places, even for people who are sophisticated in dealing with bureaucracies. For the poor, the prospect of having to maneuver among several clinics or several departments of one clinic can be daunting. Thus, the fragmentation characteristic of the health-care system makes poor people tend to avoid seeking care unless it is absolutely necessary.

Finally, medical institutions are dehumanizing, especially for poor people. This is the fourth factor inhibiting impoverished persons from getting treatment. Dehumanization can be seen in several different ways, although I shall mention only two. Health-care personnel are often brusque, impersonal, even insulting to indigent patients—who have little choice but to endure it if they desire help. Such behavior is partly because the medical staff in any large facility is often very busy and really does have very little time. But it is also partly because medical people often do not like patients who are poor, primarily because they are perceived as not being very good patients. For example, the first thing a doctor is likely to say to a poor person who has suffered for too long with an affliction, conjured up a small amount of cash, taken off from work for the day, traveled a long distance, and maneuvered through the bureaucracy to get to the right place, is "Why didn't you come in sooner?" And the tone of condemnation, of disapproval, is clearly there. After making it plain that the patient is not very wise, the same doctor then prescribes a pattern of behavior that is unrealistic; for example, "Stay in bed for at least a week and then come back and see me." But for a poor person this is a good way to lose a job or have some other financial disaster occur. While this example is obviously stereotypical, it is designed to suggest the extent to which the health-care system ignores the needs of poor people their limited resources, and the stressful situation which they are confronting.

The dehumanization of poor patients occurs in another way as well, for such persons are often used as teaching material for medical students. And that is just how they are treated, as objects of study. Sometimes the result is "only" loss of dignity. At other times, it is inferior care or unnecessary treatment. My own guess is that much of the unnecessary surgery that occurs in the United States is done to impoverished persons. After all, Medicaid pays for it, and it provides both training for students and profit for physicians. Once again, this aspect of the health-care system makes poor people hesitate to seek help unless it is absolutely necessary. No human being, rich or poor, wants to be treated as an object.

The way in which the organization of the health system affects those who live poorly can now be understood. Empirical research has shown that lower-class individuals tend to postpone visits to a doctor until a health crisis occurs, that they seem willing to tolerate symptoms of illness longer than others do, and even that they tend not to define themselves as needing care when they in fact do.[46] Although short-sighted, since necessary treatment is often delayed or not obtained at all (leading to chronic conditions or even death), these attitudes and actions do not reflect different cultural values, as suggested by the notion of a culture of poverty. Rather, as even a cursory review of the impediments to obtaining health care shows, these orientations reflect the combined effects of indigency and the structure of the health-care delivery system.[47] They are, in fact, realistic responses to a situation over which poor persons have no control.

The fundamental irony revealed by this analysis can be easily summarized. Although the manifest purpose of the health-care delivery system is to provide care, it is organized in such a way—that is, it has high costs, inconvenience, fragmentation, and dehumanizing qualities built into it—that poor people are less able to seek care and, hence, less prone to define themselves as ill. Underlying this manifest purpose is the reality that the health delivery system in the United States is designed to benefit physicians, hospitals, drug companies, and others in the medical industry rather than those who receive care, a fact that affects the poor more than any other segment of the population. This situation results from the enormous political power wielded by the medical in-dustry. The characteristics of the health delivery system already cited did not develop by accident. Rather, they reflect the priorities of those in the health care system. For example, it is not an accident that so much emphasis is placed on treating illness rather than preventing it in this country. This public policy choice, and it is a choice, is both very expen-sive, which means that costs are high, and very profitable for people in certain positions. And it is a good example of how a social structure operates on individuals (pun intended).

It should be recognized, however, that many people have personal physicians who treat their medical problems, emphasize preventive health care, and the like. Such practitioners clearly have the interests of their patients at heart. But these experiences are not generalizable; they are class related. Furthermore, the context in which even this benign form of health care occurs (the physicians' relations with insurance companies, the location and organization of their offices, their referrals to specialists, etc.) reflects the fact that each individual doctor and patient is enmeshed in a system of health care that is more oriented to the needs of providers than recipients. And this fact is not class related; it is one reason why vital statistics data show that the United States is less healthy than many other industrial societies.

There is a further irony inherent to this analysis of health and poverty. It was noted that many poor people react to their exclusion from political participation with passivity, for they do not believe that they can be effective in the political arena and feel helpless to do anything about their situation. Similarly, some impoverished individuals react to their plight by retreating into themselves; in effect, their very helplessness sometimes leads them into drugs and, because of the organization of the criminal justice system, into crime. I would like to suggest that ill-health coupled with the tendency not to seek care, even in contexts where structural impediments are minimal, constitutes an analogous response. Put differently, the social–psychological characteristics of the poor follow directly from their position in the social structure rather than from the possession of deviant cultural values. This is the topic dealt with in the next chapter.

6

CULTURAL VALUES, ANALGESIC BEHAVIOR, AND POVERTY

Many academics argue that those who live poorly also have deviant cultural values epitomized by an unwillingness to plan ahead, low aspirations, and other value orientations that are inimical to occupational success. There are two interpretations of this relationship, each of which poses the issue in causal fashion. The culture of poverty thesis sees impoverishment as caused by the possession and, most importantly, the intergenerational transmission of deviant values. The situational adaptation thesis reverses the causal arrow and sees the deviant values associated with poverty as caused by the experience of living poorly; from this angle, although values such as those noted exist, they are merely situational adaptations necessary for survival in impoverished circumstances and they are not transmitted from parents to children across generations.

As is typical in the social sciences, each of these alternative hypotheses has political implications. The culture of poverty thesis blames the poor for their impoverishment, since, it is supposed, they choose to have deviant values and pass them on to their children. This argument appeals to conservatives, academic and otherwise, because it implies that public policies designed to combat poverty cannot be effective. The situational adaptation thesis blames the society, which allows impoverishment to continue for the genesis of deviant values in each new generation of people who live poorly. This argument appeals to liberals, academic and otherwise, because it implies that public policies designed to combat poverty can be effective.

It will be shown in this chapter that both the culture of poverty and situational adaptation theses are incorrect because poor people's deviant behavior usually does not reflect deviant cultural values. Once this fact is recognized, then it becomes possible to understand some of the actions of impoverished persons in a more sociological way: In the context of dominant values, such as the work ethic, that are adhered to by all social strata, the sociological significance of class is that poor people must choose among severely restricted options, many of which are not effective problem-solving strategies. This fact, which reflects the extreme vulnerability of those who live poorly, produces deviant behavior.

I shall suggest, then, that a concatenation of factors which tend to occur together—lack of control over the social situation, pervasive frustration, low sense of self-esteem and personal efficacy, and patterns of analgesic behavior—better explain patterns of deviance engaged in by some poor people. In covariance form, the hypothesis I am putting forth is as follows: the lower the social class, *then* the less people experience control over their environment, the more frustrated they become, the lower their sense of self-esteem and personal efficacy, and the more likely they are to establish patterns of analgesic behavior that have long-term nonadaptive consequences. By analgesic behavior, I refer to coping strategies aimed at controlling distress rather than eliminating the causes of problems.[1] Thus, as will be seen, such behaviors are not goal oriented in the normal sense. While this analysis is very tentative, I shall argue that it has the merit of providing a realistic explanation of the actions of many impoverished people, actions that seem strange and incomprehensible to middle-class persons.

Accordingly, this chapter is organized into three parts. It begins with a distinction between hard-living and settled-living poor people. The focus of the analysis in this chapter is on those individuals who are best described as hard livers. Then there is a critique of the culture of poverty and situational adaptation theses. And, finally, the hypothesis already noted is explained.

HARD LIVING VERSUS SETTLED LIVING

Both the culture of poverty and the situational adaptation theses try to explain some well-known observations that are summarized in the following two paragraphs.

In many cases, poor people respond to events passively. For example, when faced with a problem they often talk tough in front of their friends but actually wait for it to go away rather than actively seeking a solution. This is because the verbal and, sometimes, the physical toughness of destitute persons often reflects their bravado rather than real self-confidence. Similarly, even when economic opportunities are available, some impoverished persons respond in nonadaptive ways that guarantee failure. For example, they may be aggressive when such behavior is inappropriate or rigid when flexibility is necessary. Further, many individuals living poorly have a history of marital instability and geographical rootlessness that prevents them from establishing enduring ties with other persons and the community in which they live. For example, they seem to develop deep emotional bonds very quickly and yet break them off just as suddenly.

In addition, many poor people are alienated from the institutions of the larger society. For example, as suggested previously, they do not belong to organizations. This separation, however, is often seen as a virtue by those living poorly, for it is accompanied by a strong sense of individualism. Such persons describe themselves as loners and emphasize the importance of self-reliance and self-direction, even though they must often depend on public aid for survival. For example, in trying to establish their individuality, they may use a distinctive language (frequently vulgar), wear distinctive clothing, or drive distinctive cars or trucks. A lot of the time, the image being fostered is one of toughness. Such people also tend to shun factory work or jobs where they cannot at least appear to be their own boss. Finally, many poverty-stricken persons act in ways which ensure that solutions to their problems cannot be found. For example, they may drink excessively or become addicted to other kinds of drugs; in extreme cases, they may withdraw into a world of make believe.

It should be emphasized that not all poor persons have these characteristics and that the qualifying words used above, "many" and "some," should be taken seriously. Nonetheless, one observer, James Howell, describes people who have traits like these as "hard livers," and he distinguishes them from other poor people whom he calls "settled livers."[2] The latter persons try to solve problems actively, hold long-term jobs, have enduring marriages, have roots in their communities, belong to organizations, and the like. Settled livers, then, are impoverished persons who have relatively stable lives. To use Merton's terminology, they ritually adapt by defining success in prosaic terms. For example, their definition of a good marriage is a long lasting one in which the husband is a good provider who does not beat his wife; happiness or emotional or sexual satisfaction are not the criteria used in evaluating a relationship.[3]

This distinction between hard livers and settled livers is an ideal type that allows observers to place poor people on a continuum, one that very roughly indicates how deviant they are. Thus, the distinction reflects a fundamental class division within poor areas. Those impoverished individuals who resemble settled livers often do not see themselves as lower class, even though they are poor and may be dependent on public aid to support themselves. When used as an epithet, by poor persons, the term lower class is reserved for the hard livers. In addition, the distinction is useful to social scientists because both the culture of poverty and situational adaptation theses aim at understanding people who resemble hard livers by postulating that they have deviant values which are reflected in their way of life.

A CRITIQUE OF THE CULTURE OF POVERTY AND SITUATIONAL ADAPTATION THESES

According to Oscar Lewis, the culture of poverty has "its own structure and rationale." It is "a way of life that is passed down from generation to generation along family lines."[4] Based on his observations, Lewis believes that while people living in a culture of poverty are aware of middle-class values and even claim to adhere to them, "on the whole they do not live by them. Thus, it is important to distinguish between what they say and what they do." And he thinks the latter reflects their true values. What many poor people do, he says, is display a low level of occupational aspiration, lack commitment to work, hold fatalistic attitudes about their health and many other aspects of their lives, prefer a present time orientation to planning ahead, seek consensual unions rather than marriage, approve of sexual promiscuity, value authoritarianism, and engage in high rates of violence, among other dubious characteristics. The similarity between these characteristics and those attributed to hard livers should be obvious.

Lewis also asserts that these cultural values have positive functions because they bring rewards that people require in order to carry on with their lives. "Living in the present," he writes, "may develop a capacity for spontaneity, for the enjoyment of the sensual, for the indulgence of impulse, which is often blunted in the middle class, future-oriented man." Furthermore, "The frequent use of violence certainly provides a ready outlet for hostility so that people in the culture of poverty suffer less from repression than does the middle class." (This is, evidently, the culture of poverty explanation for high crime rates in poor neighborhoods.) Lewis concludes by observing that "in some ways the people with a culture of poverty suffer less from alienation than do those of the middle class."[5]

This whole analysis seems ludicrous, at least to me; it appears to be little more than a projection (in a psychoanalytical sense) of middle-class ennui. But it is important to remember that Lewis' analysis does make sense to many people. For underlying much public discussion of the poverty problem is the lingering suspicion that poor persons really enjoy their impoverishment, an apprehension that receives its social scientific apotheosis in the notion of the culture of poverty. This is why economists so glibly refer to unemployment as an unpaid vacation, as leisure time.

The idea that there is a culture of poverty has been widely criticized on empirical grounds. As seen in Chapter 4, studies of the values and work behavior of the poor by Leonard Goodwin and many others indicate that impoverished persons hold work-oriented values similar to those held by other Americans. In this same vein, Chapter 3 showed that one of the most important factors in rising public assistance costs over the past 15 years has been paupers' attempts at combining work with aid whenever possible. Since Lewis makes such a point about what people do, it is important to remember that what most poor persons do is work, and this role is also characteristic of most hard livers. In addition, studies of impoverished individuals in terms of the specific values Lewis attributes to them show little support for the culture of poverty thesis.[6] Finally, most of those analyses that attribute deviant values to the poor, such as the studies of health orientations referred to in the previous chapter, do not take into account the structural restraints with which impoverished people must cope.

The culture of poverty thesis can also be criticized on purely theoretical grounds. First, it is tautologous. Thus, people who are poor and do not appear to want to work, who lower their occupational aspirations, or who continually drink themselves out of jobs or marriages are part of the culture of poverty by definition. In contrast, those poor persons who work when they can, try to plan ahead, and maintain stable families are not part of the culture of poverty, again by definition. As such, the culture of poverty thesis cannot be falsified.[7]

The second theoretical problem stems from the way in which the concept of values is used and the psychological orientations implicitly attributed to the poor. The culture of poverty literature twists the concept of values beyond all social scientific recognition. In most introductory texts, sociologists say something to the effect that values are a set of ideas about what is good and bad; as such, they provide guidelines for action and facilitate social stability. Yet the values attributed to those adhering to the culture of poverty cannot do that. Does it make sense to argue that poor people value being needy and dependent (for example, by maintaining themselves through public assistance), value not working in a society where status is defined by work, value being present time-oriented, value consensual unions, value sexual promiscuity, value authoritarianism, and value violence? I think not. This set of "values" cannot provide the foundation for a viable culture (or subculture) because they are characteristics that facilitate social and psychological disorganization rather than stability. This set of "values" cannot provide people with moral guidelines. In short, there is no culture in the culture of poverty thesis. An adequate explanation of those characteristics of the poor under consideration here must proceed on some basis other than the imputation of deviant values.

This conceptual problem occurs because certain unrealistic psychological characteristics are implicitly attributed to the poor. What needs to be remembered is that the culture of poverty thesis is an attempt at accounting for behavior that middle-class people do not understand; indeed, they think it is senseless. Thus, like the general public, academics (who are very middle class) have assumed that people who are different must have different values and that their goals in life must reflect these values. In social psychological terms, this is an example of the fundamental attribution error.[8] In this case, underlying the attribution of deviant values to the poor is an implicit psychological assumption: that the behavior of poor people, as reflected in the characteristics attributed to the culture of poverty, is goal oriented. I do not think this is always the case, as will be seen subsequently. Rather, it is more plausible to describe such characteristics as reactions to pervasive, structurally induced frustration; reactions that are patterned and predictable in a social context where people have little control over what happens to them. The significance of social class is that it indicates the quantity and effectiveness of the options individuals have. Oscar Lewis is really describing the nonlogical reactions of people with extremely limited choices. Such persons are perfectly aware of the disjunction between their life-styles and dominant values. In fact, it is this disjunction, which is forced on them by structural restraints, that causes their frustration and their resort to analgesic behaviors.

I would like to make one last comment here, the relevance of which will be suggested later. If a middle-class person, say, a college professor, were to become apathetic—letting his or her appearance go, not showing up for work on time, bouncing checks but not worrying about it, drinking too much, withdrawing from contact with family, friends, and colleagues—a clinician would probably judge that person as depressed and recommend therapy and perhaps other courses of action in order to alleviate the situation. It is ironic that when poor people display similar sorts of behaviors, they are assumed to have different values.

In opposition to the culture of poverty thesis, the situational adaptation interpretation asserts that the experience of poverty leads people to display the preferences and behaviors just cited because they have few other choices. In a very well-known essay, Hyman Rodman has tried to explain what happens by arguing that impoverished persons develop a "wider range of values" so "they need not be continually frustrated by their failure." Rodman calls this process the "lower class value stretch."[9]

The result, he says, is that poor people "come to tolerate and eventually evaluate favorably certain deviations from middle class values." For example, it can be argued that being present time oriented is simply a realistic reaction to one's impoverishment. Thus, in order to plan for the future, people not only need access to resources now, but they also need some assurance of continued access in the future. People trying to feed a family of four on $2.12 per person each day (the amount available at the poverty line, as described in Chapter 2) have little or no assurance of future resources. Hence, they do not value planning ahead. Similar ad hoc explanations can be constructed for all the traits Lewis attributes to the culture of poverty or the characteristics of those labeled here as hard livers. Thus, the situational adaptation thesis does not deny the argument that the poor have deviant values. It merely asserts that such beliefs are a realistic response to the situation in which indigent people find themselves and that each generation adopts such goals anew.

Some indication of how the process of value-stretching occurs can be seen in Elliot Liebow's, *Tally's Corner*, which is one of the most eloquent defenses of the poor ever written. The constant struggle of black street-corner men to survive with dignity in a social context in which little dignity is possible is portrayed graphically in this book. Liebow's conclusion is well known: each man's "behavior appears not so much as a way of realizing the distinctive goals and values of his own subculture, or of conforming to its models, but rather as his way of trying to achieve many of the goals and values of the larger society, of failing to do this, and of concealing his failure from others and from himself as best he can."[10] The same essential conclusion can be drawn from Howell's analysis of hard living. In effect, although Liebow does not make such an assertion, this process of attempt, failure, and self-deception—when repeated over and over again—often results in the lower-class value stretch.

There are, however, three problems with the situational adaptation thesis that make it a highly dubious analysis. First, as with the culture of poverty interpretation, the notion of values, even "stretched" values is sociologically absurd. The same question asked above is applicable here: Does it make social scientific sense to interpret the behaviors characteristic of hard livers as manifestations of values, even situationally specific values? I think not. In fairness, it should be noted that some observers who have adopted the situational adaptation thesis do not explicitly argue that the poor have deviant values. Most, like Liebow, finesse the issue. I simply think it is implicit in their work.

Second, the situational adaptation interpretation posits that people have a degree of intellectual (and perhaps emotional) flexibility which is unrealistic. Thus, by positing that the behavior and values of hard livers are merely situational adaptations which can and will change when their circumstances change, the argument ignores the socializing effect of poverty. People learn from their experiences; that is, they develop, among other characteristics, a sense of self-efficacy and patterns of responding to events that become stable parts of their personalities. And this generalization applies to all social classes. Because it cannot explain the persistence of hard living even when opportunities are available, the situational thesis is very flawed. It should be recognized here that I am not arguing change is impossible or that people do not adapt to new (nonpoverty) experiences; I am only arguing that it is difficult. This means, then, that many hard livers become—with stable jobs, enduring marriages, religious conversion, or some other significant event—settled livers. Many hard livers escape from poverty altogether. But many find it difficult to do either of these things, and they are the population of interest here.

Finally, underlying the situational thesis is the same sort of psychological assumption that characterizes the culture of poverty interpretation: Poor people are goal oriented and, as such, they are motivated to achieve both dominant as well as their peculiar stretched values. This orientation is seen clearly in Liebow's work. The streetcorner men he observed obviously felt the need to be occupationally successful, to plan ahead, to maintain stable marriages, and the like. But when achievement in the conventional sense was barred, and when (unlike settled livers) the opportunity to ritually adapt by simply scaling down their goals was also barred, then they stretched out areas of permissible behavior and values. As with the culture of poverty thesis, the assumption that hard livers are being logical and rational is made in order to understand patterns of action that are not, from a middle-class vantage point, understandable at all.

My conclusion, then, is that an adequate explanation of the characteristics of the poor under consideration here must proceed on some basis other than either the culture of poverty or the situational adaptation thesis. The irony inherent in both analyses is that while each reinforces public prejudices—conservative and liberal, respectively—neither explains very much.

Apart from the specific problems intrinsic to each interpretation, it is apparent that observers in neither camp recognize that economic deprivation and frustration usually do not produce new (that is, deviant) values in the absence of an explicit ideology. It is only when such beliefs become widespread, whether promulgated by representatives of the oppressed or developed indigenously, that there is a basis for development of a coherent value system.[11] Since this condition is clearly not satisfied in the United States, then an altogether different approach is necessary in order to understand the actions and preferences of hard livers. One way of doing this is to examine how human beings (and other animals) react to situations in which they have little control over the choices they have or the consequences of their actions. That is the topic I wish to turn to now.

ANALGESIC BEHAVIOR AND POVERTY

As described earlier, the hypothesis I am advancing is that poverty is inherently frustrating and that the attitudes and actions displayed by impoverished persons reflect their attempt, in the absence of an alternative value system, at coping with the resulting distress. I am using the term analgesic behavior to describe those practices that blunt awareness and meliorate discomfort without eliminating the source of the problem.

In order to illustrate the social significance of frustration and analgesic behavior, I am going to begin by reviewing the work of the experimental psychologist, Norman Maier, conducted in the 1940s.[12]

Maier distinguished between motivation- and frustration-instigated behavior. He defined motivation-investigated behavior as actions selected in light of the consequences they will produce. Motivated behavior, then, is a means to an end rather than an end in itself. It is flexible and adaptive: Actions that help to achieve goals are retained and those which do not are abandoned. Conversely, frustration-instigated behaviors are defined as actions that are not goal oriented; they are, rather, designed only to bring relief from aversive circumstances. Hence, I have called them analgesic. The reason such behavior seems senseless when looked at from the point of view of motivation, which is the angle most middle-class people take (including most sociologists), is because it is a terminal response. Thus, Maier argues that frustration-instigated behavior is not a means to an end, but an end in itself. This is why it is often nonadaptive. Now it should be remembered that this distinction is analytical: Organisms usually have contradictory impulses, both of which come into play from time to time.

Nonetheless, such a distinction is useful in understanding behavior, as Maier showed in a series of evocative experiments conducted over a 10-year period. Unfortunately, given the prejudices of many sociologists, Maier's work was primarily with rats. However, after describing his experiments I shall link these data with subsequent experimental research on learned helplessness in order to show their applicability to human behavior and with social psychological research on distress and coping in order to show how they help understand those who live poorly.

The experimental conditions Maier established were as follows. The rats were placed on a small stand opposite a wall containing two openings, each of which was blocked with a card bearing a distinctive symbol. Behind one of the cards was food. Thus, the location of the food could be varied by either position, regardless of the symbol on the card, or by card placement, whichever side it was on. When the animal jumped toward the correct card or position, the card fell over and food was obtained. When it jumped incorrectly, the card remained locked, and the animal received a bump on the nose and fell into a·net below.

Now following well-established tenets of ordinary learning theory, some animals were trained to jump to either a specific card or a specific position by systematically placing the food in that location (the precise reward schedule is not relevant). Hence, after trial and error, the animals learned the correct pattern and, thereafter, systematically obtained a reward by jumping to the correct location. Further, when the pattern of food placement was changed, the animals experimented and learned the new pattern very quickly. As indicated, all of this follows from learning theory. Maier labels it motivation-instigated behavior because, even when faced with uncertainty and some frustration, the animals varied their behavior until they perceived a pattern and adjusted themselves to it. Thus, their actions, even during trial-and-error periods were goal oriented. And this was a generalized response-pattern, maintained even when the reward patterned was changed.

Without pushing the analogy between infrahumans and humans too far, I would like to suggest that the rats in this situation learned that with initiative they could overcome obstacles. Their goal-oriented behavior reflected a sense that they could (within limits) control the attainment of rewards. This is similar to the experiences middle-class people have. Most observers, and this includes many social scientists, simply assume that everyone is goal oriented in the sense described here. On this basis, then, they extrapolate that there is a direct connection between attitudes and action (as described in Chapter 4) and that if the poor behave differently they must have different values. In fact, however, the sorts of experiences described here are class related. People who live poorly do not learn they can overcome obstacles. Rather, they learn that most obstacles are insurmountable.

This situation is illustrated in the next phase of Maier's experiment. For other rats were trained in an altogether different fashion: the cards were locked at random. This meant that the animals were faced with an insolvable problem in that no discernable pattern of action would systematically elicit a reward, and this fact was reflected in the nature of their actions.

After some variability in behavioral choices while apparently searching in trial-and-error fashion, the animals' first consistent response when placed in the insolvable situation was to stop jumping. Like the poor, who are often in insolvable situations, they became passive. When the animals were forced to jump, by blowing air on them, for example, the second response of some of them was to try to jump around or over the apparatus in order to get at the food. Like the poor, the animals became creative or aggressive in attempting to obtain rewards. Implementation of this strategy, however, was prevented by the installation of barriers onto the apparatus. In other words, innovative responses were met with social control measures by those in charge of the experiments.

The third consistent response was the most interesting: When forced to jump in a context where no solution was possible and where creative alternatives were eliminated, the rats chose a response from among the alternatives that were available and adhered to it rigidly even though it had no adaptive results. Thus, the animals simply selected one of the four jumping options: left side, right side, or one of the two cards regardless of the side on which it was located. While the behavior chosen could not facilitate obtaining food, that fact was irrelevant given the situation in which the animals found themselves.

This analgesic tactic had the advantage of eliminating a decision and making the rats more comfortable. Prior to this time, while still uncertain, they often had seizures. Whether for this reason or some other, the choice made was repeated over and over again regardless of what else happened. For example, even if the card was locked so that punishment occurred 100% of the time, the animals continued their selected response. Maier argues, in fact, that, having learned there was no relationship between their actions and consequences, punishment became a reward. As another example, the response was maintained even when a new option was made available. Thus, given, say, right-side jumpers, if the left-side window was left open to reveal food, the rats would sniff at it and then jump to the right. Finally, the animals developed coping strategies appropriate for the situation in which they found themselves. For example, rather than jumping head on and bumping their noses, the rats would jump sideways so as to hit their hindquarters against the locked card.

In sum, the most significant characteristics of animals' responses to inescapable aversive situations are their simplicity, their rigidity, and their analgesic quality. Simplicity is seen in the decision to cease experimenting with alternative forms of behavior. Rigidity is seen in the decision to maintain a particular response pattern regardless of what else happens. Analgesia is seen in the attempt at minimizing the pain that accompanies frustration. Maier's conclusion is that, after a period of attempting to find a solution to the problem they were faced with and after repeatedly failing in this attempt, these animals adopted behavioral strategies that were not goal oriented in the sense that they were helpful in solving the problem at hand. And it seems to me that this is precisely what poor people do: As Liebow indicates, they try to succeed, fail, and the resulting frustration produces the patterns of analgesic behavior described earlier in this chapter. I would like to suggest that the position of the poor in society is precisely analogous to the position of the rats in Maier's experiment: They have very limited options, none of which can solve the problems they face.

It is important to recognize, however, that extrapolating experimental findings dealing with nonsymbolic creatures to human beings is difficult and that these data are provocative rather than definitive. Hence, it is useful to examine briefly some of the experimental findings on learned helplessness in which people are the subjects. For this research tradition shows clearly that human beings react in ways roughly similar to the animals in Maier's work.

There is now a long literature on learned helplessness in people.[13] Although the experimental conditions vary somewhat from one study to another, they all involve exposing comparable groups of human beings, usually college students, to situations in which rewards are either contingent or noncontingent on behavior. I shall summarize the major findings in this literature with a generalized example. Readers interested in the specifics should see the sources cited in the notes.

The control group in these experiments is subjected to ordinary learning tasks. For example, when faced with a series of solvable anagrams, most people quickly learn the underlying pattern according to which the letters are mixed and then systematically discover the hidden words. Subsequently, when placed in another situation, say, one in which they can escape from hearing an aversive noise by pushing a button in a specific sequence, they readily solve this problem as well. In other words, the control group displays purposive, goal-oriented, and effective action; and their responses are generalized to new situations. In Maier's terms, their behavior is motivation instigated. As mentioned earlier, these experiences are similar to those middle-class people have.

The people in the experimental situation, however, are exposed to noncontingent reinforcement; that is, there is no relationship between their actions and rewards. For example, although told to solve the anagrams and that a solution is possible, the participants in the experiment find that they cannot discover a solution. This is because the letters are in fact random and no words can be formed. In subsequent tasks, then, three reactions have been documented: aggression, passivity, and what is called learning impairment. For example, individuals who have been exposed to the unsolvable anagram condition may become angry with the experimenter and quit.[14] Alternatively, such persons may sit passively when subsequently faced with the aversive noise situation, even when the latter problem is actually solvable. In this case, college students, few of whom come from impoverished backgrounds, make inappropriate generalizations from uncontrollable to controllable situations and display a form of "learning impairment." Having tried and failed, their behavior is frustration-instigated: It is simple, rigid, and analgesic in nature. It is not goal oriented. I would like to suggest that these experiences are similar to those poor people have all the time and that they react in much the same way participants in experimental studies of learned helplessness do; that is, they are passive, aggressive, and suffer from "learning impairment."

What needs to be remembered is that, regardless of class, psychological reactions to continual frustration and distress may produce analgesic behaviors that are not aimed at eliminating the source of the problem. In the sense of being logical or goal-oriented, these actions are not rational and cannot be understood from a point of view that equates rationality and logic. Martin Seligman, in fact, has suggested that learned helplessness is a model for depression in human beings. He speculates that the procedures used to produce this phenomenon should also produce symptoms associated with mild depression: poor self-concept, apathy, withdrawal from contact with other people, excessive drug use, and the like.[15] It seems to me that a plausible argument can be made that many poor people, rather than having deviant values, are depressed in the sense that word is used by clinicians.

I do not, however, want to push that proposition very hard in this context. Rather, I would like to suggest that by making use of the experimental findings reviewed here it is possible to understand the deviant behavior of those poor persons who have hard-living characteristics without imputing deviant values to them. Indeed, one source of their anguish is the fact that they share those values which are dominant in American society, especially those having to do with work.

It will be recalled that the hypothesis being suggested as an alternative to both the culture of poverty and situational adaptation theses is as follows: the lower the social class, *then* the less people experience control over their environment, the more frustrated they become, the lower the sense of self-esteem and personal efficacy, and the more they establish patterns of analgesic behavior that have long-term, nonadaptive consequences. The dependent variables in this hypothesis should be seen as additive functions. That is, it is not just poverty which influences the development of analgesic behaviors, especially the more debilitating forms, since many poor persons can be described as settled livers: They have a stable place in the community, however modest it may be. It is impoverishment in conjunction with the other characteristics mentioned here that leads to an emphasis on analgesic behavior by people.

On this basis, it is possible to understand the significance of some of the findings in social psychology. For there are now long literatures on the relationship between socioeconomic status and locus of control, frustration, and self-concept and personal efficacy.[16] The major finding, of course, is the lower the social class, *then* the more restricted the locus of control, the greater the frustration, and the lower the self-concept and sense of personal efficacy. What must be emphasized is that these responses are very realistic. Previous chapters have documented how little influence the poor have on the way poverty is measured; the requirements for receiving public assistance, the availability of work, the organization of the political process, the operation of the criminal justice system, or the functioning of the health-care delivery system. These data mean that people who live poorly are existing in a social environment which is characterized by very limited choices, and this situation is inherently frustrating because they perceive little connection between their actions and solutions to the problems they have. This fact reflects their extraordinary vulnerability. As a result, like the rats in Maier's experiments, some destitute people get beaten down by their daily lives and adopt patterns of action that are simple, rigid, and above all analgesic in nature. For some people, such as the hard livers described earlier, these behaviors become pervasive learned responses.

Like the other correlates of poverty dealt with in Chapters 3–5, analgesic action redounds to help cause the creation and perpetuation of a class of impoverished persons. That is the topic considered next.

7

THE CAUSES OF POVERTY

The causes of poverty can be studied from two angles, each of which provides a different kind of information. Thus, one can inquire either why individuals are poor or why ongoing social processes produce a class of impoverished persons. After briefly reviewing the problems with the first question, I shall argue that the answer to the second query produces a far more sophisticated and realistic assessment of the causes of poverty.

Most observers, and this includes many social scientists, find it easier to think about the successes and failures of individuals than to examine more general, structural characteristics of society. This is partly because the ethic of individual responsibility is so ingrained in our culture and partly because quantitative research generally focuses on individual variations.

Thus, as indicated in previous chapters, survey data show that the public has a set of easy answers to questions about the causes of poverty: It is asserted that people live poorly because they are not very thrifty, because they are lazy and do not want to work, because the "welfare" system takes care of them, because they do not have very much ability, and because they have loose morals (as signified by alcoholism and other forms of addiction, sexual promiscuity, violence, etc.). In most cases, the vast majority of the population agrees with statements like these.[1]

Similarly, many social scientific studies of employment and unemployment, political participation, voluntary association membership, crime, health-seeking behavior, and cultural values take the individual as the unit of analysis. While these happen to be the topics dealt with in previous chapters, one could pick almost any subfield in sociology and make the same assertion. As a result, the characteristics of individuals are often assumed to be the most important causal variables in the social sciences. This is why, for example, surveys of the relationship between social class and political participation have a tendency to blame the poor for their low rates of participation.[2]

The problem with those analyses which focus on individual deficiencies is that they are often neither very realistic nor very practical, and this is true whether they are promulgated by the public or by social scientists. The latter, however, are often very sophisticated in the use of quantitative methods. It is this characteristic that not only gives social scientific findings an aura of precision and objectivity but also, when individuals are the unit of analysis, often leads to unrealistic and impractical causal attributions.

The public's lack of realism becomes obvious when the stereotypes just described are juxtaposed with the facts reviewed in previous chapters. Thus, although many people believe that the poor are not very thrifty because they may purchase liquor or an expensive cut of meat or some other nonessential item and that their impoverishment often results from such lack of wisdom, the fact is that a family living at the poverty line cannot escape destitution by being thrifty. The budget depicted in Chapter 2 shows this fact clearly. Actually, as indicated in Chapter 4, my own view is that in agreeing with such assertions most people are merely expressing their values in the form of stereotypes about the poor.

The lack of realism characteristic of much social scientific research can be conveyed with a simple example. It is well known that alcoholism is inversely related to socioeconomic status; that is, the lower the social class, *then* the higher the rate of alcoholism. Both quantitative and ethnographic literature suggest this is true.[3] The question is why. One way of explaining this relationship is to suggest that poor people drink too much because they prefer the pleasure of alcohol to employment. Now such an assertion seems ludicrous when phrased in bold fashion like this, and I know of no study of alcoholism or alcohol use that would support this interpretation. But sociologists and economists make similar claims all the time: The standard wisdom is that individuals choose to seek work or not, depending on the value they place on other, presumably more desirable (but often deviant) activities; for example, drinking with their buddies. Such depictions of human behavior are just not very realistic, mainly because they do not take into account the social context in which it occurs.

The emphasis on individual deficiencies is often not very practical either, mainly because the solutions that follow are ineffectual. Poor people, some social scientists argue, should get jobs, participate in the political process, organize their neighborhoods in cooperation with the police, seek health care sooner, and be psychologically strong so as not to need alcohol or other drugs. As described previously, none of these actions, taken by poor people alone, will eliminate impoverishment. These solutions are not very practical because the individual is the unit of analysis and, as a result, they do not take into account the social context in which each person must act.

It should be emphasized here that I am not arguing individual behaviour is unimportant. Quite the opposite is the case: Social contexts do not act, people do. But, as shown in Chapters 5 and 6, pepople choose among socially structured alternatives. This means that a sociological analysis of the causes of poverty must take this fact into account.

From this point of view, a realistic and practical assessment of the causes of poverty has to be structural in nature; that is, it should get at the way in which the organization of socciety systematically produces a class of poor persons. For once the social facts circumscribing individual choice are made clear, then it is possible to address solutions to problems. In this regard, it should be remembered that a focus on the significance of social structure does not involve arcane reasoning. For example, even though the public emphasizes the importance of individual initiative in eliminating poverty, it is also aware of the social context in which such behavior must occur. Thus, after agreeing with the stereotypes cited at the beginning of this chapter, well over half of all respondents also assent to the following statements: "People are poor because there just aren't enough good jobs for everybody" and "Poor people didn't have a chance to get a good education—schools in poor neighborhoods are much worse than other schools."[4] These assertions show a clear awareness of the way in which individuals' choices are circumscribed by social facts they do not control.

A sociological analysis should explain how these structural processes work. Hence, in the remainder of this chapter I shall examine four characteristics of American society that cause the existence of poverty:

1. The way in which the correlates of poverty create a vicious circle that often traps the poor and prevents them from changing their situation
2. The way the class system reproduces itself over time
3. The organization of the economy
4. The continuation of institutionalized discrimination against blacks and women

The point of this analysis is to show that most impoverished people live poorly for structural reasons, very few of which have to do with their motivations, skills, or other personal traits.

THE VICIOUS CIRCLE OF POVERTY AND PAUPERISM

✓ Being poor is more than merely an economic status. It combines with other spheres of life in a reciprocal cause and effect way. This reciprocity can be described by seeing poverty as part of a vicious circle that snares people and prevents their escape. In addition to lack of money, some of the components of this circle are public assistance, the political system, the criminal justice system, the health-care delivery system, and the patterns of analgesic behavior engaged in by the poor. In other words, the correlates of poverty are not merely the unfortunate results of having little income; they also help to perpetuate living poorly. In this *elements* way, then, they cause the creation and perpetuation of a class of poverty-stricken persons.

1) The first element in the vicious circle is pauperism. Rather than stimulating impoverished households to extricate themselves from poverty, public assistance is designed to keep people poor. This is because the difficulties involved in maintaining a normal family life are so great and the penalties for obtaining employment or increasing wages are so severe. Conservatives like to argue that employed persons should not get public aid because they ought to remain economically independent. And, as seen in Chapter 3, this policy has been implemented in the past few years. Nonetheless, it is a shameful orientation, for the hard fact is that an intact family of four can hardly survive (legally) when the head earns $3.35 per hour, or $6,968 a year. The choices a family in this situation has are very limited and do not generate much optimism for the future. Here are some examples of the options available ot such a household.

In order to get AFDC the family has to break up. Another way of proceeding, of course, is to commit public assistance fraud by pretending to have an absent father or cohabiting without being married. Although these strategies are degrading, many families use them because they are the only way to survive. Two implications of such behavior ought to be mentioned. First, underlying observations by Oscar Lewis and other culture of poverty theorists that poor people prefer consensual unions to marriage is the reality of the public aid system, which structures the choices available to such persons. These are not college students having a fling before marriage, and to assert that impoverished women and men value cohabiting as a permanent life-style is puerile. Second, control of both the livelihood and the continued existence of such a family does not rest with the persons involved, but with a third party: the social worker. Although midnight raids looking for a man in the house ceased some years ago, social workers still make home visits for various reasons. It is my impression that they often see evidence of AFDC mothers cohabiting;

some just overlook it, others terminate public aid (including food stamps and Medicaid). Hence, the future of such a household depends utterly on the orientation of a stranger. Piven and Cloward have argued that one of the functions of public assistance has always been to regulate the lives of the poor, and this is still true today.[5] This is one reason why many impoverished persons resort to analgesic behavior.

Let us return to the example of a formally (that is, married) intact family: If this household is lucky enough to live in one of the 17 states that extend Medicaid coverage to intact poor families, then its health-care needs can be met. In the other 33 states, the household must (a) break apart so as to qualify for AFDC and become eligible for Medicaid that way; (b) plead for charity at a local hospital; or (c) avoid getting sick or having accidents. In most states, then, if intact families with low incomes choose to stay together, they often perpetuate their poverty simply because they cannot obtain medical care. This is because untreated acute conditions easily become chronic. Note again that the choices such households have are dictated by policies over which they have no control.

Although this family is eligible for food stamps, what it cannot do is increase its income by, say, the head getting a better job or the unemployed spouse going to work. For under the current rules, the household will have to choose between public assistance and wage income. Thus, as described in Chapter 3, a family with an income above 130% of the poverty line is automatically ineligible for food stamps, even if the expenses involved in getting to work and arranging for child care reduce net income to a figure below poverty level. A similar process occurs with Medicaid. Such families have very difficult choices to make, for they are faced with what economists call high marginal tax rates. That is, they get no rewards for attempting to increase their income above a certain level. They are, then encouraged to stay poor by the public assistance system. In this context, street crime becomes a realistic option. But the penalties for getting caught are substantial. The stress inherent in living in these circumstances is such that many families (whether married or cohabiting) do not have to pretend to break apart. Yet the impoverished mother faces many of the same problems especially the imperative to stay dependent in order to retain eligibility for public aid.

Prior to 1981, the public assistance system was not very good; it was fragmented, inefficient, and inequitable; and it encouraged families to break up and remain paupers. Since that time, all these tendencies have been exacerbated. As a result, pauperism forms part of a vicious circle that creates and perpetuates a class of indigent persons. What is truly amazing is that so many people keep trying. This fact shows not only the importance of status considerations and the salience of dominant American values, but also how remarkable the human spirit is. It is easy to see why a few individuals just give up. Yet the sad fact is that it really does not matter whether people are beaten down or not, for the likelihood of their escaping poverty is almost totally dependent on events beyond their control. This fact can be seen when the other correlates of poverty are examined.

The second element in the vicious circle is political disenfranchisement. As indicated in Chapter 5, destitute persons are politically disenfranchised because they do not have the resources necessary to participate in the legitimate political arena and because the major parties make no effort to mobilize impoverished persons. As a result, "welfare" policy benefits the middle classes and penalizes the poor for working; public assistance does not promote family stability; street crime is not controlled; and the health-care delivery system does not meet the needs of indigent people. It is important to remember that these results reflect the political choices of upper- and middle-class people. As such, while the public policies producing them are not immutable, it is unlikely that any changes which occur will benefit the poor unless they also benefit those who are not poor. This is because the political process is run by and for upper- and middle-class people, in about that order of importance, since these are the individuals who contribute money to campaigns and vote in the greatest numbers. For example, it has been estimated that 90% of all campaign contributions come from just 1% of the population and that 60% of all donations are in amounts greater than $500.[6] Very few people can afford to contribute even this small amount of money.

Now this situation can be changed. For example, by enacting legislation to limit campaign contributions, especially by political action committees, and by making it easier to register and vote, then the ability of indigent people to participate (without violence) would be vastly increased. Their influence on public policy would be greater as well. However, because the implementation of such changes depends on the non-poor, since they are the dominant actors in the current system, it is not likely that the means to increase political participation (i.e., political power) will be sponsored by middle- and upper-class people. This is why the formation of public policy is dependent on events beyond the control of the poor. Thus, as with public assistance, the organization of the political process helps to create a class of impoverished people.

The third element in the vicious circle is crime and the criminal justice system. When the emphasis in considering this issue is placed on crime and criminals, then it can be seen that the relative inability to attain either economic or occupational success through legal means induces high rates of street crime among the poor. In addition, the criminal justice system is organized in a way that perpetuates the relationship between crime and poverty; it dehumanizes its subjects while in jail and severely restricts their options afterward.

When the emphasis is placed on the victims of crime, then it can be seen that the pervasiveness of street crime in poor neighborhoods means that such areas are disorganized and unsafe, and that there are plenty of criminal role models available for children. The main sociological implication of endemic social disorganization and the existence of deviant role models is that poor persons can never have the illusion of control over their immediate environment: When people's own bodies and homes are not safe, then it is very difficult to plan ahead or be goal oriented; and when parents find it difficult to control their children's socialization, then it is very difficult to have faith in the future. The result, in Norman Maier's terms, is that motivation-instigated behavior becomes more difficult and, hence, less likely.

Yet the poor do not have either the economic or political means to change this situation for either the criminal or the victim. One consequence of political disenfranchisement is that the people who have the greatest incentive to alter criminal justice policy are least capable of doing so. Furthermore, the poor are relatively helpless in this matter because the rich benefit from the failure of the criminal justice system to control crime. In its lack of success, the criminal justice system perpetuates the illusion that the most costly and most dangerous acts are those committed by the poor, thus directing attention away from the harmful behaviors of upper-class people. In sum, then, elimination or alleviation of the adverse effects of crime and the criminal justice system is dependent on events beyond the control of the poor. As with public assistance and political disenfranchisement, the organization of the criminal justice system helps to perpetuate a class of impoverished people.

The fourth element in the vicious circle is ill health and the health-care delivery system. It was seen in Chapter 5 that a health gap exists such that, by every measure, the poor are significantly worse off than any other segment of the population. At the same time, impoverished people tend to ignore symptoms and wait too long before defining themselves as ill, mainly because the organization of the health-care system impedes their access to medical help.

The long-term result of the structure of the health delivery system is the creation and perpetuation of a class of indigent people. Here is an example of how this process can occur, taken from the Children's Defense Fund's analysis of the health of the poor children.[7]

Archie was a full-term, normal healthy baby. He received his health care during infancy from a city clinic. When he was eighteen months old, he had a fever and an earache. His mother, relying on her mother's advice, rocked him to soothe his crying and ease Archie's pain, gave him half an aspirin every few hours, and used a commercial ear-drop preparation. While rocking him, his mother noticed that some fluid began draining from his ear. Archie seemed less distressed after the fluid drained, and he recovered completely within a few days.

Three months later the fever and the earache recurred. This time both ears were affected. Home remedies brought no relief and Archie was taken to the clinic. The doctor diagnosed bilateral otitis media. This is a common childhood illness, easily diagnosed, and easily and effectively treated by antibiotics. [Archie's mother] was able to pay $15 for antibiotics only by deferring her rent payment. Because Archie seemed to recover in a few days, his mother discontinued the medication prescribed by the doctor before the full antibiotic regimen was completed. Within a month, the condition returned, and this time rocking, ear drops, and a few left over antibiotic pills were administered and Archie seemed to recover.

According to the Children's Defense Fund, Archie is now 8-years-old, burdened by a hearing loss and speech impediment due to his early bouts with otitis media. As a result, he has flunked the first grade twice, needs remedial education, and has become something of a behavioral problem in school. The long-term prospects for this child are dismal, for his ability to support himself as an adult is now doubtful. Yet his problem could have been prevented.

This example illustrates how the health-care system creates and perpetuates poverty on a mass scale by showing the problems poor families face when the need for medical help arises. Organizations like the Children's Defense Fund argue that Archie's experience is common. The inconsistent coverage provided by Medicaid, as outlined in Chapter 3, along with the structural analysis of the health-care delivery system, depicted in Chapter 5, lend credence to this claim.

Like most poor mothers, Archie's is evidently a caring person who, quite simply, cannot take her child to the doctor unless it is absolutely necessary, a fact that has had tragic results. In the illustration, the main problem is cost, although other elements of the health delivery system are undoubtedly issues, too. It should be noted that health education would be useful in this case, since the mother should not have terminated Archie's antibiotics prematurely. Here is a good example, however, of the perverse results that occur when poor persons try to plan ahead, for it is not unreasonable to think that when Archie's symptoms disappeared his mother tried to save the remaining medicine in order to have some available for the future. She simply did not know about the long-term consequences. And this ignorance may reflect the fact that the way medicine is dispensed is at least partly dependent on having understood the physician's instructions, assuming any were given. It is not farfetched to suppose that the prescription was accompanied by little or no explanation to Archie's mother of the importance of completing the antibiotic regimen.[8]

Now the process of creating a class of poor persons due to the operation of the health-care system applies even more to adults, of course, for parents are more likely to obtain treatment for their children than for themselves. It will be recalled from Chapter 4 that half of all householders (family heads) living below the poverty line did not work in 1981. Census data also show that one-third of those who were unemployed all year gave illness or disability as the main reason.[9] These are people with chronic conditions, many of which could have been prevented with early screening, diagnosis, and treatment. Unfortunately, the likelihood of this occurring is very low. This is why poor people, given the fact that they are more likely to be exposed to dangerous and unhealthy conditions, have more chronic health problems and disabilities. This is why, then, that the health-care system creates and perpetuates the existence of a class of impoverished people.

It is important to recognize that this situation is not immutable. Yet any conceivable solution is dependent on the exercise of political power. In sum, then, in a context in which they are disenfranchised, the elimination or alleviation of the adverse effects of the health-care delivery system is dependent on events beyond the control of the poor. As with public assistance, political disenfranchisement, and the criminal justice system, the organization of the health-care delivery system helps to perpetuate a class of impoverished people.

The fifth element in the vicious circle is analgesic behavior and its correlates: restricted locus of control, and low self-esteem and personal efficacy. It was argued in Chapter 6 that when people's experiences teach them that their actions cannot produce solutions to their problems, then they are prone to engage in what Norman Maier called frustration-instigated behavior; that is, actions are aimed at controlling stress rather than eliminating or resolving problems. The image used in the chapter was that of analgesic behavior and the hypothesis suggested there was the following: the lower the social class, *then* the less people experience control over their environment, the lower their sense of self-esteem and personal efficacy, and the more likely they are to establish patterns of analgesic behavior that have long-term nonadaptive consequences. It was suggested in Chapter 6 that the dependent variables are related to each other in additive fashion.

This hypothesis, to the extent it reflects the experiences of impoverished persons, gives new meaning to W.I. Thomas' dictum that when people define things as real they are real in their consequences.[10] For to the extent that analgesic behavior becomes a learned response, solutions to the problems destitute people face become less likely. For example, patterns of withdrawal into drugs, television, or other forms of escape impede people's ability to solve problems. Similarly, aggression often prevents problem solving because it is nonadaptive; it can lead to jail, a deterioration of family relations (e.g., as in spouse beating or abuse of children), and other deleterious results.

This angle of vision also allows us to interpret certain findings in social psychology with more understanding; for example, the relationship between social class and psychological distress. Kessler and Cleary replicate a long-established finding by showing that lower-class people experience higher levels of psychological distress because they are more exposed to stressful life events. The authors take this finding one step further, however, by also demonstrating that even when exposure to stressful events is controlled (that is, when the effect of the same event or the same rate of events is examined), lower-class people still display more psychological distress.[11] They argue that this is because poor persons have fewer intrapsychic resources and means of social support. If Kessler and Cleary are correct, and I think they are, this is why impoverished people engage in various forms of frustration-instigated behavior. It is why they develop simplistic, rigid, and analgesic coping strategies. This mode of analysis seems far more reasonable than that which attributes deviant values to the poor.

The organization and stability of the correlates of poverty mean that they function as a sort of vicious circle. For example, when people begin receiving public assistance (especially AFDC) their life chances as well as their life-styles diminish, and they are more likely to become politically apathetic, to get caught up in the criminal justice system, to suffer from chronic ill-health, and to learn analgesic responses. Similarly, when people are caught and convicted of their particular street crime or when they live with a pervasive fear of victimization and are in fact victimized repeatedly, then their life chances as well as their life-styles diminish, and they (or their families) are more likely to end up on the public-aid rolls, to become politically apathetic, to suffer from chronic ill health, and to learn analgesic responses. In other words, when people get caught at any point in the vicious circle, the likelihood of their being snared by some other aspect of it greatly increases. When this fact is recognized, then one can see how the class system reproduces itself.

THE REPRODUCTION OF THE CLASS SYSTEM

It has been emphasized repeatedly that people choose among socially structured alternatives. What this means in terms of class stability is that people use their resources to protect their relative positions in society. They do this both as individuals and as members of status groups. The result is that the class structure reproduces itself over time and a stratum of impoverished persons is continually recreated.

In order to gain a preliminary understanding of how this process occurs, I am going to begin this section by asking readers to think about a game of Monopoly, both as it is actually played and as it might appear if it were organized to reflect reality.[12] The purpose of this little fantasy is not only to suggest how the class system reproduces itself but also to indicate how research findings on social mobility and status attainment can be understood when viewed in a structural context. On that basis, data on occupational mobility and status attainment will be reviewed. Finally, I shall suggest, following Max Weber, why the class system reproduces itself by limning the way in which the educational process and family experiences of lower-class people create and perpetuate poverty.

The game of Monopoly embodies many Americans' fundamental values, especially their beliefs about equality of opportunity and the virtue inherent in competitive striving for success. In the game as it is actually played, each participant begins with an equal amount of money, $1,500. By combining luck (symbolized by the roll of the dice) and shrewdness (symbolized by purchase and auction decisions), competitors seek economic success. The point to remember about the game is that everyone really does start off with the same chance of winning. After all, a game is only fair under such conditions and no one wants to participate in a contest in which some of the players have an unfair advantage. Many people believe that life is like a game of Monopoly and that their socioeconomic position represents their reward for hard work. Unfortunately, the real world does not conform to this fantasy, mainly because some people have more advantages than others and the results of their hard work vary accordingly.

Here is a fictional version of Monopoly, one that is more analogous to the real world than the actual game. Begin by imagining that four groups of people are participating and that they compete both as individuals against all other individuals and, in certain situations, as members of their respective groups. Also, imagine that the game board is much larger than is usual because there are so many contestants. The first group of participants is very small, statistically insignificant in fact, but its members are relatively advantaged at the start: They begin the game already owning some property and possessing lots of money, say $3,000 each. The second group is very large but its members have considerably fewer advantages to begin with: They have no property and about $1,500 each. The third group is also very large but its members are even more disadvantaged: They have no property and only about

$1,000 each. The last group is smaller but still significant in size; its members are the most disadvantaged of all: They not only own no property and have very little money, about $500 each, they also do not know all the rules of the game. One final point: No one can quit competing. Any players who run out of money or go to jail are required to beg for more cash, pay their penalties, and continue playing.

In this context, then, the competition begins. Now Monopoly is a game played by individuals, and it would be easy to describe the process by which each participant acquired income and property, and thereby found a place in the game. (This would be the Monopoly equivalent of status attainment, of course.) But such an analysis would be completely misleading because it did not take into account the fact that the competitors' opportunities are socially structured and that the members of each group occasionally help each other out.

From this latter point of view, it is possible to sketch the results of the game in a plausible way. The members of Group 1, the rich, will generally remain well off unless they are very unlucky or unwise. This is because they begin competing with many built in advantages and share some of them; for example, they pool their "get out jail free cards." Similarly, the members of Group 2 will, with some variation, maintain their positions. Although upward mobility into Group 1 will occur occasionally, most movement will be within Group 2 and of relatively short distance. The members of Groups 3 and 4 are obviously in the most precarious positions. While some upward mobility into Group 2 will occur occasionally, most movement will be short distance, usually within or between the lower-level groups. Security is always uncertain for these participants in the game, mainly because the resources available to the members of the bottom groups are so minimal that it is difficult, on their own, to make much headway. As a result, because the competitors are not allowed out of the game, some readjust their goals and only play by going through the motions (this is what Merton called ritualism). Others, however, pull out guns and use them to alter their economic situation. Still others just sit at the game board passively while their tokens are moved for them.

With apologies to Peter Blau and Otis Dudley Duncan, this fictional vignette reflects the major findings in their study of social mobility.[13] Although Blau and Duncan's results are well known to most sociologists, I shall briefly summarize them here.

They found that, at least among males, there are three great strata in the United States: white-collar workers, blue-collar workers, and farm workers. The boundaries of these strata form semipermeable barriers to social mobility such that upward and downward movement tends to be within each of the two main classes (blue- and white-collar workers) and of relatively short distance. In short-hand terms, then, the mode is for white-collar parents to have white-collar sons and for blue-collar parents to have blue-collar sons. The implication underlying these findings, of course, is that when poor people escape from poverty by becoming, say, stable blue-collar workers, their security is very precarious (no matter how hard they work) since the members of this stratum are usually the most affected by economic changes.

In this context, it should be pointed out that Blau and Duncan also found the United States to be a dynamic nation in that mobility across strata lines occurs rather frequently (just how often will be noted later). The causal factors, however, are instructive; for the most important historical causes of upward mobility (which has occurred more frequently than downward) have been structural: technological change, class differences in fertility rates, and migration. Technological changes have opened up white-collar occupations over the past century and have thus been a "pull" factor stimulating upward mobility. At the same time, the higher fertility rates characteristic of families in lower prestige occupations have been a "push" factor stimulating upward mobility. As the authors summarize the situation, the pressure of displaced manpower at the bottom of the class system (*The American Occupational Structure* is a study of male mobility) coupled with job opportunity at the top has been the historical context in which "a chain reaction of short-distance movements throughout the occupational structure" has occurred.[14] Even though class differences in fertility have declined somewhat in recent years, Blau and Duncan argue that such differentials are endemic to industrial societies and that, along with technological change, will continue to produce internal migration and occupational mobility.[15]

As an aside, it should be recognized that these findings are inherently misleading in at least one respect: They do not reflect the existence of an additional stratum, the rich. What is significant about this small aggregate of people is their possession of income-producing assets and their enormous political power. These factors, which have an ascriptive basis, make their occupations relatively unimportant as determinants of status.[16] This is what distinguishes the property-owning classes from those who do not own property, for the latter depend on the prestige of their jobs as determinants of status.

This historical milieu (technological change and class differences in fertility) is the context within which the status attainment process must be placed. Failure to do this, which is typical in status attainment research, leads to misunderstanding because the analysis focuses on individuals without ascertaining the socially structured alternatives that are available to them. As a research tradition, the literature on status attainment is now very long.[17] In simplified form, the process of attaining occupational statuses is pictured as an interrelated chain of ascribed and achieved factors: family background and native ability, along with assorted social–psychological variables, decisively affect educational attainment and the jobs one obtains in early adulthood; while family background, native ability, educational attainment, and early jobs decisively influence subsequent occupational attainment.

The emphasis in the literature, however, is that while the importance of ascribed factors (family and ability) is greatest when one is young, the importance of achieved factors (education and job performance) becomes steadily greater with age. Thus, the usual interpretation of these findings is to assert that the process of stratification is based mainly, but not wholly, on achievement. In Blau and Duncan's words, "Whenever the stratification system of any moderately large and complex society is described, it is seen to involve both ascriptive and achievement principles. [But] in a liberal democratic society we think of the more basic principle as being that of achievement. Some ascriptive features of the system may be regarded as vestiges of an earlier epoch, to be extirpated as rapidly as possible."[18]

However, when both the historical milieu in which this process takes place and the nature of the data Blau and Duncan used are recognized, then their findings can be interpreted somewhat differently. First, the rewards of hard work go mostly to those who start off with some advantages. This is why the authors found that the mode is occupational stability—from blue collar to blue collar and from white collar to white collar: It is also why ascribed factors systematically influence status attainment. Thus, even though "superior status cannot any more be directly inherited" and even though status "must be legitimated by actual achievements that are socially acknowledged," ascription remains important: People's family background is significant mainly because it allows them to obtain educational credentials that qualify them for better jobs.[19] I shall return to this relationship below.

Second, over the past century or so, American society has been organized in a way that men's hard work could pay off in the form of upward mobility. This is why Blau and Duncan (along with many others) have found that achieved factors are of great importance among adult males—technological change and class differences in fertility rates have opened up channels for achievement and produced a chain reaction of moves, both inter- and intragenerationally.

Third, not everyone has been able to take advantage of the opportunities available even when they worked very hard. Basically, the social structure has had a large number of open channels for achievement by white males but considerably fewer and shorter ones for those individuals with the greatest ascriptive disadvantages. This is why research in the status attainment tradition has also found that blacks, women, and others who come from poor backgrounds because they were born to the wrong parents, worked in the wrong industry, or lived in the wrong region of the country, have achieved less.[20] As Michael Harrington observed, people who have disadvantaged parents can be paragons of hard work and morality but most of them will remain poor or live on the edge of poverty.[21] Mobility, it should be recalled, is nearly always short distance.

What these findings mean is that when poor people get jobs and become economically independent, it is nearly always a result of hard work combined with opportunities provided by others (who nearly always benefit even more). In general, as has been emphasized before, impoverished persons are rarely able to create their own opportunities. According to Vaz Pato and Williamson, the importance of family background is so great for impoverished and other disadvantaged persons that it is best to construct separate path models to describe the process of socioeconomic achievement for the poor and the nonpoor, respectively.[22] My own guess is that this is also true for the very rich, mainly because income-producing property rather than occupation determines their status in society.

Nonetheless, Blau and Duncan, along with most others who write in the status attainment tradition, are impressed with the extent to which occupational mobility occurs in American society, especially in comparison with other Western industrial nations. For example, they found that about 10% of the white male sons originating in "manual-class" occupations end up in "elite-class" jobs in the United States and that this figure is much higher than what occurs in Europe and Japan.[23] While they are right to be impressed and probably correct in suggesting that the possibility for upward mobility keeps class consciousness and class conflict low in this country, this finding means that 90% of the white male sons originating in the "manual class" end up in somewhat less prestigious occupations. By the way, elite, as used by Blau and Duncan, means professional and technical work. Most persons in such occupations —whether they be teachers or physicians or playground superintendents —are not usually considered elites in the political science literature. In the Monopoly vignette described earlier, people in these occupations would be placed in Group 2, white-collar jobs because they do not own property. In any case, what should be kept in mind is that most sons of manual workers end up as manual workers; if they move at all it is only within the blue-collar hierarchy. As such, they are always economically insecure, always prone to poverty, regardless of how hard they work. This is the blunt fact that must be understood. One last point: It is worth remembering that the 10%:90% ratio cited here would change significantly if all those in the labor force other than white males were included in the analysis; that is, the proportion of children coming from blue-collar backgrounds that is upwardly mobile into professional occupations would decline precipitiously.

Max Weber has argued that while classes and status groups are analytically separable bases for stratification, in practice they coalesce such that meaningful social strata are formed.[24] This is because the life-style that expresses people's status in society is dependent on their economic circumstances (class in Weber's terminology), and vice versa. Furthermore, even though they are not formally organized as groups, the members of various social strata act together to protect their positions in society. They do this in several ways. For example, members of a social stratum usually extend hospitality to social equals. This is accomplished by the choice of leisure-time activities, neighborhood residences, schools, even eating partners. It is not an accident (and it is not, by the way, merely symbolic) that corporate executives eat together in private dining rooms and expensive restaurants, or that white-collar workers eat with one another rather than with blue-collar employees.

In addition, Weber said that members of a social stratum usually restrict marriage partners to social equals and, of course, he was correct. The tendency toward class homogamy with regard to marriage is a well-known empirical generalization in sociology.[25]

Finally, the members of each social stratum try to monopolize "privileged modes of acquisition." This process is both direct and indirect. Thus, people at all status levels try to curb economic competition: They organize to protect their jobs and incomes. This is the motivation underlying the behavior of property owners who defend low taxes on capital gains by means of campaign contributions. It is also the motivation of physicians, clinical psychologists, and automobile workers who organize to restrict entry into such jobs. In modern societies, Weber noted, the game of curbing the competition and protecting status is played (and legitimated) in the political arena in ways similar to that depicted in Chapter 5. In this contest, as was shown, the poor are effectively disenfranchised and politically apathetic as a result. In addition, privileged modes of acquisition are monopolized indirectly as well, by education and socialization. It does matter if one goes to Phillips Exeter Academy (a prep school) or to a public high school, and it does matter if one attends Harvard or a local community college. The difference, however, is both educational and experiential, and the result reflects not just income and occupation but also power.

Without belaboring the point, the last task in this section is to suggest how the family lives and educational experiences of poor people influence the status attainment process and thereby lead to the reproduction of the class system and the perpetuation of poverty. Once again, the vulnerability of the poor and the way in which their choices are restricted will be seen.

One of the main reasons why people usually move around in the same status hierarchy as their parents did (or do) is their family background. Here is an empirical generalization dealing with the relationship between socioeconomic status and family formation: the lower the social class, *then* the younger the age at marriage, the sooner in the marriage children arrive, and the larger the family size.[26] What I want to do here is suggest how the family experiences of poor and working-class children increase the likelihood of their being impoverished themselves by sketching some of the consequences of the relationship between social class and family formation.

This empirical generalization implies that the children of young parents, especially when the parents are themselves from poor or near poor backgrounds, often spend at least the early years of their lives in an environment in which economic want without satisfaction is everywhere.[27] What children learn, then, is that their parents cannot control what happens to the family: how much there is to eat, what kind of house they live in, etc. Even when such households stay together and a stable standard of living is eventually achieved, the family's life-style is always precarious. And children know this. These are the people who must continually delay gratification, not the middle class, and the effect is for children to learn that they are vulnerable and that they do not control their environment.

In addition, this empirical generalization also means that children are often raised by parents who are still, in years and experience, children themselves. Because such parents pass from girl and boy to wife and husband to mother and father so swiftly, they do not have time to integrate and assimilate the psychological orientations and behaviors necessary for their new roles.[28] One indicator of this fact is they lack both marriage and parenting skills. As mentioned, this means that children's early years are spent in an environment in which want without satisfaction is everywhere, only in this case the thing wanted is psychological security. Thus, to be raised by people who are unsure of their own adulthood can mean that children are responded to in very inconsistent ways; for example, loving care may be combined with periods of neglect and episodes of physical abuse. It should be recalled here that some of the effects of lack of predictability were outlined in Chapter 6: People become frustrated, aggressive, passive, and tend to engage in analgesic behavior. When children are placed in a similar environment, they react in many of the same ways. Poor children are more likely to be exposed to such conditions early in life.

Finally, this empirical generalization also means that family breakup is a constant threat. This fact can be phrased in covariance fashion: The lower the social class and the younger the age at marriage, *then* the higher the rate of marital instability—as indicated by separation, desertion, and divorce.[29] Again, what children learn from this experience is that they are vulnerable and that they have little control over what happens to them. As seen in previous chapters, this lesson is often repeated over and over again throughout their lives.

Now this sketch does not do justice to the full range of familial experiences poor and blue-collar children have. I would only claim that the types of events depicted here are class related and that they help to account for the reproduction of the class system and the perpetuation of poverty. Recognition of the importance of factors such as these should make it clear that when poor parents have children who are also impoverished, this result does not reflect the intergenerational transmission of deviant values. In addition, when considering the vexing issue of destitution continuing from one generation to another, it is good to remember the studies of AFDC use discussed in Chapter 4 and the mobility data already described: Most people are on the public assistance rolls for short periods in their lives and most children of poor parents are not impoverished themselves.

Another reason why people usually move around in the same status hierarchy as their parents did (or do) is their level of educational attainment.

Blau and Duncan explain the significance of education in two rather different ways. The dominant image, one that subsequent researchers in the status attainment tradition have emphasized, is that the educational system is a kind of sorting agency in which the most talented individuals rise to the top. This vision of American society as a meritocracy is clearly what Blau and Duncan have in mind when they explain the significance of education in allowing 10% of the sons of manual class fathers to achieve "elite" status in the United States.[30] They observe that "it is the under-privileged class of manual sons that has exceptional chances for mobility into the elite in this country. There is a grain of truth in the Horatio Alger myth. The high level of popular education in the United States, perhaps reinforced by the lesser emphasis on formal distinctions of social status, has provided the disadvantaged lower strata with outstanding opportunities for long-distance upward mobility." In assessing this assertion one has to allow for a certain amount of academic hyperbole.

In the same chapter, however, Blau and Duncan also recognize the importance of ascription.[31] They note, for example, that "given the existing family structure it is hardly conceivable that men in the elite [that is, in professional occupations] would not attempt to assure that their sons remain in the top stratum, and their resources and power often enable them to do so." One way this task is accomplished is through education: "Superior family origins increase a man's chances of attaining superior occupational status in the United States in large part because they help him to obtain a better education." In short, Blau and Duncan, along with all subsequent researchers in the status attainment tradition, found that the best predictor of children's educational attainment is their social class background. This finding has also been replicated in the sociology of education literature, the most famous example of which is the Coleman Report.[32]

In covariance form, these data can be summarized with the following well-known empirical generalization: the higher the parents' social class, *then* the higher the educational attainment of children. In plain language, what this assertion means is that the educational system reproduces the class system. As in the description of family life, all I want to do here is suggest how the educational experiences of poor and working-class children increase the likelihood of their being impoverished by sketching some of the characteristics of the school system.

One implication of this empirical generalization is that the educational resources available to children varies by social class. For example, Christopher Jencks has estimated that youngsters whose parents are in the top fifth of the income distribution (i.e., who have incomes above $37,000 in 1981) benefit from twice the educational resources, in simple dollar terms, as children whose parents are the bottom fifth (below $11,000).[33] Although the effects of differences in resources are a matter of some controversy, such variation means that poor children have fewer opportunities to learn. Thus, it is my impression that the availability of computers in the classroom is directly related to the socioeconomic status of the students served, both in the school and in the district as a whole. In addition, exposure to computers outside the school—at computer camps, private after-school workshops, or at home—is undoubtedly class related. The budget described in Chapter 2 does not allow for the purchase of computer time or personal computers. Yet such knowledge probably will be an essential form of literacy in the next few years.

This empirical generalization also implies that there is a "hidden curriculum" in schools; that is, school grades and, hence, success, are not solely dependent on cognitive skills but also on such personality characteristics as self-discipline, the ability to take direction, intellectual (as opposed to emotional) oriented behavior, and hard work independent of intrinsic task orientation.[34] These are just the characteristics that poor children are least likely to have (especially when they are the children of young parents), and there is considerable evidence that the educational system does little to build such traits. Rather, to be poor in the public schools is often to be stigmatized, precisely because such students are often behind academically and have negatively charged personality characteristics. As a result, what they learn in school, often from the very first day, is that their ability and effort do not count for very much. Just as the subjects in the experiments on learned helplessness came to believe they could not solve simple anagrams, so do poor children come to think they cannot learn, with the result that they react inappropriately in other contexts.[35] Hence, a vicious circle is created.

As a caveat, I want to emphasize that many individual teachers try very hard to help impoverished children. Nontheless, what facts like those reported here mean is that poor children often enter school behind other children and when this occurs they usually do not catch up. This means, in turn, that the educational system functions to weed out a certain proportion of the population, who will fill dead-end and low-paying jobs — at least when they are available. That is the topic I wish to turn to next.

THE ORGANIZATION OF THE ECONOMY

Full employment means, or should mean, that everyone who can and wants to work has a job which pays a livable income. Previous chapters, however, have shown that the economy is not organized with this goal in mind. Rather, there are two sets of contradictory expectations built into the American economy. The first is this: Although people are expected to have a job and every person understands and internalizes this duty, the society is under no obligation to provide employment. This is true even though the federal government occasionally enacts job programs for the poor. For these are always temporary palliatives, and it remains the case that programs started this year can (and probably will) be terminated next year. Ultimately, each individual is on her or his own in this matter. The second contradictory expectation is this: while all adults who work are expected to earn wages that are sufficient to provide for their own and their families' livelihood, the society is under no obligation to ensure that income earned on the job can actually support one's household. This fact constitutes the logic (such as it is) underlying the changes in public assistance programs that were portrayed in Chapter 3. Again, each individual is on her or his own. And the overall result has been sketched in the two previous sections: Poverty and pauperism constitute a vicious circle that traps some people, and the reproduction of the class system helps to perpetuate the existence of a stratum of poor persons.

However, it can also be argued that the organization of the economy helps to cause poverty. Writers in the emerging dual economy tradition assert that some people are more likely to be poor than others, even when they have the same skills, simply because of the industry in which they work. This point of view contradicts the orthodox economic wisdom, which postulates that people's wages reflect the value of their skills as determined by competition in the market place. In order to put this argument in perspective, I shall begin by briefly reviewing the way in which orthodox economists explain the distribution of jobs and wages, and then sketch the dual economy hypothesis. In each case, the cause of poverty is seen differently.

The dominant theoretical orientation in economics is called marginal productivity theory. In the economists' terminology, the marginal productivity of labor is the extra output added by each additional worker. The idea is that in contexts where there is perfect competition, everyone at the same skill level receives wages equal to those of the last person hired. Phrased formally, the theory can be stated in the following way: the higher workers' marginal productivity, *then* the higher their wages.[36] In general, deviations from a condition of perfect competition are treated as "aberrations" or "complications" that will be reduced over the long run as market mechanisms (supply and demand) produce wage and price equilibrium. In effect, orthodox economists assume that, like Adam Smith's "invisible hand," market processes in advanced industrial societies are sufficiently competitive so that people's wages reflect their productivity; and their productivity, of course, is a function of their skills. Thus, if some persons earn low incomes it is because they are unskilled or their skills are in low demand.

This explanation of the distribution of wages leads to a straightforward interpretation of the causes of poverty that focuses on expectations about individual behavior. The basic issues are unemployment and low-wage work, each of which will be examined before noting the causal attribution orthodox economists make.

The empirical generalization about the relationship between socioeconomic status and being out of work is well known: The lower the social class, *then* the higher the rate of unemployment.[37] For example, the average unemployment rate for white-collar workers was 4% in 1981, compared to 10% for blue-collar workers. This means that people with lower prestige and lower income-producing jobs are always more uncertain about their employment, a fact that adds a great deal of stress to their daily lives because the specter of impoverishment is always present.

What should be remembered in considering these figures is that the unemployment rate does not reflect the total number of people experiencing job loss in any year. That is, since most unemployment is of relatively short duration, the average was about 14 weeks in 1981, the total number of persons who are in the labor force and experience some unemployment during a year is three or four times the overall rate. Most of these people are blue-collar workers and many of them are impoverished.

In addition, because the labor force is defined as those persons who have jobs or are actively looking for employment, individuals who have become so discouraged that they no longer believe work is available and, hence, no longer seek jobs are not counted as unemployed. While data on the number of discouraged workers are very difficult to obtain, it is safe to say that millions of people who have given up looking for employment would re-enter the labor force if opportunity presented itself. This tendency to come back into the labor force when jobs appear is reflected in the curious headlines we all see   once in a while in the newspaper. Let us say that a plant opens or re-opens and word gets out that 200 jobs will be available. It is very common for there to be 2,000 or even more applicants for the positions. When jobs open up, real jobs that pay livable wages, people seem to come out of the woodwork to apply for them and this fact becomes a news event.

Unfortunately, even though many observers think that employment is the best solution to poverty, many jobs do not pay livable wages. Among poor families, 22% are headed by a person who worked all year long in 1981.[38] For these households, the problem is not lack of work, it is low wages.

What these data mean in cash terms is shown in Table 7.1, which depicts the income of working poor households in 1980.[39] Of those impoverished families in which the head worked full time all year long, half earned less than $7,500. In those poor households in which the head worked all year long at a part time job, 60% earned less than $7,500. The thing to remember about these income figures is that they are for entire families and, hence, include the contributions of employed spouses, children, and any cash public-assistance the households received. Table 7.1 makes it clear that there are more than 5 million families whose heads work very hard and still find it difficult to provide for themselves and their children. This is why it is sound public policy to allow poor households to combine jobs and public assistance.

Many of the families represented in Table 7.1 have heads who are underemployed in the sense that, no matter how hard they work, they find it difficult to earn a livable wage. Many are working part time when they would prefer being employed full time. Most are caught in a self-perpetuating cycle composed of a series of unstable low-wage jobs punctuated by periods of unemployment and public assistance. As a result, they have an erratic work history that makes them unsuitable for more stable jobs, and the cycle continues.

When orthodox economists attempt to explain the causes of poverty,

TABLE 7.1: Work Experience and Income among Poor Families, 1980

Income level	Head worked full time		Head worked part time	
	50–52 weeks	1–49 weeks	50–52 weeks	1–49 weeks
< $2,500	13%	9%	8%	16%
$2,500–$4,999	9	19	19	27
$5,000–$7,499	28	36	34	29
$7,500–$9,999	51	36	40	27
	101%*	100%	101%*	99%
Total families:	1,995,000	1,991,000	431,000	965,000

*Rounding error.

they usually focus on the twin problems of jobs and wages. In so doing, they nearly always adopt an individualistic orientation; that is, they emphasize the obligations of the job hunter and wage earner. Thus, when they are asked why there are not enough jobs for every person to have one, the response by orthodox economists is likely to be "at what wage?" Their point is that the minimum wage is an aberration in a perfectly competitive economy and if wages were allowed to find their "natural" level there would be plenty of jobs for everyone. And when asked why wages are sometimes so low that households find survival difficult, the response of orthodox economists is likely to be that in a competitive society "people's wages reflect their marginal productivity," or skills. What this assertion implies is that the range of income in American society reflects the range of skills and that the relative success or failure of individuals results from the level of competence they bring into the marketplace. Thus, if workers are poor it is because they either do not have very much human capital (that is, their "natural" ability augmented by education, job experience, and the like) or they do not have a very strong commitment to the labor force. The image underlying orthodox economics is of American society as a meritocracy in which people are sorted in terms of their skills and appropriately rewarded.

From this point of view, then, the causes of poverty in a competitive society are perfectly clear: people's failure to work (or seek employment) and their failure to develop marketable skills. Basically, orthodox economists argue that rational low-wage workers should, and will if they are desperate enough, either find a job or add to their human capital so that they can be more productive and earn higher incomes. This is their solution to the problem of poverty. Implicit in this point of view are some rather harsh judgments. Individuals who appear to choose neither of the two options noted here (get a job or augment skills) must have different values and must, therefore, accept the consequences. It is assumed that they prefer leisure time or drinking with their buddies to working and, hence, that they deserve to be poor. As previously indicated, such analyses are neither very realistic nor very practical. The fascinating thing about assertions like these, and they are very common among economists, is that they are often made by people whose jobs and incomes are protected by the tenure system. It is always easier to argue that other people should compete.

In contrast to the orthodox view, the nascent literature on the dual economy offers an alternative means for understanding the distribution of jobs and wages, one that takes into account the consequences of the fact that perfect competition does not exist in the economy.[40] Writers in this area have argued, in various ways, that the economy can be divided into at least two sectors, core and periphery, and that workers' location in one or the other systematically affects their earnings even when they have similar skills (human capital). In so doing, most studies in this tradition focus on the characteristics of companies in each sector. Those industries dominated by large, capital intensive, and oligopolistic firms are seen as forming the core, while industries dominated by small, labor intensive, and competitive firms make up the periphery. An oligopoly is a market situation in which a few producers dominate but do not fully control the market, with the result that there is less competition. The implicit hypothesis in the dual economy literature, phrased in covariance form, is: the larger, more capital intensive, and more oligopolistic enterprises are, *then* the higher the imcome of employees at all skill levels, the greater their job stability, and the lower their rate of poverty.

The findings in this literature dramatically confirm the hypothesis. Among them are the following: There are significant differences in the characteristics of the labor force making up the core and periphery sectors: workers in core industries earn more money, have lower rates of unemployment, endure lower rates of poverty, have more education, and are disproportionately white and male. Now it is possible to argue that the reason employees in the core sector earn more and experience less poverty is because they have more skills. However, when skill level and such ascriptive factors as race and sex are controlled, there are still significant differences in earnings, job stability, and poverty rates between workers in the core and those in periphery sectors. What this finding means is that "a change in sectoral placement without altering the racial, sexual, human capital, or occupational characteristics of the average periphery worker, would yield a substantial increase in annual earnings" and a significant decrease in the likelihood that such a person would be impoverished.[41]

Thus, unlike orthodox analyses, the dual economy explanation for the cause of poverty is structural: Those persons employed in peripheral industries are much more likely to have incomes below the poverty line, even if they have similar skills. This is because wages are lower and jobs are often intermittently available. A large proportion of the individuals shown in Table 7.1 are poor simply because they are working in the peripheral sector of the economy.

Some additional findings in the dual economy literature are also worth noting here. While, as indicated, human capital variables (education, job training) produce higher wages in core industries, another factor that significantly affects income is union membership, which also produces higher incomes in core industries. At the same time, however, for those people employed in the periphery sector the most important factor reducing the likelihood of having an income below the poverty line appears to be union membership. Yet these industries are precisely those which are the most difficult to organize. Finally, a point I shall return to in the concluding section of this chapter, sexual and racial discrimination in income appears to be greater in the core than in the periphery industries.

Before leaving this topic, a few qualifying words are in order. The literature on the dual economy is still emerging, both empirically and conceptually. In addition, it should be clear to all observers that the American economy is undergoing enormous changes, mainly due to the decline of smokestack industries, the historical backbone of the American economy. For these reasons, I referred to the dual economy hypothesis rather than labeling it an empirical generalization.

Nonetheless, although taking into account these qualifications, it seems reasonable to conclude that writers in this tradition are on to something: Regardless of the skills people have, the nature of the jobs available to them decisively influences the likelihood of their living poorly. Hence, it seems reasonable to argue that one cause of the existence of a class of impoverished persons in American society is the organization of the economy.

RACIAL AND SEXUAL DISCRIMINATION

The last topic to be dealt with in this chapter is the manner in which racial and sexual discrimination causes poverty. Despite the efforts of some conservative observers, both academic and popular, to portray the problem of discrimination as a past issue that has been resolved, the data on poverty are a sobering reminder of the reality of racism and sexism.[42] This section begins with a brief description of the number of blacks and women who live poorly in America and some of their characteristics. I shall then argue that the pattern revealed is not accidental and suggest some of the structural mechanisms by which race and sex discrimination produces a class of impoverished persons. Conceptually, patterns of racial and sexual discrimination simply reflect the ability of a class system dominated by white males to reproduce itself over time. However, the problem of discrimination is so pervasive in the United States that it merits a separate discussion.[43]

In Chapter 2 it was noted that 34% of all black Americans live poorly and that blacks are three times more likely than whites to be impoverished. These figures have remained relatively stable since about 1970, despite some progress in implementing civil rights legislation and considerable decline in normatively sanctioned racism.[44] Although there has recently been some disagreement as to the extent and significance of class divisions that now exist within the black community (and I do not wish to enter that debate here), racial discrimination remains an important cause of the disproportionate amount of poverty among blacks, regardless of people's individual efforts.[45] This fact is vividly protrayed in Table 7.2, which compares black and white poor families in terms of some human capital variables: achievement and labor force participation.[46]

There are two patterns of interest in the table. The first can be summarized in the following way: for both blacks and whites, the higher the level of achievement and the greater the labor-force participation, *then* the lower the rate of poverty. As a variable, and apart from its official definition, labor-force participation can be crudely conceptualized in three steps: total nonparticipation (regardless of reason), unemployment, and employment.

The table shows that educational attainment pays off; college educated people of both races live poorly at lower rates. Similarly, occupational attainment produces a lower incidence of poverty. In addition, when families of both races have more members who are employed and when the head works more, they have lower poverty rates. And the range among the figures is dramatic. For example, regardless of race, households with no worker in them are two or two and one-half times more likely to be impoverished than families with workers. This kind of pattern is precisely what would be expected in an open-class system that emphasizes achievement and the necessity for self-support.

However, the second pattern depicted in Table 7.2 is not what would be expected in an open-class system or one in which racism is no longer a problem. The pattern can be summarized in this manner: Regardless of level of achievement or degree of labor-force participation, blacks are much more likely to live below the poverty line than whites. The differences by race are very wide and systematic. Thus, for example, in every

TABLE 7.2: Selected Characteristics of Families by Poverty Status and Race, 1981

Characteristics	*Percentage below poverty line*	
	White	*Black*
Education of head		
Less than 8 years	21%	40%
High-school degree	8%	26%
1 year or more of college	3%	12%
Occupation of head		
Professional and technical	3%	6%
Clerical and sales	5%	15%
Crafts	5%	8%
Operatives	7%	16%
Service	14%	32%
Nonfarm laborers	11%	18%
Farmers and farm laborers	28%	50%
Number of workers in family		
No workers	23%	75%
One worker	12%	32%
Two workers	4%	10%
Three workers	3%	11%
Work experience of head		
Worked full time: 50–52 weeks	3%	7%
Worked 1–49 weeks	16%	37%

category—education and occupation of head, number of workers in the family, and work experience of the head—blacks are two to three times as likely to be poor as whites. These differences would remain even after controlling for such other variables as age and marital status, or examining breakdowns by detailed occupation or specialization within occupations. From this angle of vision, then, it is still the case that neither achievement nor labor-force participation counts as much for blacks as for whites, at least in terms of the likelihood of living poorly in America. Table 7.2 depicts the effects of systematic racial discrimination: A class of poor black Americans exists (and will continue to exist) regardless of the efforts or skills of individuals.

A similar conclusion can be drawn when sexual differences in poverty rates are examined. In Chapter 2 it was observed that 35% of all female-headed households are poor. In addition, it should also be recognized that 47% of all impoverished families are headed by women.[47] As with blacks, these figures have remained relatively stable during the 1970s, despite some progress in implementing civil rights legislation (with the obvious

TABLE 7.3: Selected Characteristics of Female-Headed Families with No Husband Present and All Other Families by Poverty Status, 1981

Characteristics	*Percentage below poverty line*	
	Female head, no husband	*All other*
Education of head		
Less than 8 years	49%	20%
High-school degree	28%	6%
1 year or more of college	17%	3%
Occupation of head		
Professional and technical	8%	2%
Clerical and sales	15%	2%
Crafts	16%	5%
Operatives	27%	6%
Service	40%	7%
Nonfarm laborers	33%	11%
Farmers and farm laborers	B[a]	30%
Number of workers in family		
No workers	73%	16%
One worker	29%	10%
Two workers	13%	4%
Three workers	8%	3%
Work experience of head		
Worked full time: 50–52 weeks	3%	7%
Worked 1–49 weeks	16%	37%

B[a] = Base too small to calculate percentage.

exception of the ERA). Regrettably, I do not think that normatively sanctioned sexism has declined very much. Just as with racial differences, sexual discrimination is an important factor in the excessive poverty rates characteristic of female-headed families. This fact is shown clearly in Table 7.3, which compares rates of impoverishment in female-headed households with all other families in terms of the same human capital variables used previously.[48] The important fact to remember, of course, is that virtually all families falling into the "other" category have two adults in them because the number of male-headed households with no wife present remains statistically insignificant. I shall return to this point later.

Again, there are two patterns of interest in the table, each of which can be summarized as mentioned in the previous section. The first is: for both female-headed households with no husband present and all other families, the higher the level of achievement and the greater the labor-force participation, *then* the lower the rate of poverty. Both educational and occupational attainment pay off in the sense that they reduce the likelihood of a household being poor regardless of whether it is female headed or has two adults in it. Further, when families have more members who are employed and when the head works more, they also have lower poverty rates regardless of whether they are female headed. Just as with racial differences, the range among the figures in Table 7.2 is dramatic. And as noted previously, this pattern is just what would be expected in an open class, achievement-oriented society that values self-support.

The second pattern also mimics the findings with regard to race and poverty in that it is precisely what would not be expected in an open-class system, only in the case of sex and poverty the differences displayed in the table are much greater: Regardless of the level of achievement or degree of labor-force participation, female-headed households are much more likely to be poor than all other families. These differences would remain even after controlling for age and race, or when examining detailed occupational breakdowns or specialization within occupations. While there is some literature which shows that black women have made significant income gains over the past few years, it remains the case that families headed by women of either race are much more likely to be poor than all other households.[49] Table 7.3 depicts the consequences of systematic sexual discrimination: A class of poor, female-headed households exists (and will continue to exist) regardless of the efforts of individuals.

The racial and sexual differences depicted in Tables 7.2 and 7.3 cannot be considered accidental. These data make it difficult to assert that blacks and women who live poorly do so because of their deviant values or their laziness or any other individual characteristics. For people of both sexes and races who work hard to obtain an education or to advance occupationally, who remain employed, and who make sure that everyone in the household has a job, still suffer from a greater likelihood of being poor merely because they are women or black. Thus, it seems more reasonable to look for the structural mechanisms by which disproportionate numbers of blacks and women are channelled into poverty, regardless of their individual efforts. I shall focus on three such mechanisms, two of which deal with discrimination in employment: recruitment and screening practices.[50] These factors affect both blacks and women. In addition, however, the extraordinary proportion of poor families headed by women with no husband present clearly indicates that divorce has rather different consequences for men and women in American society. This issue will be the third mechanism discussed.

The recruitment practices used by employers, especially in private industry, are such that blacks and women are less likely to hear about jobs and, hence, less likely to get them. The result is that blacks and women are disproportionately assigned to the periphery sector of the economy and, more generally, have lower occupational prestige and lower incomes, on the average, than do white males.[51] One indicator of these facts is the higher rates of impoverishment displayed in Tables 7.1 and 7.2.

As seen in Chapter 4, most studies show that a majority of people find out about jobs through word of mouth.[52] What this fact means is that, directly or indirectly, most firms use white male employees as the primary source of referrals for jobs. The exceptions involve sex-stereotyped jobs and companies located in minority areas. With these qualifications noted, it can be hypothesized that at all skill levels, the greater the number of blacks currently employed, *then* the greater the number of black applicants and the greater the rate at which they will be hired.[53] This is because blacks and whites usually participate in different social networks. What this hypothesis means is that the best predictor of the rate at which blacks apply for and obtain jobs is the current racial composition of a firm's workforce. The same hypothesis, of course, can be applied to women. As long as the primary source of knowledge about jobs is male employees, informal referral patterns will probably reflect the job-related sex-role stereotypes such persons have.

Additional frequently used methods of recruitment discriminate against blacks and women in other ways. For example, the choice of whether to rely on "walk-in" job applicants can be used to maintain the racial composition of an employer's workforce. Thus, firms located in suburban areas populated mainly by whites (partly as a result of housing discrimination), may accept applications from walk-ins, while those located in or near black communities may choose to rely on responses to formal advertisements. What is interesting is that, regardless of tactic, as long as it is systematically adhered to without regard to race, then it appears to be a nonracist, universalistic criterion.

There are, however, equally overt but less justifiable strategies that can be used; for example, selective advertisements: In large cities, firms can publicize low-paying jobs in newspapers primarily serving the black community while confining ads for higher paying, more stable positions to newspapers read mainly by whites.[54] Similarly, sex-segregated job advertisements or, where these have been eliminated, the language used in describing work, influence the sex of job applicants and, hence, the sexual composition of a firm's labor force.[55] Finally, the use of employment agencies for job referrals allows considerable leeway for informal understandings as to the kinds of persons wanted in particular jobs.

There is a natural tendency to believe, since racial and sexual discrimination in employment and income is both illegal and immoral, that few people would engage in it—especially those who own and operate respectable enterprises. Unfortunately, such a belief would be naive, as the data presented previously suggest. What must be remembered, here, is that a fundamental bureaucratic task in all organizations is to justify what one wishes to do in universalistic terms, no matter how invidious the goal may be. The recruitment strategies mentioned here (there are others, of course) allow managers to do just that, with the result that racial and sexual discrimination in employment and income remains pervasive and disproportionate numbers of blacks and women live poorly in America. In this way, the class structure is recreated.

The screening processes used by employers are such that, having learned about jobs, blacks and women are less likely to get them if they are not stereotypically filled by such persons. In nearly all cases, potential employees must go through some sort of screening procedure, which can involve an evaluation of a person's job application form and other credentials, an interview, a background check, and an intelligence or some other aptitude test.

Some people are not interviewed simply because they are judged not to have the qualifications necessary for a job, such as a stable employment record or a high school diploma. These criteria appear to be universalistic. But for those people who have been in the periphery labor market where intermittent employment is a fact of life no matter how hard they work, their ability to change their situation is limited by this fact. Sometimes then, they do not even get interviewed. As indicated previously, blacks and women are much more likely to be employed in periphery industries.

Leniency in evaluating people's qualifications is often allowed or required. For example, in some cases formal educational requirements are artificial barriers to jobs; such criteria are useful because they have the aura of objectivity. But they are often waived—selectively, based on an interview. In such contexts, however, screening criteria are often very subjective. An evaluator's judgments about people's "appearance," "self-confidence," "emotional makeup," and many other characteristics are freely used.[56] Thus, employers' stereotypes about minorities and women can easily enter into the decision-making process; for the difference between a white male who has "self-confidence" and a woman or black who is "pushy" is very subtle. But the result can be very discriminating.

Similarly, when a background check reveals a criminal record, a person can be denied a job. Finally, those people who do not perform well on paper and pencil tests can be denied jobs, even if their actual work performance might be excellent.

What needs to be remembered here is that while employers want qualified people to work for them, their notions as to who is capable are determined according to very subjective criteria: what customers expect or want, who would best fit in, the nature of the job in question, and their (usually hidden) attitudes toward certain kinds of people. In general, the screening process is often used to justify decisions made on a racist or sexist basis. When the process appears objective, yet the workforce remains racially and sexually segregated, then observers can be sure that hidden criteria underlie the appearance. The result is that racial and sexual discrimination remains pervasive and disproportionate numbers of blacks and women live poorly. This is how the class structure is continually recreated.

In addition to direct occupational and income discrimination that affects both blacks and whites, an additional cause of poverty among females is sex-role norms that still dictate women's obligations in American society. Although these norms influence behavior in many areas, I shall focus on childrearing obligations here.[57]

It was noted earlier that nearly half of all poor families are headed by women without husbands and that a third of all female-headed households are poor. In general, these figures reflect the high divorce rate that is now characteristic of the United States and prevailing norms as to which sex can and should care for children, both during marriage and after it dissolves. The result is that while divorce can free a man from family responsibility and poverty, it often results in poverty and dependence on public aid for women.

The impoverishment of women and female-headed families occurs because the social imperative to rear children influences their educational decisions, job or career choices, and labor-force participation rates. For girls from impoverished backgrounds, the decision to drop out of school in order to have children and get married alters forever their occupational and income prospects. While the wisdom of such decisions can be debated, there are often strong social and psychological pressures that influence this choice.[58] Similarly, among those who do obtain a high-school diploma, decisions about whether to continue their education and the choice of major are often made in light of the importance of the mothering role. Finally, young women's job and career decisions also tend to be made in these terms.[59] Boys and young men, I would suggest, are less prone to make educational and job decisions in terms of the salience of the parental role.

The long-term impact of this state of affairs is that women are led to develop skills and take jobs in light of the needs of their husbands and their children. This is one reason, although not the only reason, why women are often confined to the periphery labor market. Furthermore, because females are more likely to work part-time "voluntarily" and to move in and out of the labor force over the years, their skills either do not develop or deteriorate with the passage of time. Thus, when divorce occurs, it is often the case that the parent with the fewest job skills and options is deemed the most capable of providing child care. This is an additional source of sex discrimination and an important reason why so many female-headed families live poorly in America.

8

SUMMARY

In describing what it is like to live poorly in America, I have tried to correct some of the myths people have about those who are impoverished and to explain some of the correlates and causes of poverty. In so doing, I have emphasized the limited choices indigent people have and their resulting vulnerability.

Some persons think that the official measure of poverty is too high, that those living at the poverty threshold can live reasonably well—if they have the will. Conservative analysts have presented an even more extreme version of this argument by claiming that the poverty cut-off is too high because the Census Bureau does not count the effect of in-kind income which public assistance beneficiaries receive. From this point of view, "welfare" programs eliminate a great deal of impoverishment. Chapter 2 refutes such arguments and shows that the line of reasoning undergirding them is misbegotten.

The analysis of family budgets in Chapter 2 shows clearly that a household living at the poverty line lives poorly in an absolute sense; that is, such a family has great difficulty surviving in American society. Another way of illustrating that the poverty line is a realistic indicator of impoverishment is by comparing it to relative measures, such as Bureau of Labor Statistics budgets and survey respondents' perceptions of the minimum income that families need. These data show that an economic chasm separates those who are judged to be poor in an absolute sense from those who are relatively deprived.

Furthermore, studies of the "anti-poverty effectiveness of in-kind tranfers," which constitute the main body of evidence for the conservative version of the argument, are flawed logically, methodically, and substantively. Chapter 2 identified the following problems inherent in these studies: (1) they fail to recognize that public assistance eligibility requires continual destitution, (2) they count medicaid income twice, (3) they produce unrealistic estimates of the "value" of food stamps and other forms of noncash income, and (4) they count the in-kind income received by the poor while ignoring the far greater amounts received by the nonpoor. Such analyses must be wrong; they confuse methodological sophistication with science. In fact, despite the impression created by these studies, there is no scientific way of identifying the rate of impoverishment. The poverty line is useful because it provides a realistic criterion for identifying those who live poorly in America.

When the family budgets of impoverished people are depicted, then their extreme vulnerability becomes clear. Providing for even the simplest necessities of life in the United States—food, clothing, shelter, and education—is extremely difficult for those living poorly. In addition, they are unable to prepare for and are unable to prevent changes in their economic situation caused by revised public assistance rules, accident or illness, job termination, criminal victimization, racial or sexual discrimination, and many other things. This is the reason that they often engage in analgesic behavior.

Some persons are confused about the intent of such "welfare" programs as Aid for Families with Dependent Children, Supplementary Security Income, Food Stamps, and Medicaid; they believe that these programs are designed to eliminate impoverishment. As noted above, some academicians (who should know better) share this viewpoint. Many people also think that public assistance costs a great deal of money—too much, in fact. Chapter 3 refutes these arguments.

It is important to distinguish between the anti-poverty programs instituted during the war on poverty and the public assistance programs that were initiated and expanded during those same years. As shown in Chapter 3, the intent of the former was to eliminate poverty while the purpose of the latter was (and is) to alleviate some of the problems associated with living poorly. In addition, the requirements of the four programs described in Chapter 3 show clearly that they cannot eliminate poverty even in principle.

Public assistance programs do not, in fact, cost very much. This point was illustrated in Chapter 3 by comparing expenditures for public aid to the total budget, to outlays for social insurance, and to special interest subsidies. It is possible to place the cost of public assistance into perspective by recognizing two interrelated facts. First, the higher the social class, *then* the greater the economic benefits received from government. This occurs because political power is a function of class in American society and the application of political power produces economic benefits for people. Second, and this follows from the first, public assistance has dual functions: it provides income support for both the poor and the nonpoor. Sometimes this support is direct: AFDC benefits are paid directly to the poor and Medicaid benefits (that is, income) go directly to the providers of health and health care. Sometimes this support is indirect: all the public assistance cash paid to the poor trickles up to the rest of the population and leaves those who are impoverished just where they began.

The detailed description of public assistance programs that makes up the bulk of Chapter 3 also shows that the problems endemic to them—inefficiency, inequitability, work disincentives, and fraud—have been exacerbated in recent years. Turning these programs over to the states will make them more inefficient and inequitable. Restricting the eligibility of low wage workers increases work disincentives and does nothing about the two previous problems. While public concern about fraud is reasonable, only the federal government has the resources to detect and prosecute it, especially when attention focuses on those people who have the opportunity and the skills to commit large scale crime: third parties.

When the characteristics of public assistance programs are depicted, then, once again, the exteme vulnerability of the poor becomes clear. For example, the antifamily bias inherent to the AFDC program means that those who live poorly are less able than any other segment of the population to simply stay married and raise their children. They are less able to maintain satisfactory (if informal) family relationships because of the ever present possibility of investigations by "welfare" workers. They are less able to influence those public policies affecting their lives. They are less able to change their social situation based on their own hard work. In short, they are less able to do almost everything that the nonpoor think they ought to be doing.

Some people, including some academics, believe that the poor do not want to work and that public assistance has destroyed the incentive to get jobs and to keep them. Chapter 4 refutes these assertions.

The work ethic is a pervasive American value, and Chapter 4 shows clearly that there are no differences between the poor and the nonpoor with regard to this cultural standard. Furthermore, when employment rates, responses to job announcements, and other indicators of work activity are examined, then it becomes plain that wages constitute the most important source of income for nearly all of those who live poorly in the United States. Surprisingly, this assertion is also true for public assistance recipients.

When the attitudes and employment rates of impoverished persons are depicted, it becomes obvious, as above, how awfully vulnerable the poor are. Given their educational background and skills, and given the lack of realistic training programs, poverty-stricken persons can only work when there are jobs available; as it turns out, most of these jobs are in the secondary labor market. There are, of course, illegal options, some of which are fairly remunerative. Without condoning such actions, some combination of low wage work and "hustling" is often the only choice indigent people have. As it turns out, regardless of the moral position one takes, such activities clearly reflect the salience of the work ethic in the lives of impoverished persons.

Chapter 5 describes some of the correlates of poverty: political disenfranchisement and apathy, street crime, and ill health. In all three cases, attention focuses on the manner in which people's choices are socially structured.

Political disenfranchisement and the resulting apathy of the poor are not simply free choices that reflect their priorities in life. Rather, the economic resources available to impoverished persons sharply limit their ability to participate in the legitimate political arena. Apart from lack of money, poor people usually do not participate in voluntary organizations of all sorts, mainly because they do not have social skills, transportation, freedom from criminal victimization, and many other personal and social characteristics necessary to belong. Finally, of course, neither of the major political parties tries to enlist or mobilize the poor, primarily because the parties are dominated by nonpoor persons who benefit from the existence of a class of impoverished people. The unexpected implication of this analysis is that some form of political unruliness is often the most realistic way for the poor to call attention to their interests. As in every other sphere of life, however, there are structural limitations on this mode of action. In general, impoverished people have no influence over political decisions, even when these decisions affect their opportunity to participate.

Although criminal behavior is not correlated with class, the type of crime is: impoverished people commit a higher proportion of street crime. It follows that they are also victimized at a much higher rate than other segments of the population. The correlation between street crime and poverty is mainly due to the kinds of criminal opportunities available to poor persons, the limited means they have for achieving occupational (and, thereby, economic) success, the presence of role models who can teach others how to commit such crimes, and the organization of the criminal justice system. Once again, impoverished people have no influence over these factors.

Health is class-related in America, mainly because of the organization of the health care delivery system: its cost, inconvenience, fragmentation, and dehumanizing qualities have a far greater impact on the poor than any other segment of the population. Yet, as above, impoverished people have no influence over these factors.

When the structural characteristics of American society are depicted, as in Chapter 5, the limited choices available to the poor and their corresponding vulnerability to changes in public policy become clear once again. While a "rational" person will vote, not commit a crime, and seek health care promptly, these options are often closed off to impoverished people. From this angle of vision, it is possible to understand the behavior of the poor in a realistic way.

Because impoverished people sometimes act in ways that are clearly not effective problem-solving strategies, and because their behaviors often seem to be at odds with mainstream American values, it is frequently asserted that there is a culture of poverty or that lower class persons "stretch" dominant values. Despite the appealing nature of these ideas, Chapter 6 shows that the attribution of deviant values to the poor is an inadequate and unrealistic way of explaining their behavior. This is because each explanation is flawed both conceptually and empirically.

In Chapter 6, I argued that social class is significant in American society because it indicates the number of options people have available and their effectiveness as problem-solving strategies. When these facts are recognized, then the social psychological characteristics and behaviors of many poor persons become more understandable. A reasonable hypothesis is the following: the lower the social class, *then* the less the people experience control over their environment, the more frustrated they become, the lower their sense of self-esteem and personal efficacy, and the more they establish patterns of analgesic behavior that have long-term nonadaptive consequences. The evidence adduced to illustrate the hypothesis included Norman Maier's analysis of frustration-instigated behavior in animals, studies of learned helplessness in human beings, and research into the relationship between social class and locus of control, self esteem and the like. From this point of view, class differences in values are not very relevant. Rather, what appears to happen is that the inability to control or influence one's own life leads some impoverished persons to adopt patterns of action that are simple, rigid, and analgesic in nature. To the extent that such behaviors become pervasive learned responses, they redound to help cause the perpetuation of poverty.

Some people prefer to see poverty as a problem faced by individuals. From this angle of vision, the cause of poverty lies in each person's characteristics: her or his desire to work, willingness to move in order to obtain a job, thriftiness, morality, etc. And there is little doubt that these issues are important factors influencing whether an individual lives poorly or not.

But this angle of vision is incomplete for two reasons. First, most poor people work very hard whenever and wherever they can. Second, knowledge of individual characteristics is not very helpful in explaining why a class of impoverished people lives poorly in America. The latter is a sociological question, and it has been the topic of Chapter 7.

When the causes of impoverishment are analyzed in structural terms, it becomes apparent that elimination of poverty in America is not a very realistic goal. Those living at the bottom of the class system are always more likely to be snared in the vicious circle described above; many of them are going to be left behind as, over time, the class system reproduces itself; many of them are going to be channelled into the secondary labor market regardless of their skill levels; and many of them are going to continue being victimized by racial and sexual discrimination. For individuals, this analysis means that their chance of escaping from poverty is nearly always dependent on events beyond their control.

Nonetheless, it seems to me that it is possible to alleviate some of the problems associated with impoverishment, and to do so in such a way that everyone benefits. Although there are many (implicit and explicit) suggestions for public policy contained in this book, I would like to conclude by mentioning only the following four:

• First, the United States should set full employment as a national priority. And this target should be defined so as to mean that everyone who can work and wants a job has one. That everyone, not just the poor, will benefit from a fully employed, active population should be obvious.

• Second, public assistance should be streamlined, stripped of its anti-family bias, and coupled with a negative income tax. I am convinced that this money is well spent; for not only would the public aid system be more equitable and efficient, but recipients would be able to maintain family ties and be employed. Apart from the overall social benefits that would accompany such policies, the trickle up effect that is intrinsic to public assistance programs would redound to provide economic benefits to other members of the community.

• Third, it is imperative that girls and women be allowed, indeed encouraged, to practice birth control. Current strictures are not only inequitable, they constitute poor policy: they injure parents, they injure children, and by extrapolation they injure the state.

• Finally, the opportunity for political participation should be increased by making it easier to vote. Piven and Cloward, for example, have recently suggested that voter registration occur in public assistance offices. This is a thoroughly practical plan that promises enormous public benefit because it holds open the possibility of including the dispossessed in our political process. Unfortunately, its chances of being enacted are not very great.

Notes

Chapter 1: Introduction

1. Lyndon Johnson, *Public Papers of the President, 1963-64* (Washington, D.C.: U.S. Government Printing Office, 1972), Vol. 2, p. 988.

2. Hazel Erskine, "The Polls: Government Role in Welfare," *Public Opinion Quarterly*, 39 (Summer, 1975): 257-74.

3. Herbert Gans, "The Positive Functions of Poverty," *American Journal of Sociology* 78 (September, 1972): 275-89.

4. Burton R. Clark, "The 'Cooling Out' Function in Higher Education," *American Journal of Sociology* 65 (May, 1960): 569-76.

5. Martin Anderson, *Welfare: The Political Economy of Welfare Reform in the United States* (Stanford, Cal.: Hoover Institution Press, 1978).

6. *Ibid.*, p. 15.

7. *Ibid.*, pp. 19-20.

8. *Ibid.*, p. 43.

9. *Ibid.*, p. 47.

10 *Ibid.*, p. 59.

11. *Ibid.*, pp.67-132.

12. *Ibid.*, pp. 88-89, 101.

13. Arthur Stinchcombe, "Merton's Theory of Social Structure." Pp. 11-34 in L. Coser (ed.), *The Idea of Social Structure* (New York: Free Press, 1975).

14. Joe R. Feagin, *Subordinating the Poor* (Englewood Cliffs, N.J.: Prentice-Hall, 1976), pp. 95-97. See also Michael Morris and John B. Williamson, "Stereotypes

and Social Class: A Focus on Poverty," Chapter 9 in Arthur G. Miller (ed.), *In the Eye of the Beholder: Contemporary Issues in Stereotyping* (New York: Praeger, 1982).

15. Michael Harrington, *The Other America* (Baltimore, MD: Penguin Books, 1971; first printing: 1962), pp. 15–16.

Chapter 2: Poverty

1. Michael Harrington, *The Other America* (Baltimore, MD: Penguin Books, 1971; first printing: 1962).

2. Citizens Board of Inquiry, *Hunger, U.S.A.: A Report by the Citizens Board of Inquiry into Hunger and Malnutrition in the United States* (Boston: Beacon Press, 1968). See also Robert Coles, *Still Hungry in America* (New York: World Publishing Co., 1969).

3. Mollie Orshansky, "How Poverty Is Measured," *Monthly Labor Review* 92 (February, 1969). See also Mollie Orshansky, *Documentation of Background Information and Rationale for Current Poverty Matrix*, Technical Paper #1 for *The Measure of Poverty* (Washington, D.C.: U.S. Department of Health, Education, and Welfare, 1976), pp. 233–36.

4. Mollie Orshansky, "How Poverty Is Measured," p. 37.

5. Table 2.1 is from the U.S. Bureau of the Census, "Money Income and Poverty Status of Families and Persons in the United States, 1981," *Current Population Reports*, Series P-60, No. 134 (Washington, D.C.: U.S. Government Printing Office, 1982), Table A-1. See text for an explanation of the changes in the poverty definition.

6. *Ibid.*, Table 15.

7. *Ibid.*, Table 14.

8. *Ibid.*, Tables 14 and 18.

9. Larry E. Salathe, *Household Expenditure Patterns in the United States*, Technical Bulletin No. 1603 (Washington, D.C.: U.S. Department of Agriculture, 1979).

10. U.S. Bureau of the Census, "Money Income and Poverty Status of Families and Persons in the United States, 1980 (Advance Report)," Tables 6 and 20.

11. "Family Budgets," *Monthly Labor Review* 105 (July, 1982): 44–46.

12. "Family of Four Needs Record $277 Per Week," *The Gallup Report* 185 (February, 1981): 20–21.

13. Mollie Orshansky, "How Poverty is Measured," p. 38.

14. See E. Coter, E. Grossman, and F. Clark, *Family Food Plans and Food Costs* (Washington, D.C.: U.S. Department of Agriculture, 1962). See also Betty Peterkin, *Food Plans for Poverty Measurement*, Technical Paper XII for *The Measure of Poverty* (Washington, D.C.: U.S. Department of Health, Education, and Welfare, 1976).

15. U.S. Dept. of Health, Education, and Welfare, *The Measure of Poverty*, pp. 74–77; Mollie Orshansky, *Update of the Orshansky Index*, Technical Paper XI for *The Measure of Poverty* (Washington, D.C.: Social Security Administration, 1976).

16. Jill King, *The Consumer Price Index*, Technical Paper V for *The Measure of Poverty* (Washington, D.C.: U.S. Department of Health, Education, and Welfare, 1976).

17. Congressional Budget Office, *Indexing with the Consumer Price Index: Problems and Alternatives* (Washington, D.C.: U.S. Government Printing Office, 1981).

18. U.S. Bureau of the Census, "Money Income of Households, Families, and Persons in the United States: 1980," *Current Population Reports*, Series P-60, No. 132 (Washington, D.C.: U.S. Government Printing Office, 1982), Table 1.

19. *Ibid.*, pp. 220–26.

20. *Ibid.*, pp. 230–31.

21. Edgar K. Browning, *Redistribution and the Welfare System* (Washington, D.C.: American Enterprise Institute, 1975); Roger A. Freeman, *The Growth of American Government: A Morphology of the Welfare State* (Stanford, Cal.: Hoover Institution Press, 1975); Morton Paglin, *Poverty and Transfers In-Kind* (Stanford, Cal.: Hoover Institution Press, 1980); Timothy Smeeding, *Alternative Methods for Valuing Selected In-Kind Transfer Benefits and Measuring Their Effect On Poverty* (Washington, D.C.: U.S. Bureau of the Census, 1982). This literature is now very long. For a relatively complete review, see Smeeding's analysis.

22. Thomas Joe, *Profiles of Families in Poverty: Effects of the 1983 Budget Proposals on the Poor* (Washington, D.C.: Center for the Study of Social Policy, 1982).

23. Timothy Smeeding, *Alternative Methods for Valuing Selected In-Kind Transfer Benefits and Measuring their Effect on Poverty*, pp. 49 and 78–102.

24. *Ibid.*, p. 56.

25. Timothy Smeeding and Marilyn Moon, "Valuing Government Expenditures: The Case of Medical Care Transfers and Poverty," *Review of Income and Wealth* 26 (September, 1980): 305–24. See also Morton Paglin, *Poverty and Transfers In-Kind*.

26. Timothy Smeeding, *Alternative Methods for Valuing Selected In-Kind Transfers and Measuring their Effect on Poverty*, pp. 58–63. See also Kenneth Clarkson, "Welfare Benefits of the Food Stamp Programs," *Southern Economic Journal* 34 (1976): 864–78; Janice Peskin, *In-Kind Income and the Measurement of Poverty*, Technical Paper VII for *The Measure of Poverty* (Washington, D.C.: U.S. Department of Health, Education, and Welfare, 1976); Timothy Smeeding, "The Anti-Poverty Effectiveness of In-Kind Transfers," *Journal of Human Resources* 12 (Summer, 1977): 360–78.

27. Timothy Smeeding, *Alternative Methods for Valuing Selected In-Kind Transfers and Measuring Their Effect on Poverty*, pp. 69–71.

28. Timothy Smeeding and Marilyn Moon, "Valuing Government Expenditures: The Case of Medical Care Transfers and Poverty," p. 306.

29. Timothy Smeeding, *Alternative Methods for Valuing Selected In-Kind Transfers and Measuring Their Effect on Poverty*, pp. 49–51. The quote is on p. 51.

30. *Ibid.*, p. 6.

31. *Ibid.*, pp. 8 and 106–09. Table 2.5 is a simplified version of Smeeding's two presentations, both of which are obtuse.

32. Eugene Smolensky, Leanna Stiefel, Maria Schmundt, and Robert Plotnick, "In-Kind Transfers and the Size Distribution of Income." Chapter 7 in Marilyn Moon and Eugene Smolensky (eds.), *Improving Measures of Economic Well-Being* (New York: Academic Press, 1977).

33. Martin Anderson, *Welfare* (Stanford, Cal.: Hoover Institution Press, 1980).

Chapter 3: Public Assistance

1. See Advisory Commission on Intergovernmental Relations, *Public Assistance: The Growth of a Federal Function* (Washington, D.C.: U.S. Government Printing Office, 1980); and Advisory Commission on Intergovernmental Relations, *Tax Capacity of the Fifty States* (Washington, D.C.: U.S. Government Printing Office, 1982).

2. Congressional Budget Office, *Indexing with the Consumer Price Index: Problems and Alternatives* (Washington: D.C.: U.S. Government Printing Office, 1981).

3. Executive Office of the President, *Budget of the United States Government, Fiscal 1983* (Washington, D.C.: Office of Management and Budget, 1982), pp. 5-130, 5-143, and 9-3. Executive Office of the President, *Budget of the United States Government, Fiscal 1984* (Washington, D.C.: Office of Management and Budget, 1983): pp. 5-103, 5-114, and 9-3.

4. U.S. Bureau of the Census, *Statistical Abstract of the United States, 1980*

(Washington, D.C.: U.S. Department of Commerce, 1981), p. 330.

5. Executive Office of the President, *Budget of the United States Government, Fiscal 1983,* pp. 5–130, 5–143, and 5–166. Executive Office of the President, *Budget of the United States Government, Fiscal Year 1984,* pp. 5–103, 5–114, and 5–131.

6. William J. Lawrence and Stephen Leeds, *An Inventory of Federal Income Transfer Programs* (Institute for Socioeconomic Studies: White Plains, N.Y., 1978), p. 14.

7. Congressional Budget Office, *Agricultural Price Support Programs: A Handbook* (Washington, D.C.: U.S. Government Printing Office, 1980), p. 14. For the cost of price supports, see Executive Office of the President, *Budget of the United States Government, Fiscal 1983,* p. 5–60.

8. Congressional Budget Office, *Five Year Budget Projections and Alternative Budgeting Strategies for Fiscal Years 1980–1984: Supplemental Report on Tax Expenditures* (Washington, D.C.: U.S. Government Printing Office, 1979), pp. 15–22.

9. Gail R. Wilensky, *Government and the Financing of Health Care* (Washington, D.C.: National Center for Health Services Research, 1982).

10. In an interview with the Associated Press (January 2, 1982), Wilensky estimated that tax expenditures for health care ballooned to $22 billion in 1981.

11. The number of recipients comes from *Social Security Bulletin* 44 (September 1981): 41. The level of payment comes from "Departments of Labor, Health and Human Services, Education, and Related Agencies Appropriations for 1982, *Hearings before a Subcommittee of the Community on Appropriations,* House of Representatives, Part 5 (Washington, D.C.: U.S. Government Printing Office, 1981), p. 440.

12. U.S. Department of Health and Human Services, *Aid to Families with Dependent Children, 1977 Recipient Characteristics Study,* Part I (Washington, D.C.: U.S. Government Printing Office, 1980), p. 28.

13. Robert Pear, "States Disregarding Federal Law Limiting Welfare Families Assets," *New York Times,* January 26, 1982, p. 1.

14. Executive Office of the President, *Fiscal Year 1982 Budget Revisions: Additional Details on Budget Savings* (Washington, D.C.: Office of Management and Budget, 1981), p. 141.

15. Department of Health and Human Services, *Characteristics of State Plans for Aid to Families with Dependent Children: Need, Eligibility, Administration* (Washington, D.C.: U.S. Government Printing Office, 1981), pp. 235–36. It should be noted that states establish a need level and then authorize maximum benefits as some proportion of that amount. Thus, some states pay 100% of their need level, some 75%, and some specify a specific dollar amount.

16. Executive Office of the President, *Fiscal Year 1982 Budget Revisions,* p. 141.

17. Ferrel Guillory, "Managing Budget Cuts at the State Level," *North Carolina Insight* 4(No. 4, 1981): 26–30.

18. Thomas Joe, *Profiles of Families in Poverty: Effects of the FY 1983 Budget Proposals on the Poor* (Washington, D.C.: Center for the Study of Social Policy, 1982).

19. Executive Office of the President, *Fiscal Year 1982 Budget Revisions: Additional Details on Budget Savings,* p. 140.

20. Thomas Joe, *Profiles of Families in Poverty.*

21. *Ibid.*

22. See U.S. Department of Health and Human Services, *Characteristics of State Plans for Aid to Families with Dependent Children* (Washington, D.C.: U.S. Government Printing Office, 1981); U.S. Department of Health and Human Services, *Research Tables Based on Characteristics of State Plans for Aid to Families with Dependent Children* Washington, D.C.: U.S. Government Printing Office, 1980). The next two paragraphs are based on these two sources.

23. Congressional Budget Office, *Indexing with the Consumer Price Index,* pp. 113–16.

24. Unless otherwise specified, the facts reported in the next few paragraphs come from U.S. Department of Health and Human Services, *Aid to Families with Dependent Children: A Chartbook* (Washington, D.C.: U.S. Government Printing Office, 1980). See also John Williamson, "Beliefs about the Welfare Poor," *Sociology and Social Research* 58 (January, 1974): 163–75.

25. Donald J. Bogue, "A Long-Term Solution to the AFDC Problem: Prevention of Unwanted Pregnancy," *Social Service Review* 49 (December, 1975): 539–52.

26. U.S. Bureau of the Census, *Statistical Abstract of the United States, 1980,* p. 358.

27. See Select Committee on Aging, U.S. House of Representatives, *SSI (Supplementary Security Income): Questions and Answers* (Washington, D.C.: U.S. Government Printing Office, 1975); Alicia Munnell, "Federalizing Welfare: The Fiscal Impact of the SSI Program," *New England Economic Review* (Sept. – Oct., 1977): 3–28; U.S. Department of Health, Education, and Welfare, *A Guide to Supplemental Security Income* (Washington, D.C.: U.S. Government Printing Office, 1979).

28. *Social Security Bulletin* 44 (January, 1982): 49.

29. On SSI payment levels, see *Social Security Bulletin* 44 (June, 1981): 1. On the

savings, see Executive Office of the President, *Fiscal Year 1982 Budget Revisions*, p. 178.

30. Thomas Tissue, "Response to Recipiency under Public Assistance and SSI," *Social Security Bulletin* 41 (November, 1978): 3–15.

31. *Indiana Public Welfare Programs* (Indianapolis, Ind.: Department of Public Welfare, 1982), pp. D–3, D–11. See also U.S. Bureau of the Census, *Characteristics of Households and Persons Receiving Noncash Benefits: 1979* (Washington, D.C.: U.S. Government Printing Office), pp. 12–13.

32. Loretta Schwartz-Nobel, *Starving in the Shadow of Plenty* (New York: G. P. Putnam & Sons, 1981).

33. Conference Report, *Omnibus Budget Reconciliation Act of 1981* (Washington, D.C.: U.S. Government Printing Office, 1981), pp. 2–11.

34. Executive Office of the President, *Fiscal Year 1982 Budget Revisions*, pp. 37–38.

35. Maurice MacDonald, *Food, Stamps, and Income Maintenance* (New York: Academic Press, 1977).

36. Kathryn Longen, *Domestic Food Programs: An Overview* (Washington, D.C.: U.S. Department of Agriculture, 1980); "Oversight Hearings on Child Nutrition," *Hearings before the Subcommittee on Elementary, Secondary, and Vocational Education of the Committee on Education and Labor*, March, 1980 (Washington, D.C.: U.S. Government Printing Office, 1980), pp. 96–169.

37. See Milton Kotelchuck, *1980 Massachusetts Special Supplemental Program for Women, Infants and Children (WIC) Evaluation Project* (Boston, MA: Department of Public Health, 1982); Joseph C. Endozien, Boyd R. Switzer, and Rebecca B. Brian, "Medical Evaluation of the Special Supplemental Food Program for Women, Infants and Children," *American Journal of Clinical Nutrition* 32 (March, 1979): 677–92.

38. Kathryn Longen, *Domestic Food Programs: An Overview;* "Reagan seeks Medicaid Fee and School Lunch Cutback," *New York Times* (December 30, 1981), p. 9.

39. Food Resource and Action Center, *The Impact of Child Nutrition Budget Cuts: A Look at the States and Selected School Districts* (Washington, D.C.: Food Resource and Action Center, 1982).

40. Subcommittee on Nutrition, *Hearing before the Subcommittee on Nutrition of the Committee on Agriculture, Hunger in America: Ten Years Later*, Senate, April 30, 1979 (Washington, D.C.: U.S. Government Printing Office, 1979).

41. Karen Davis and Cathy Schoen, *Health and the War on Poverty* (Washington,

D.C.: Brookings Institution, 1978).

42. Medicaid/Medicare Management Institute, *Data on the Medicaid Program: Eligibilty, Services, Expenditures* (Washington, D.C.: U.S. Department of Health, Education, and Welfare, 1979).

43. *Indiana Public Welfare System*, p. C–7.

44. "Waste and Abuse in Social Security Act Programs," *Hearing before the Subcommittee on Public Asistance of the Committee on Finance*, Nov. 16, 1979 (Washington, D.C.: U.S. Government Printing Office, 1980), pp. 88–89; "Department of Labor and Health, Education, and Welfare Appropriations for 1979," *Hearings before a Subcomittee of the Committee on Appropriations*, Part 6, House of Representatives (Washington, D.C.: U.S. Government Printing Office, 1979), pp. 1258–79.

45. Thomas J. Anton, *An Estimate of the Fiscal Impact of President Reagan's Budget Proposals* (Ann Arbor, MI: Institute for Social Research, 1981). See also Advisory Commission on Intergovernmental Relations, *Tax Capacity of the Fifty States*.

46. "Administration of the AFDC Program," *Third Report by the Committee on Government Operations*, July 18, 1979, p. 40. See also U.S. Department of Health and Human Services, *Disposition of Public Assistance Cases involving Questions of Fraud, Fiscal Year 1979* (Washington, D.C.: U.S. Government Printing Office, 1981).

47. U.S. Department of Justice, *Fraud and Abuse in Government Benefit Programs* (Washington, D.C.: U.S. Government Printing Office, 1979); "Waste and Abuse in Social Security Act Programs;" "Medicaid and Medicare Frauds, "*Hearing before the Subcommittee on Long-Term Care of the Special Committee on Aging*, U.S. Senate, August 30, 1976 (Washington, D.C.: U.S. Government Printing Office, 1977); "Fraud and Racketeering in Medicare and Medicaid," *Hearing before Select committee on Aging*, House of Representatives, October 4, 1978 (Washington, D.C.: U.S. Government Printing Office, 1979).

48. "Administration of the AFDC Program," p. 40.

Chapter 4: Poverty, Public Assistance, and Work

1. Joe R. Feagin, *Subordinating the Poor* (Englewood Cliffs, N.J.: Prentice-Hall, 1972), pp. 91–130. See also Joan Huber and William H. Form, *Income and Ideology* (New York: Free Press, 1973); Lee Rainwater, *What Money Buys* (New York: Basic Books, 1974).

2. George Gilder, *Wealth and Poverty* (New York: Basic Books, 1981), p. 68.

3. Robert K. Merton, "Social Structure and Anomie," in *Social Theory and Social Structure* (New York: Free Press, 1968), pp. 185–215.

4. This is one of those stereotypes that social science has affirmed. See Peter Blau and Otis Dudley Duncan, *The American Occupational Structure* (New York: Wiley, 1967). For a compact review of the literature on status attainment, see Chapter 6.

5. Leonard Goodwin, *Do the Poor Want to Work?* (Washington, D.C.: Brookings Institution, 1972); Leonard Goodwin, *Can Social Science Help Resolve National Problems?* (New York: Free Press, 1975). There are many other studies of poor people's attitudes toward work and all of them point in the same direction; see Mary Bryna Sanger, *Welfare of the Poor* (New York: Academic Press, 1979) for a review of this literature.

6. See Elliot Liebow, *Tally's Corner* (Boston: Little, Brown, 1967); Joseph T. Howell, *Hard Living on Clay Street* (New York: Anchor Books, 1973); Edward J. Walsh, *Dirty Work, Race and Self-Esteem* (Ann Arbor, MI: Institute of Labor and Industrial Relations, 1975). The quotation below is from Liebow, p. 63, and the sentence following the quote is a paraphrase from p. 54.

7. Morris Rosenberg and Leonard I. Pearlin, "Social Class and Self-Esteem among Children and Adults," *American Journal of Sociology* 84(July, 1978): 53-77.

8. U.S. Bureau of the Census, "Money Income and Poverty Status of Families and Persons in the United States: 1981," *Current Population Reports*, Series P-60, No. 134 (Washington, D.C.: U.S. Government Printing Office, 1982), pp. 27-28.

9. *Ibid.*, p. 26. Only 3% gave some reason for not working other than those cited in the text.

10. See Herbert E. Meyer, "Jobs and Want Ads: A Look Behind the Words," *Fortune* (November 20, 1978), pp. 88-96; Bradley R. Schiller, "Want Ads and Jobs for the Poor," *Manpower* 6(January, 1974); 11-13.

11. Mary Corcoran, Linda Datcher, and Greg J. Duncan, "Most Workers Find Jobs Through Word of Mouth," *Monthly Labor Review* 103 (August, 1980):33-36.

12. See Francis Fox Piven and Richard Cloward, *Regulating the Poor: The Functions of Public Welfare* (New York: Vintage Books, 1971).

13. Martin Rein nad Lee Rainwater, "Patterns of welfare Use,"*Social Service Review* 52 (December, 1978): 511-34; David W. Lyon, *The Dynamics of Welfare Dependency: A Survey* (New York: Ford Foundation, 1977). See also Greg J. Duncan and James N. Morgan (eds.), *Five Thousand American Families: Patterns of Economic Progress,* Volumes 1-8 (Ann Arbor, MI: Institute for Social Research, 1974-78.)

14. The studies cited in Note 13 are all longitudinal. For a cross-sectional analysis, see Richard M. Devens, "Unemployment among Recipients of Food Stamps and AFDC," *Monthly Labor Review* 102 (March, 1979):47-53.

15. See Carol Stack, *All Our Kin* (New York: Harper & Row, 1974); Robert Coles, *Children of Crisis*, Vol. I (Boston, Little Brown, 1964), 368–69.

16. See Bradley R. Schiller, "Lessons from WIN: A Manpower Evaluation," *Journal of Human Resources* 13 (Fall, 1978): 502–23; Leonard Goodwin, *The Work Incentive (WIN) Program and Related Experiences* (Washington, D.C.: U.S. Department of Labor, 1977); and Charles Garvin, Audrey D. Smith, and William J. Reid (eds.), *The Work Incentive Experience* (Montclair, NJ: Allenheld, Osmun & Co., 1978).

17. Leonard Goodwin, *The Work Incentive (WIN) Program and Related Experiences.*

18. See Kenneth J. Newbeck and Jack L. Roach, "Income Maintenance Experiments, Politics, and the Perpetuation of Poverty," *Social Problems* 28 (February, 1981): 308–20.

19. Martin Anderson, *Welfare* (Stanford, Cal.: Hoover Institution Press, 1978), pp. 67–87.

20. Robert A. Moffitt, "The Negative Income Tax: Would It Discourage Work?" *Monthly Labor Review* 104(April, 1981): 23–27.

21. One of the strangest findings to emerge from the negative income tax experiments is that they were associated with an increase in family dissolution; see Michael Hannon, *et. al.*, "Income and Independence Effects on Marital Dissolution," *American Journal of Sociology* 84(November, 1978): 611–33. Unfortunately, the authors do not provide a really satisfactory explanation of this finding. In addition, it has been strongly challenged by Leonard Goodwin, "Limitations of the Seattle and Denver Income Maintenance Analysis," *American Journal of Sociology* 85 (November, 1979): 653–57.

22. President's Commission for a National Agenda for the Eighties, *Government and the Advancement of Social Justice, Health, Welfare, Education, and Civil Rights in the Eighties* (Washington, D.C.: U.S. Government Printing Office, 1980).

23. Milton Friedman, *Capitalism and Freedom* (Chicago, Ill.: University of Chicago Press, 1962). For a background on the history of the negative income tax experiments, see Robert A. Levine, "How and Why the Experiment Came About." Pp. 15–25 in J. A. Pechman and P. M. Timpane (eds.) *Work Incentives and Income Guarantees: The New Jersey Negative Income Tax Experiment* (Washington, D.C.: Brookings Institution, 1975); Peter N. Rossi and Katherine C. Lyall, *Reforming Public Welfare: A Critique of the Negative Income Tax Experiment* (New York: Russell Sage Foundation, 1976).

24. Peter H. Rossi and Katherine C. Lyall, *Reforming Public Welfare.*

25. *Ibid.*

26. Robert A. Moffitt, "The Negative Income Tax: Would It Discourage Work?"

27. Sonia Wright, "Work Response to Income Maintenance: Economic, Sociological, and Cultural Perspectives," *Social Forces* 53(June, 1975): 553–62.

Chapter 5: Some Correlates of Poverty

1. The phrase comes from an essay by Arthur Stinchcombe, who uses it to describe Robert Merton's theoretical orientation. I think, however, that it is a general statement of the theoretical basis for sociology as an academic discipline, one that is pointed out in every introductory textbook. Its significance in Merton's work is that he is one of the few practicing sociologists who take it seriously. See Arthur Stinchcombe, "Merton's Theory of Social Structure." Pp. 11–34 in L. A. Coser (ed.), *The Idea of Social Structure* (New York: Free Press, 1975).

2. Louis Schneider, "Ironic Perspective and Sociological Thought." Pp. 323–38 in L. A. Coser (ed.), *The Idea of Social Structure* (New York: Free Press, 1975).

3. Sidney Verba and Norman H. Nie, *Participation in America: Political Democracy and Social Equality* (New York: Harper & Row, 1972).

4. The theoretical basis for this idea is in Max Weber's writings, especially *Economy and Society* (New York: Bedminister, 1968). The most well-known exponent of the pluralist view is Robert A. Dahl, *Pluralist Democracy in the United States: Conflict and Consent* (Chicago: Rand McNally, 1967).

5. Sidney Verba and Norman H. Nie, *Participation in America*, pp. 125–37.

6. Leonard Beeghley, Ellen Van Velsor, and E. Wilbur Bock, "The Correlates of Religiosity among Black and White Americans," *Sociological Quarterly* 22 (Summer, 1981): 403–12; Russell L. Curtis and Louis A. Zurcher, "Voluntary Associations and the Social Integration of the Poor," *Social Problems* 18 (Winter, 1971): 339–57. The relationship between class and membership is actually curvilinear: Participation rates also decline among upper-class people.

7. See the studies in S. M. Lipset and S. Rokkan (eds.), *Party Systems and Voter Alignments* (New York: Free Press, 1967).

8. John F. Zipp, Richard Landerman, and Paul Luebke, "Political Parties and Political Participation: A Reexamination of the Standard Socioeconomic Model," *Social Forces* 60 (June, 1982): 1140–53.

9. Robert F. Kennedy, *New York Times*, October 24, 1966, p. 16; quoted in Lewis A. Coser, *Continuities in the Study of Social Conflict* (New York: Free Press, 1967), p. 74.

10. Francis Fox Piven and Richard A. Cloward, *Poor People's Movements: Why They Succeed, How They Fail* (New York: Pantheon, 1977), p.26.

11. *Ibid.*, p. 25.

12. Lewis A. Coser, *Continuities*, p. 84.

13. Francis Fox Piven and Richard Cloward, *Poor Peoples Movements.* See also William A. Gamson, *The Strategy of Protest* (Homewood, Ill.: Dorsey, 1975); Joe R. Feagin and Harlan H. Hahn, *Ghetto Revolts* (New York: Macmillan, 1973).

14. See Law Enforcement Assistance Administration, *Survey of Inmates of Local Jails, 1972* (Washington, D.C.: U.S. Government Printing Office, 1974) and Law Enforcement Assistance Administration, *Survey of Inmates of State Correctional Facilities, 1974* (Washington, D.C.: U.S. Government Printing Office, 1976). Although the empirical generalization given in the text is the most common conclusion, there is a rather puerile academic controversy over whether class is related to crime specifically and to deviance generally. For the latest episode, see Terence P. Thornberry and Margaret Farnworth, "Social Correlates of Criminal Involvement: Further Evidence on the Relationship between Social Status and Criminal Behavior," *American Sociological Review* 47 (August, 1982): 505–18. The first problem with this entire literature is that crime is, in effect, defined as street crime. Even with these sorts of crimes, however, it is difficult to show a relationship to poverty; see Charles R. Tittle, Wayne J. Villemez, and Douglas A. Smith, "The Myth of Social Class and Criminality: An Assessment of the Empirical Evidence," *American Sociological Review* 43 (October, 1978): 643–56. Hence, the usual strategy is to emphasize statistically significant differences in low-frequency crimes. The second, and more serious, problem with this literature is that it tacitly assumes both white-collar crime and types of deviance that harm others but are not defined as criminal do not exist (see text). The lesson we ought to learn from Merton's work is that the form deviance takes is a function of the opportunities available.

15. Robert K. Merton, *Social Theory and Social Structure*, pp. 185–214. The reader familiar with Merton's essay, "Social Structure and Anomie" will recognize that I define "ritualism" in a way rather differently than he does.

16. See Edward J. Walsh, *Dirty Work, Race, and Self-Esteem* (Ann Arbor, MI: Institute of Labor and Industrial Relations, 1975), Lillian Rubin, *Worlds of Pain* (New York: Basic Books, 1976), p. 36.

17. Robert K. Merton, *Social Theory and Social Structure*, pp. 199–200.

18. The theoretical basis for this point is elaborated in Edwin H. Sutherland, *Principles of Criminology* (New York: J. B. Lippincott Co., 1947). See also the readings in Ronald A. Farrell and Victoria Lynn Swigart, *Social Deviance*, 2nd ed. (New York: J. B. Lippincott, Co., 1978).

19. See John Allen, *Assault with a Deadly Weapon: The Autobiography of a Street Criminal* (New York: Pantheon Books, 1977); Claude Brown, *Manchild in the Promised Land* (New York: Signet, 1965).

20. Joseph Califano, *The 1982 Report on Drug Abuse and Alcoholism* (New York: Warner Books, 1982), pp. 77–81.

21. Law Enforcement Assistance Administration, *Criminal Victimization in the United States* (Washington, D.C.: U.S. Government Printing Office, 1976); U.S. Department of Justice, *Criminal Victimization in the United States, 1978* (Washington, D.C.: U.S. Government Printing Office, 1980).

22. Barbara Becnel, "The Crime–Unemployment Cycle," *AFL-CIO Federationist* 85 (November, 1978): 9–14. See also Suzanne Barclay, *et. al., Schooling and Work among Youth from Low Income Households* (Washington, D.C.: U.S. Department of Labor, 1980).

23. The quotation is from James W. Hunt, James E. Bowers, and Neal Miller, *Laws, Licenses, and the Offender's Right to Work* (Washington, D.C.: American Bar Association, 1973). In addition, see Richard A. Berk, Kenneth J. Lenihan, and Peter Rossi, "Crime and Poverty," *American Sociological Review* 45 (October, 1980): 766–86; the historical studies cited in President's Commission on Law Enforcement and the Administration of Justice, *Task Force Report: Corrections* (Washington, D.C.: U.S. Government Printing Office, 1967), pp. 2–4; Daniel Glaser, *The Effectiveness of a Prison and Parole System* (Indianapolis: Bobbs-Merrill, 1964); George Pownall, *Employment Problems of Released Prisoners* (Washington, D.C.: U.S. Department of Labor, 1969).

24 James W. Hunt, *et al., Laws, Licenses, and the Offender's Right to Work*, p. 18.

25. Quoted in Jeffrey H. Reiman, *The Rich Get Richer and the Poor Get Prison* (New York: John Wiley, 1979), p. 35. The next four paragraphs are indebted to this source.

26. President's Commission on Law Enforcement and the Administration of Justice, *The Challenges of Crime in a Free Society* (Washington, D.C.: U.S. Government Printing Office, 1967), p. 15.

27. The best recent study of white-collar crime is Marshall B. Clinard, *Illegal Corporate Behavior* (Washington, D.C.: U.S. Department of Justice, 1979). The self-report data cited in the text is from the President's Commission on Law Enforcement and the Administration of Justice, *The Challenge of Crime in a Free Society*, p. v. A recent critique has argued that self-report studies are flawed because they focus on offenses that are less serious; see Michael J. Hindelang, *et. al.,* "Correlates of Delinquency: The Illusion of Discrepancy between Self-Report and Official Measures," *American Sociological Review* 44 (December, 1979): 995–1014. Nonetheless,

such research is very useful because it taps into the extent of unrecorded deviant behavior.

28. Victoria Lynn Swigert and Ronald L. Farrell, "Normal Homicides and the Law," *American Sociological Review* 42 (February, 1977): 16-31.

29. Jeffrey H. Reiman, *The Rich Get Richer and the Poor Get Prison*, p. 119; Marshall B. Clinard, *Illegal Corporate Behavior*, p. 16; U.S. Chamber of Commerce, *White Collar Crime* (Washington, D.C.: U.S. Chamber of Commerce, 1974).

30. Jerome Carlin, Jan Howard, and Sheldon Messinger, *Civil Justice for the Poor* (New York: Russell Sage, 1967).

31. Executive Office of the President, *Budget of the United States Government—Fiscal Year, 1983* (Washington, D.C.: Office of Management and Budget, 1982), p. 8-145; Legal Services Corporation, *Characteristics of Field Programs Supported by the Legal Services Corporations* (Washington, D.C.: Legal Services Corporation, 1982).

32. Karen Davis and Cathy Schoen, *Health and the War on Poverty* (Washington, D.C.: Brookings Institution, 1978), pp. 27-35.

33. U.S. Bureau of the Census, *Stastical Abstract of the United States* (Washington, D.C.: U.S. Government Printing Office, 1981), pp.73 and 77.

34. Kyriakos S. Markides and Connie McFarland,"A Note on Recent Trends in the Infant Mortality–Socioeconomic Status Relationship," *Social Forces* 61 (September, 1982): 268-76; C.H. Brooks, "Path Analysis of Socioeconomic Correlates of County Infant Mortality Rates," *International Journal of Health Services* 5, no. 3 (1975): 499-514; C. H. Brooks, "The Changing Relationship between Socioeconomic Status and Infant Mortality: An Analysis of State Characteristics," *Journal of Health and Social Behavior* 16, no. 3 (1975): 291-303.

35. U.S. Department of Health, Education, and Welfare, *Health Status of Minorities and Low Income Groups,* (Washington, D.C.: U.S. Government Printing Office, 1978), pp. 37-39. See also Steven L. Gortmaker, "Poverty and Infant Mortality in the United States," *American Sociological Review* 44 (April, 1979): 280-97; Nigel Paneth "Infant Mortality Reexamined," *Journal of the American Medical Association* 247 (February 19, 1982): 1027.

36. U.S. Department of Health and Human Services, *Selected Health Characteristics by Occupation* (Washington D.C.: U.S. Government Printing Office, 1980), pp. 31-32.

37. Karen Davis and Cathy Schoen, *Health and the War on Poverty*, p. 35.

38. U.S. Department of Health, Education, and Welfare, *Health Status of Minori-*

ties and Low Income Groups, p. 137; Karen Davis and Kathy Schoen, *Health and the War on Poverty,* p. 38.

39. U.S. Department of Health, Education, and Welfare, *Health Status of Minorities and Low Income Groups,* p. 214.

40. U.S. Bureau of the Census, *Statistical Abstract of the United States* (Washington, D.C.: U.S. Government Printing Office, 1981), p. 119.

41. Children's Defense Fund, *EPSDT: Does it Spell Health Care for the Poor Children* (Washington D.C.: Children's Defense Fund, 1977).

42. M. H. Becker, C. A. Nathanson, R. H. Drachman, and J. P. Kirscht, "Mothers' Health Beliefs and Children's Clinic Visits: A Prospective Study." *Journal of Community Health* 3 (1975):125–35; E. Berkanovic and L. G. Reeder, "Can Money Buy the Appropriate Use of Services? Some Notes on the Meaning of Utilization Data," *Journal of Health and Social Behavior* 15 (1974):93–99.

43. U.S. Department of Human Services, *Selected Health Characteristics by Occupation,* pp. 59–60.

44. Barbara Ehrenreich and John Ehrenreich, *The American Health Empire* (New York: Random House, 1960).

45. L. A. Aday, "Economic and Noneconomic Barriers to the Use of Needed Medical Services." *Medical Care* 13 (1975):447–56.

46. See Lee Rainwater, "The Lower Class: Health, Illness and Medical Institutions." Pp. 250–77 in I. Deutscher and E. Thompson (eds.), *Among the People: Encounters with the Poor* (New York: Basic Books, 1968); E. L. Koos, *The Health of Regionville* (New York: Columbia University Press, 1954); Irving K. Zola, "Culture and Symptoms: An Analysis of Patients' Presenting Complaints," *American Sociological Review* 31 (October, 1966):615–30.

47. See Diane B. Dutton, "Explaining the Low Use of Health Services By the Poor: Costs, Attitudes, or Delivery Systems?" *American Sociological Review* 43 (June, 1978): 348–68; and the exchange of comments between Dutton and James A. Neff *American Sociological Review* 47 (August, 1982): 554–61. See also Lee A. Crandall and R. Paul Duncan, "Attitudinal and Situational Factors in the Use of Physicians Services by Low Income Persons," *Journal of Health and Social Behavior* 22 (March, 1981): 64–77.

Chapter 6: Cultural Values, Analgesic Behavior, and Poverty

1. I have taken the image of analgesic behavior from Richard A. Ball, "A Poverty Case: The Analgesic Subculture of the Southern Appalachians," *American*

Sociological Review 33 (December, 1968): 885–96. This article is very provocative because the author uses an image that is arresting and then draws exactly the wrong conclusion from the experimental research he cites: that frustration-instigated behavior reflects a subculture. It is Ball who called my attention to Norman Maier's work, discussed in the text.

2. James T. Howell, *Hard Living on Clay Street* (Garden City, N.Y.: Anchor Books, 1973). I should note that my analysis is a loose extrapolation of Howell's distinction. He might not agree with the way I have phrased the differences between hard and settled livers.

3. See Lillian Breslow Rubin, *Worlds of Pain* (New York: Basic Books, 1976).

4. Oscar Lewis, "The Culture of Poverty." Pp. 187–200 in D. P. Moynihan (ed.), *On Understanding Poverty* (New York: Basic Books, 1969), p. 187.

5. *Ibid.* p. 197.

6. See Barbara E. Coward, J. Allen Williams, and Joe R. Feagin, "The Culture of Poverty Debate: Some Additional Data," *Social Problems* 21 (June, 1974): 621–33; Lola M. Ireland, Oliver C. Moles, and Robert M. O'Shea, "Ethnicity, Poverty, and Selected Attitudes; A Test of the 'Culture of Poverty' Thesis," *Social Forces* 47 (June, 1969): 405–13. The most well-known critiques of the culture of poverty thesis are Charles A. Valentine, *Culture and Poverty* (Chicago, Ill.: University of Chicago Press, 1978) and Eleanor Burke Leacock, *The Culture of Poverty: A Critique* (New York: Simon and Schuster, 1971).

7. It is possible to extrapolate some testable hypotheses from the culture of poverty thesis; see L. Richard Della Fave, "The Culture of Poverty Revisited: A Strategy for Research," *Social Problems* 21 (June, 1974): 609–62. However, this task requires considerable creativity.

8. See Thomas Pettigrew, "Social Psychology's Potential Contributions to an Understanding of Poverty." Pp. 189–233 in Vincent T. Covello (ed.), *Poverty and Public Policy: An Evaluation of Social Scientific Research* (Cambridge, MA: Schenkman Publishing Co., 1980).

9. Hyman Rodman, "The Lower Class Value Stretch," *Social Forces* 42 (December, 1963): 205–15.

10. Elliot Liebow, *Tally's Corner* (Boston: Little, Brown, 1967), p. 222.

11. See Jonathan H. Turner and Leonard Beeghley, *The Emergence of Sociological Theory* (Homewood, Ill.: Dorsey Press, 1981), pp. 146–54 and 170–90.

12. Norman R. F. Maier, *Frustration: The Study of Behavior without a Goal* (New York: McGraw-Hill, 1949).

13. See Donald S. Hiroto, "Locus of Control and Learned Helplessness," *Journal of Experimental Psychology* 102 (February, 1974): 187–93; Donald S. Hiroto and Martin E. P. Seligman, "Generality of Learned Helplessness in Man," *Journal of Personality and Social Psychology* 31 (February, 1975): 311–27; Susan Roth and Larry Kubal, "Effects of Noncontingent Reinforcement on Tasks of Differing Importance: Facilitation and Learned Helplessness," *Journal of Personality and Social Psychology* 32 (October, 1975): 680–91; Shelley E. Taylor, "Hospital Patient Behavior: Reactance, Helplessness, or Control?" *Journal of Social Issues* 35 (No. 1, 1979): 156–84. Strangely, nowhere in this literature is there a citation to Norman Maier's work.

14. Susan Roth and R. R. Bootzin, "The Effects of Experimentally Induced Expectancies of External Control: An Investigation of Learned Helplessness," *Journal of Personality and Social Psychology* 29 (February, 1974): 253–64. This article is interesting because the authors interpret an aggressive response as inconsistent with the learned helplessness hypothesis and, as such, try to explain it away. Perhaps if they had been familiar with Maier's study or recalled the frustration–aggression hypothesis, they would have adopted a different point of view.

15. This point is taken from Donald S. Hiroto and Martin Seligman, "The Generality of Learned Helplessness in Man." For a full exposition of Seligman's argument, see his *Helplessness* (San Francisco, Cal.: Freeman, 1976).

16. See E. Jerry Phares, *Locus of Control in Personality* (Morristown, N.J.: General Learning Press, 1976); Morris Rosenberg and Leonard I. Pearlin, "Social Class and Self-Esteem among Children and Adults," *American Journal of Sociology* 84 (July, 1978): 53–77; Ronald C. Kessler and Paul D. Cleary, "Social Class and Psychological Distress," *American Sociological Review* 45 (June, 1980): 463–78.

Chapter 7: The Causes of Poverty

1. See Joe R. Feagin, *Subordinating the Poor* (Englewood Cliffs, N.J.: Prentice-Hall, 1976); John B. Williamson, "Beliefs about the Motivation of the Poor and Attitudes toward Poverty Policy," *Social Problems* 21 (June, 1974): 634–48; Joan Huber and William H. Form, *Income and Ideology* (New York: Free Press, 1973).

2. For a good critique of this tendency, see John Zipp, Richard Landerman, and Paul Luebke, "Political Parties and Political Participation: A Reexamination of the Standard Socioeconomic Model," *Social Forces* 60 (June, 1982): 1140–53.

3. See Joseph Howell, *Hard Living on Clay Street* (Garden City, N.Y.: Anchor Books, 1973); Leonard I. Pearlin and Clarice W. Radabaugh, "Economic Strains and the Coping Functions of Alcohol," *American Journal of Sociology* 82 (November, 1976): 652–63.

4. Linda Birzotta Nilson, "Reconsidering Ideological Lines: Beliefs about Poverty in America," *Sociological Quarterly* 22 (Autumn, 1981): 531–48.

5. Francis Fox Piven and Richard A. Cloward, *Regulating the Poor: The Functions*

of Public Welfare (New York: Vintage Books, 1971).

6. See Philip M. Stern, *The Rape of the Taxpayer* (New York: Vintage Books, 1974), p. 382. For a concise summary of the way in which wealth and politics combine, see Leonard Beeghley, *Social Stratification in America: A Critical Analysis of Theory and Research* (New York: Random House, 1978), pp. 224–31.

7. Children's Defense Fund, *EPSDT: Does It Spell Health Care for Poor Children?* (Washington, D.C.: Children's Defense Fund, 1977), p. 23.

8. A good ethnographic account of the quality of interaction between doctors and poor patients is in Joseph T. Howell, *Hard Living on Clay Street.* (Garden City, N.Y.: Anchor Books, 1973).

9. U.S. Bureau of the Census, "Money Income and Poverty Status of Famiies and Persons in the United States: 1981," *Current Population Reports* (Series P–60, No. 134, 1982).

10. William I. Thomas, *The Unadjusted Girl* (Boston: Little, Brown & Co., 1923).

11. Ronald C. Kessler and Paul D. Cleary, "Social Class and Psychological Distress," *American Sociological Review* 45 (June, 1980): 463–78.

12. The word *Monopoly* is the trademark of Parker Brothers for its Real Es-Trading Game (Beverly, MA: Parker Brothers Division of General Mills Fun Group, Inc., 1935, 1946, 1961).

13. Peter Blau and Otis Dudley Duncan, *The American Occupational Structure* (New York: John Wiley, 1967). Their findings have been replicated by David L. Featherman and Robert M. Hauser, *Opportunity and Change* (New York: Academic Press, 1978).

14. *Ibid.*, p. 66.

15. *Ibid.*, pp.425–32.

16. See anything by E. Digby Baltzell, but especially his *Puritan Boston and Quaker Philadelphia* (New York: Free Press, 1979). See also Robert Coles, *The Privileged Ones* (Boston: Little, Brown, 1977).

17. For a concise review of this literature, see Leonard Beeghley, *Social Stratification in America*, pp. 301–23.

18. Peter Blau and Otis Dudley Duncan, *The American Occupational Structure*, p. 163.

19. *Ibid.*, pp. 163 and 430.

20. For example, Blau and Duncan also found that while education pays off for black men and southern men, their achievement levels are much less than for white men and nonsouthern men. Others have come up with similar findings for women (black and white); see Mary E. Ayella and John B. Williamson, "The Social Mobility of Women: A Causal Model of Socioeconomic Success," *Sociological Quarterly* 17 (Autumn, 1976): 534–54.

21. Michael Harrington, *The Other America* (Baltimore, MD: Penguin Books, 1971; first printing, 1962), pp. 15–16. See also Robert W. Hodge and Barbara Laslett, "Poverty and Status Attainment." Pp. 126–63 in Vincent T. Covello (ed.), *Poverty and Public Policy* (Cambridge, MA: Schenkman Publishing Co., 1980).

22. Manuel Vaz Pato and John Williamson, "Socioeconomic Achievement: The Case of the Working Poor," *Journal of Sociology and Social Welfare* 6 (March, 1979): 245–64. See also Robert W. Hodge and Barbara Laslett, "Poverty and Status Attainment."

23. Peter Blau and Otis Dudley Duncan, *The American Occupational Structure*, p. 434.

24. Max Weber, *Economy and Society* (Totowa, NJ: Bedminister Press, 1968), pp. 284–306 and 901–38. For a concise summary of Weber's analysis of social stratification in modern society, see Jonathan H. Turner and Leonard Beeghley, *The Emergence of Sociological Theory* (Homestead, Ill: Dorsey Press, 1981), pp. 232–46.

25. Gerald R. Leslie, *The Family in Social Context*, 5th ed. (New York: Oxford University Press, 1982).

26. See Leonard Beeghley, *Social Stratification in America*, pp. 148–49.

27. Lillian Breslow Rubin, *Worlds of Pain* (New York: Basic Books, 1976), Robert Coles, *The South Goes North* (Boston: Little, Brown and Co., 1967); Sandra L. Hofferth and Kristin A. Moore, "Early Childrearing and Subsequent Economic Well-Being," *American Sociological Review* 44 (October, 1979): 784–815.

28. Lillian Breslow Rubin, *Worlds of Pain.*

29. Phillips Cutright, "Income and Family Events: Marital Stability," *Journal of Marriage and the Family* 33 (May, 1971): 291–306.

30. Peter Blau and Otis Dudley Duncan, *The American Occupational Structure*, p. 435.

31. *Ibid.*, pp. 435 and 418.

32. James S. Coleman *et al.*, *Equality of Educational Opportunity* (Washington, D.C.: U.S. Government Printing Office, 1966). For a good review of this litera-

ture, see Rodman B. Webb, *Schooling and Society* (New York: Macmillan, 1981).

33. Christopher Jencks *et al.*, *Inequality: A Reassessment of the Effect of Family and Schooling in America* (New York: Harper & Row, 1972), p. 48. The income data are from the U.S. Bureau of the Census, "Money Income and Poverty Status of Families and Persons in the United States: 1981," *Current Population Reports*, Series P–60, No. 134 (Washington, D.C.: U.S. Government Printing Office, 1982), Table 4.

34. Samuel Bowles and Herbert Gintis, *Schooling in Capitalist America* (New York: Basic Books, 1976), p. 40.

35. Adele Thomas, "Learned Helplessness and Expectancy Factors: Implications for Research in Learning Disabilities" *Review of Educational Research* 49 (Spring, 1979): 208–21.

36. See any introductory economics text. For a critical view, see David M. Gordon, *Theories of Poverty and Underemployment* (Lexington, MA: D.C. Heath & Co., 1972).

37. The data in this and the following paragraph are from *Monthly Labor Review* 105 (September, 1982): 53–67.

38. U.S. Bureau of the Census, "Money Income and Poverty Status of Families and Persons in the United States, 1981," *Current Population Reports*, Series P–60, No. 134 (Washington, D.C.: U.S. Government Printing Office, 1982), p. 27.

39. U.S. Bureau of the Census, "Characteristics of the Population Below the Poverty Level: 1980," *Current Population Reports*, Series P-60, No. 133 (Washington, D.C.: U.S. Government Printing Office, 1982), p. 128.

40. In what follows, I rely on two main sources: Robert Bibb and William Form, "The Effects of Industrial, Occupational, and Sex Stratification on Wages in Blue Collar Markets," *Social Forces* 55 (June, 1977): 974–96; E. M. Beck, Patrick M. Horan and Charles M. Tolbert, "Stratification in a Dual Economy," *American Sociological Review* 43 (October, 1978): 704–20. These authors are sociologists. It should be recognized that the notion of a dual economy (or segmented labor market, as it is also called) originated in economics. See David M. Gordon, *Theories of Poverty and Underemployment*; David M. Gordon (ed.), *Problems in Political Economy* (Boston, MA: D.C. Heath & Co., 1977). For a conservative critique of this literature, see Glen G. Cain, The Challenge of Segmented Labor Market Theories to Orthodox Theory," *Journal of Economic Literature* 14 (December, 1977): 1215–56.

41. E. M. Beck, Patrick M. Horan, and Charles M. Tolbert, "Stratification in a Dual Economy," p. 713.

42. See Edward G. Banfield, *The Unheavenly City Revisited* (Boston: Little,

Brown, 1974) and George Gilder, *Wealth and Poverty* (New York: Basic Books, 1981).

43. For chapter-length treatments of the problems of racial and sexual inequality, see Leonard Beeghley, *Social Stratification in America*. For a good general sketch of the dimensions of racial inequality, see Hubert M. Blalock, *Racial and Ethnic Relations* (Englewood Cliffs, N.J.: Prentice-Hall, 1982). For similar analyses of the dimensions of sexual inequality, see Ann Stromburg and Shirley Harkess (eds.). *Women Working* (Palo Alto, Cal.: Mayfield, 1978); Judith Long Laws, *The Second X* (New York: Elsevier, 1979).

44. U.S. Bureau of the Census, "Money Income and Poverty Status of Families and Persons in the United States, 1981," p. 22. By the phrase "normatively sanctioned racism," I mean overt racial epithets and discriminatory policies.

45. See William Julius Wilson, *The Declining Significance of Race,* 2nd ed. (Chicago: University of Chicago Press, 1980) and Charles Vert Willie, *The Caste and Class Controversy* (Bayside, N.Y.: General Hall, 1979).

46. U.S. Bureau of the Census, "Money Income and Poverty Status of Families and Persons in the United States, 1981," p. 27.

47. *Ibid.,* calculated from pp. 22–23.

48. *Ibid.,* pp. 26–27.

49. E. M. Beck, Patrick M. Horan, and Charles M. Tolbert, "Industrial Segmentation and Labor Market Discrimination," *Social Problems* 28 (December, 1980): 113–30.

50. Joe R. Feagin and Clairece Booher Feagin, *Discrimination American Style: Institutional Racism and Sexism* (Englewood Cliffs, N.J.: Prentice-Hall, 1978). The next few paragraphs are indebted to this source.

51. E. M. Beck, Patrick M. Horan, and Charles M. Tolbert, "Industrial Segmentation and Labor Market Discrimination."

52. See Mary Corcoran, Linda Datcher, and Greg J. Duncan, "Most Workers Find Jobs Through Word of Mouth," *Monthly Labor Review* 103 (August, 1980): 33–36.

53. There is at least one study which indicates that there is variation by skill level, with current racial composition of the work force better predicting the number of black applicants for white-collar than blue-collar jobs. See Bettye Kirkpatrick Eidson, "Institutional Racism: Minority Group Manpower Policies of Major Urban Employers," Ph.D. dissertation, Johns Hopkins University, 1971.

54. See Joe R. Feagin and Clairece Booher Feagin, *Discrimination American Style: Institutionalized Racism and Sexism.*

55. Sandra L. Bein and Daryl L. Bein, "Sex-Segretated Want Ads: Do They Discourage Female Job Applicants?," in Catherine R. Simpson (ed.), *Discrimination Against Women* (New York: R.R. Bowker & Co., 1973)

56. Joe R. Feagin and Clairece Booher Feagin, *Discrimination American Style: Institutional Racism and Sexism.*

57. See Leonard Beeghley, *Social Stratification in America;* National Advisory Council on Economic Opportunity, *The American Promise: Equal Justice and Economic Opportunity* (Washington, D.C.: U.S. Government Printing Office, 1981).

58. Lillian Rubin, *Worlds of Pain* (New York: Basic Books, 1978).

59. See Ann Stromberg and Shirley Harkess, *Women Working;* Judith Long Laws, *The Second X.*

Bibliography

Aday, L. A. "Economic and Noneconomic Barriers to the Use of Needed Medical Services." *Medical Care* 13 (1975): 447–56.

Advisory Commission on Intergovernmental Relations. *Public Assistance: The Growth of a Federal Function.* Washington, D.C.: U.S. Government Printing Office, 1980.

Advisory Commission on Intergovernmental Relations. *Tax Capacity of the Fifty States.* Washington, D.C.: U.S. Government Printing Office, 1982.

Allen, John. *Assault with a Deadly Weapon: The Autobiography of a Street Criminal.* New York: Pantheon Books, 1977.

Anderson, Martin. *Welfare: The Political Economy of Welfare Reform in the United States.* Stanford, Cal.: Hoover Institution Press, 1978.

Anton, Thomas J. *An Estimate of the Fiscal Impact of President Reagan's Budget Proposals.* Ann Arbor, MI: Institute for Social Research, 1981.

Ayella, Mary E., and John B. Williamson. "The Social Mobility of Women: A Causal Model of Socioeconomic Success." *Sociological Quarterly* 17 (Autumn, 1976): 534–54.

Ball Richard A. "A Poverty Case: The Analgesic Subculture of the Southern Appalachians." *American Sociological Review* 33 (December, 1968): 885–96.

Baltzell, E. Digby. *Puritan Boston and Quaker Philadelphia.* New York: Free Press, 1976.

Banfield, Edward G. *The Unheavenly City Revisited.* Boston: Little, Brown, 1974.

Barclay, Suzanne, *et al. Schooling and Work among Youth from Low Income Households.* Washington, D.C.: U.S. Department of Labor, 1980.

Beck, E. M., Patrick M. Horan, and Charles M. Tolbert. "Industrial Segmentation and Labor Market Discrimination." *Social Problems* 28 (December, 1980): 113–30.

——— "Stratification in a Dual Economy." *American Sociological Review* 43 (October, 1978): 704–20.

Becker, M. H., C. A. Nathanson, R. H. Drachman, and J. P. Kirscht. "Mothers' Health Beliefs and Children's Clinic Visits: A Prospective Study." *Journal of Community Health* 3 (1975): 125–35.

Becnel, Barbara. "The Crime–Unemployment Cycle." *AFL–CIO Federationist* 85 (November, 1978): 9–14.

Beeghley, Leonard. *Social Stratification in America: A Critical Analysis of Theory and Research.* New York: Random House, 1978.

Beeghley, Leonard, Ellen Van Velsor, and E. Wilbur Bock. "The Correlates of Religiosity among Black and White Americans." *Sociological Quarterly* 22 (Summer, 1981): 403–12.

Bein, Sandra L., and Daryl L. Bein. "Sex-Segregated Want Ads: Do They Discourage Female Job Applicants?" In *Discrimination against Women,* Catherine R. Simpson (ed.). New York: R. R. Bowker and Co., 1973.

Berk, Richard A., Kenneth J. Lenihan, and Peter H. Rossi. "Crime and Poverty." *American Sociological Review* 45 (October, 1980): 766–86.

Berkanovic, E., and L. G. Reeder. "Can Money Buy the Appropriate Use of Services? Some Notes on the Meaning of Utilization Data." *Journal of Health and Social Behavior* 15 (1974): 93–99.

Bibb, Robert, and William Form. "The Effects of Industrial, Occupational, and Sex Stratification on Wages in Blue Collar Markets." *Social Forces* 55 (June, 1977): 974–96.

Blalock, Hubert M. *Racial and Ethnic Relations.* Englewood Cliffs, N.J.: Prentice-Hall, 1982.

Blau, Peter and Otis Dudley Duncan. *The American Occupational Structure.* New York: Wiley, 1967.

Bogue, Donald J. "A Long-Term Solution to the AFDC Problem: Prevention of Unwanted Pregnancy." *Social Service Review* 49 (December, 1975): 539–52.

Bowles, Samuel, and Herbert Gintis. *Schooling in Capitalist America.* New York: Basic Books, 1976.

Brooks, C. H. "The Changing Relationship between Socioeconomic Status and Infant Mortality: An Analysis of State Characteristics." *Journal of Health and Social Behavior* 16, no. 3 (1975): 291–303.

Brown, Claude. *Manchild in the Promised Land.* New York: Signet, 1965.

Browning, Edgar K. *Redistribution and the Welfare System.* Washington, D.C.: American Enterprise Institute, 1975.

Cain, Glen G. "The Challenge of Segmented Labor Market Theories to Orthodox Theory." *Journal of Economic Literature* 14 (December, 1977): 1215–56.

Califano, Joseph. *The 1982 Report on Drug Abuse and Alcoholism.* New York: Warner Books, 1982.

Carlin, Jerome, Jan Howard, and Sheldon Messinger. *Civil Justice for the Poor.* New York: Russell Sage, 1967.

Children's Defense Fund. *EPSDT: Does it Spell Health Care for Poor Children.* Washington, D.C.: Children's Defense Fund, 1977.

Citizens Board of Inquiry. *Hunger, U.S.A.: A Report by the Citizens Board of Inquiry into Hunger and Malnutrition in the United States.* Boston: Beacon Press, 1968.

Clark, Burton R. "The 'Cooling Out' Function in Higher Education." *American Journal of Sociology* 65 (May, 1960): 569–76.

Clarkson, Kenneth. "Welfare Benefits of the Food Stamp Programs." *Southern Economic Journal* 34 (1976): 864–78.

Clinard, Marshall B. *Illegal Corporate Behavior.* Washington, D.C.: U.S. Department of Justice, 1979.

Coleman, James S., *et al. Equality of Educational Opportunity.* Washington, D.C.: U.S. Government Printing Office, 1966.

Coles, Robert. *Children of Crisis.* Vol. I. Boston: Little, Brown, 1964.

——— *The Privileged Ones.* Boston: Little, Brown, 1977.

——— *The South Goes North.* Boston, Little, Brown, and Co., 1967.

——— *Still Hungry in America.* New York: World Publishing Co., 1969.

Conference Report. *Omnibus Budget Reconciliation Act of 1981.* Washington, D.C.: U.S. Government Printing Office, 1981.

Congressional Budget Office. *Agricultural Price Support Programs: A Handbook.* Washington, D.C.: U.S. Government Printing Office, 1980.

Congressional Budget Office. *Five Year Budget Projections and Alternative Budgeting Strategies for Fiscal Years 1980–1984: Supplemental Report on Tax Expenditures.* Washington, D.C.: U.S. Government Printing Office, 1979.

Congressional Budget Office. *Indexing with the Consumer Price Index: Problems and Alternatives.* Washington, D.C.: U.S. Government Printing Office, 1981.

Corcoran, Mary, Linda Datcher, and Greg J. Duncan. "Most Workers Find Jobs through Word of Mouth." *Monthly Labor Review* 103 (August, 1980): 33–36.

Coser, Lewis A. *Continuities in the Study of Social Conflict.* New York: Free Press, 1967.

Coter, E., E. Grossman, and F. Clark. *Family Food Plans and Food Costs.* Washington, D.C.: U.S. Department of Agriculture, 1962.

Coward, Barbara E., J. Allen Williams, and Joe R. Feagin. "The Culture of Poverty Debate: Some Additional Data." *Social Problems* 21 (June, 1974): 621–33.

Crandall, Lee A., and R. Paul Duncan. "Attitudinal and Situational Factors in the Use of Physicians Services by Low Income Persons." *Journal of Health and Social Behavior* 22 (March, 1981): 64–77.

Curtis, Russell L., and Louis A. Zurcher. "Voluntary Associations and the Social Integration of the Poor." *Social Problems* 18 (Winter, 1971): 339–57.

Cutright, Phillips. "Income and Family Events: Marital Stability." *Journal of Marriage and the Family* 33 (May, 1971): 291–306.

Dahl, Robert A. *Pluralist Democracy in the United States: Conflict and Consent.* Chicago: Rand McNally, 1967.

Davis, Karen, and Cathy Schoen. *Health and the War on Poverty.* Washington, D.C.: Brookings Institution, 1978.

Della Fave, L. Richard. "The Culture of Poverty Revisited: A Strategy for Research." *Social Problems* 21 (June, 1974): 609–62.

Devens, Richard M. "Unemployment among Recipients of Food Stamps and AFDC." *Monthly Labor Review* 102 (March, 1979): 47–53.

Duncan, Greg J., and James N. Morgan (eds.). *Five Thousand American Families: Patterns of Economic Progress,* Volumes 1–8. Ann Arbor, MI: Institute for Social Research, 1974–1978.

Dutton, Diane B. "Explaining the Low Use of Health Services By the Poor: Costs, Attitudes, or Delivery Systems?" *American Sociological Review* 43 (June, 1978): 348–68.

Ehrenreich, Barbara, and John Ehrenreich. *The American Health Empire.* New York: Random House, 1960.

Eidson, Bettye Kirkpatrick. "Institutional Racism: Minority Group Manpower Policies of Major Urban Employers." Ph.D. dissertation, Johns Hopkins University, 1971.

Endozien, Joseph C., Boyd R. Switzer, and Rebecca B. Brian. "Medical Evaluation of the Special Supplemental Food Program for Women, Infants, and Children. *American Journal of Clinical Nutrition* 32 (March, 1979): 677–92.

Erskine, Hazel. "The Polls: Government Role in Welfare." *Public Opinion Quarterly* 39 (Summer, 1975): 257–74.

Executive Office of the President. *Budget of the United States Government, Fiscal 1983.* Washington, D.C.: Office of Management and Budget, 1982.

Executive Office of the President. *Fiscal Year 1982 Budget Revisions: Additional Details on Budget Savings.* Washington, D.C.: Office of Management and Budget, 1981.

"Family Budgets." *Monthly Labor Review* 105 (July, 1982): 44–46.

"Family of Four Needs Record $277 Per Week." *The Gallup Report* 185 (February, 1981): 20–21.

Farrell, Ronald A. and Victoria Lynn Swigert. *Social Deviance,* 2nd ed. New York: J. B. Lippincott Co., 1978.

Feagin, Joe R. *Subordinating the Poor.* Englewood Cliffs, N.J.: Prentice-Hall, 1976.

Feagin Joe R., and Clairece Booher Feagin. *Discrimination American Style: Institutional Racism and Sexism.* Englewood Cliffs, N.J.: Prentice-Hall, 1978.

Feagin, Joe R., and Harlan H. Hahn. *Ghetto Revolts.* New York: Macmillan, 1973.

Featherman, David L., and Robert M. Hauser. *Opportunity and Change.* New York: Academic Press, 1978.

Food Resource and Action Center. *The Impact of Child Nutrition Budget Cuts: A Look at the States and Selected School Districts.* Washington, D.C.: Food Resource and Action Center, 1982.

Freeman, Roger A. *The Growth of American Government: A Morphology of the Welfare State.* Stanford, Cal.: Hoover Institution Press, 1975.

Friedman, Milton. *Capitalism and Freedom.* Chicago: University of Chicago Press, 1962.

Gamson, William A. *The Strategy of Protest.* Homewood, Ill.: Dorsey, 1975.

Gans, Herbert. "The Positive Functions of Poverty." *American Journal of Sociology* 78 (September, 1972): 275–89.

Garvin, Charles, Audrey D. Smith, and William J. Reid (eds.). *The Work Incentive Experience*. Montclair, N.J.: Allenheld, Osmun and Co., 1978.

Gilder, George. *Wealth and Poverty*. New York: Basic Books, 1981.

Glaser, Daniel. *The Effectiveness of a Prison and Parole System*. Indianapolis: Bobbs-Merrill 1964.

Goodwin, Leonard. *Can Social Science Help Resolve National Problems?* New York: Free Press, 1975.

—— *Do the Poor Want to Work?* Washington, D.C.: Brookings Institution, 1972.

—— "Limitations of the Seattle and Denver Income Maintenance Analysis." *American Journal of Sociology* 85 (November, 1979): 653–57.

—— *The Work Incentive (WIN) Program and Related Experiences*. Washington, D.C.: U.S. Department of Labor, 1977.

Gordon, David M. (ed.). *Problems in Political Economy*. Boston, MA: D.C. Heath and Co., 1977.

—— *Theories of Poverty and Underemployment*. Lexington, MA: D.C. Heath and Co., 1972.

Gortmaker, Steven L. "Poverty and Infant Mortality in the United States." *American Sociological Review* 44 (April, 1979): 280–97.

Guillory, Ferrel. "Managing Budget Cuts at the State Level." *North Carolina Insight* (No. 4, 1981): 26–30.

Hannon, Michael, *et al.* "Income and Independence Effects on Marital Dissolution." *American Journal of Sociology* 84 (November, 1978): 611–33.

Harrington, Michael. *The Other America*. Baltimore, MD: Penguin Books, 1971. First printing: 1962.

Hindelang, Michael J., *et al.* "Correlates of Delinquency: The Illusion of Discrepancy between Self-Report and Official Measurers." *American Sociological Review* 44 (December, 1979): 995–1014.

Hiroto, Donald S. "Locus of Control and Learned Helplessness." *Journal of Experimental Psychology* 102 (February, 1974): 187–93.

Hiroto, Donald S., and Martin E. P. Seligman. "Generality of Learned Helplessness in Man." *Journal of Personality and Social Psychology* 31 (February, 1975): 311-27.

Hodge, Robert W., and Barbara Laslett. "Poverty and Status Attainment." Pp. 126-63 in *Poverty and Public Policy*, Vincent T. Covello (ed.). Cambridge, MA: Schenkman Publishing Co., 1980.

Hofferth, Sandra L., and Kristin A. Moore. "Early Childrearing and Subsequent Economic Well-Being." *American Sociological Review* 44 (October, 1979): 784-815.

Howell, James T. *Hard Living on Clay Street*. Garden City, N.Y.: Anchor Books, 1973.

Huber, Joan, and William H. Form. *Income and Ideology*. New York: Free Press, 1973.

Hunt, James W., James E. Bowers, and Neal Miller. *Laws, Licenses, and the Offender's Right to Work*. Washington, D.C.: American Bar Association, 1973.

Ireland, Lola M., Oliver C. Moles, and Robert M. O'Shea. "Ethnicity, Poverty, and Selected Attitudes: A Test of the 'Culture of Poverty' Thesis." *Social Forces* 47 (June, 1969): 405-13.

Jencks, Christopher, *et al. Inequality: A Reasssessment of the Effect of Family and Schooling in America*. New York: Harper and Row, 1972.

Joe, Thomas. *Profiles of Families in Poverty: Effects of the 1983 Budget Proposals on the Poor*. Washington, D.C.: Center for the Study of Social Policy, 1982.

Johnson, Lyndon. *Public Papers of the President, 1963-64*, Vol. 2. Washington, D.C.: U.S. Government Printing Office, 1972.

Kessler, Ronald C., and Paul D. Cleary. "Social Class and Psychological Distress." *American Sociological Review* 45 (June, 1980): 463-78.

King, Jill. *The Consumer Price Index*. Technical Paper V for *The Measure of Poverty*. Washington, D.C.: U.S. Department of Health, Education, and Welfare, 1976.

Koos, E. L. *The Health of Regionville*. New York: Columbia University Press, 1954.

Kotelchuck, Milton. *1980 Massachusetts Special Supplemental Program for Women, Infants and Children (WIC) Evaluation Project*. Boston, MA: Department of Public Health, 1982.

Law Enforcement Assistance Administration. *Criminal Victimization in the United States*. Washington, D.C.: U.S. Government Printing Office, 1976.

Law Enforcement Assistance Administration. *Survey of Inmates of Local Jails, 1972.* Washington, D.C.: U.S. Government Printing Office, 1974.

Law Enforcement Assistance Administration. *Survey of Inmates of State Correctional Facilities, 1974.* Washington, D.C.: U.S. Government Printing Office, 1976.

Lawrence, William J., and Stephen Leeds. *An Inventory of Federal Income Transfer Programs.* White Plains, N.Y.: Institute for Socioeconomic Studies, 1978.

Laws, Judith Long. *The Second X.* New York: Elsevier, 1979.

Leacock, Eleanor Burke. *The Culture of Poverty: A Critique.* New York: Simon and Schuster, 1971.

Legal Services Corporation. *Characteristics of Field Programs Supported by the Legal Services Corporation.* Washington, D.C.: Legal Services Corporation, 1982.

Leslie, Gerald R. *The Family in Social Context,* 5th ed. New York: Oxford University Press, 1982.

Levine, Robert A. "How and Why the Experiment Came About." Pp. 15–25 in *Work Incentives and Income Guarantees: The New Jersey Negative Income Tax Experiment,* J. A. Pechman and P. M. Timpane (eds.). Washington, D.C: Brookings Institution, 1975.

Lewis, Oscar. "The Culture of Poverty." Pp. 187–200 in *On Understanding Poverty,* D. P. Moynihan (ed.). New York: Basic Books, 1969.

Liebow, Elliot. *Tally's Corner.* Boston: Little, Brown, 1967.

Lipset, S. M., and S. Rokkan (eds.). *Party Systems and Voter Alignments.* New York: Free Press, 1967.

Longen, Kathryn. *Domestic Food Programs: An Overview.* Washington, D.C.: U.S. Department of Agriculture, 1980.

Lyon, David W. *The Dynamics of Welfare Dependency: A Survey.* New York: Ford Foundation, 1977.

MacDonald, Maurice. *Food, Stamps, and Income Maintenance.* New York: Academic Press, 1977.

Maier, Norman R. F. *Frustration: The Study of Behavior Without a Goal.* New York: McGraw-Hill, 1949.

Markides, Kyriakos S., and Connie McFarland. "A Note on Recent Trends in the Infant Mortality–Socioeconomic Status Relationship." *Social Forces* 61 (September, 1982): 286–76.

Medicaid/Medicare Management Institute. *Data on the Medicaid Program: Eligibility, Services, Expenditures.* Washington, D.C.: U.S. Department of Health, Education, and Welfare, 1979.

Merton, Robert K. "Social Structure and Anomie." Pp. 185–215 in *Social Theory and Social Structure.* New York: Free Press, 1968.

Meyer, Herbert E. "Jobs and Want Ads: A Look Behind the Words." *Fortune* (November 20, 1978): 88–96.

Moffitt, Robert A. "The Negative Income Tax: Would It Discourage Work?" *Monthly Labor Review* 104 (April, 1981): 23–27.

Morris, Michael, and John B. Williamson. "Stereotypes and Social Class: A Focus on Poverty." Chapter 9 in *In the Eye of the Beholder: Contemporary Issues in Stereotyping,* Arthur G. Miller (ed.). New York: Praeger, 1982.

Munnell, Alicia. "Federalizing Welfare: The Fiscal Impact of the SSI Program." *New England Economic Review* (Sept.–Oct., 1977): 3–28.

National Advisory Council on Economic Opportunity. *The American Promise: Equal Justice and Economic Opportunity.* Washington, D.C.: U.S. Government Printing Office, 1981.

Newbeck, Kenneth J., and Jack L. Roach. "Income Maintenance Experiments, Politics, and the Perpetuation of Poverty." *Social Problems* 28 (February, 1981): 308–20.

Nilson, Linda Birzotta "Reconsidering Ideological Lines: Beliefs about Poverty in America." *Sociological Quarterly* 22 (Autumn, 1981): 531–48.

Orshansky, Mollie. *Documentation of Background Information and Rationale for Current Poverty Matrix.* Technical Paper No. 1 for *The Measure of Poverty.* Washington, D.C.: Department of Health, Education, and Welfare, 1976.

——— "How Poverty Is Measured." *Monthly Labor Review* 92 (February, 1969).

——— *Update of the Orshansky Index.* Technical Ppaer XI for *The Measure of Poverty.* Washington, D.C.: Social Security Administration, 1976.

"Oversight Hearings on Child Nutrition." *Hearings before the Subcommittee on Elementary, Secondary, and Vocational Education of the Committee on Education and Labor,* March 1980. Washington, D.C.: U.S. Government Printing Office, 1980.

Paglin, Morton. *Poverty and Transfers In-Kind.* Stanford, Cal.: Hoover Institution Press, 1980.

Paneth, Nigel. "Infant Mortality Reexamined." *Journal of the American Medical Association* 247 (February 19, 1982).

Pearlin, Leonard I., and Clarice W. Radabaugh. "Economic Strains and the Coping Functions of Alcohol." *American Journal of Sociology* 82 (November, 1976): 652–63.

Peskin, Janice. *In-Kind Income and the Measurement of Poverty.* Technical Paper VII for *The Measure of Poverty.* Washington, D.C.: U.S. Department of Health, Education, and Welfare, 1976.

Peterkin, Betty. *Food Plans for Poverty Measurement.* Technical Paper XII for *The Measure of Poverty.* Washington, D.C.: U.S. Department of Health, Education, and Welfare, 1976.

Pettigrew, Thomas. "Social Psychology's Potential Contributions to an Understanding of Poverty." Pp. 189–233 in *Poverty and Public Policy: An Evaluation of Social Scientific Research,* Vincent T. Covello (ed.). Cambridge, MA: Schenkman Publishing Co., 1980.

Phares, E. Jerry. *Locus of Control in Personality.* Morristown, N.J.: General Learning Press, 1976.

Piven, Francis Fox, and Richard Cloward. *Poor People's Movements: Why They Succeecd, How They Fail.* New York: Pantheon, 1977.

——— *Regulating the Poor: The Functions of Public Welfare.* New York: Vintage Books, 1971.

Pownall, George. *Employment Problems of Released Prisoners.* Washington, D.C.: U.S. Department of Labor, 1969.

President's Commission for a National Agenda for the Eighties. *Government and the Advancement of Social Justice, Health, Welfare, Education, and Civil Rights in the Eighties.* Washington, D.C.: U.S. Government Printing Office, 1980.

President's Commission on Law Enforcement and the Administration of Justice. *The Challenge of Crime in a Free Society.* Washington, D.C.: U.S. Government Printing Office, 1967.

President's Commission on Law Enforcement and the Administration of Justice. *Task Force Report: Corrections.* Washington, D.C.: U.S. Government Printing Office, 1967.

Rainwater, Lee. "The Lower Class: Health, Illness and Medical Institutions. Pp. 250–77 in *Among the People: Encounters with the Poor,* I. Deutscher and E. Thompson (eds.). New York: Basic Books, 1968.

―――― *What Money Buys.* New York: Basic Books, 1974.

Reiman, Jeffrey H. *The Rich Get Richer and the Poor Get Prison.* New York: John Wiley, 1979.

Rein, Martin, and Lee Rainwater. "Patterns of Welfare Use." *Social Service Review* 52 (December, 1978): 511–34.

Rodman, Hyman. "The Lower Class Value Stretch." *Social Forces* 42 (December, 1963): 205–15.

Rosenberg, Morris, and Leonard I. Pearlin. "Social Class and Self-Esteem among Children and Adults." *American Journal of Sociology* 84 (July, 1978): 53–77.

Rossi, Peter N., and Katherine C. Lyall. *Reforming Public Welfare: A Critique of the Negative Income Tax Experiment.* New York: Russell Sage Foundation, 1976.

Roth, Susan, and R. R. Bootzin. "The Effects of Experimentally Induced Expectancies of External Control: An Investigation of Learned Helplessness." *Journal of Personality and Social Psychology* 29 (February, 1974): 253–64.

Roth, Susan, and Larry Kubal. "Effects of Noncontingent Reinforcement on Tasks of Differing Importance: Facilitation and Learned Helplessness." *Journal of Personality and Social Psychology* 32 (October, 1975): 680–91.

Rubin, Lillian. *Worlds of Pain.* New York: Basic Books, 1976.

Salathe, Larry E. *Household Expenditure Patterns in the United States,* Technical Bulletin No. 1603. Washington, D.C.: U.S. Department of Agriculture, 1979.

Sanger, Mary Bryna. *Welfare of the Poor.* New York: Academic Press, 1979.

Schiller, Bradley R. "Lessons from WIN: A Manpower Evaluation." *Journal of Human Resources* 13 (Fall, 1978): 502–23.

―――― "Want Ads and Jobs for the Poor." *Manpower* 6 (January, 1974): 11–13.

Schneider, Louis. "Ironic Perspective and Sociological Thought." Pp. 323–38 in *The Idea of Social Structure,* L. A. Coser (ed.). New York: Free Press, 1975.

Schwartz-Nobel, Loretta. *Starving in the Shadow of Plenty.* New York: G. P. Putnam and Sons, 1981.

Select Committee on Aging, U.S. House of Representatives. *SSI (Supplementary Security Income): Questions and Answers.* Washington, D.C.: U.S. Government Printing Office, 1975.

Seligman, Martin. *Helplessness.* San Francisco, Freeman, 1976.

Smeeding, Timothy. *Alternative Methods for Valuing Selected In-Kind Transfer Benefits and Measuring Their Effect on Poverty.* Washington, D.C.: U.S. Bureau of the Census, 1982.

────── "The Anti-Poverty Effectiveness of In-Kind Transfers." *Journal of Human Resources* 12 (Summer, 1977): 360–78.

Smeeding, Timothy, and Marilyn Moon. "Valuing Government Expenditures: The Case of Medical Care Transfers and Poverty." *Review of Income and Wealth* 26 (September, 1980): 305–24.

Smolensky, Eugene, Leanna Stieffel, Maria Schmundt, and Robert Plotnick. "In-Kind Transfers and the Size of Distribution of Income." Chapter 7 in *Improving Measures of Economic Well-Being,* Marilyn Moon and Eugene Smolensky (eds.). New York: Academic Press, 1977.

Stack, Carol. *All Our Kin.* New York: Harper and Row, 1974.

Stern, Philip M. *The Rape of the Taxpayer.* New York: Vintage Books, 1974.

Stinchcombe, Arthur. "Merton's Theory of Social Structure." Pp. 11–34 in *The Idea of Social Structure,* L. Coser (ed.). New York: Free Press, 1975.

Stromberg, Ann, and Shirley Harkess (eds.). *Women Working.* Palo Alto, Cal.: Mayfield, 1978.

Subcommittee on Nutrition. *Hearing before the Subcommittee on Nutrition of the Committee on Agriculture, Hunger in America: Ten Years Later,* Senate, April 30, 1979. Washington, D.C.: U.S. Government Printing Office, 1979.

Sutherland, Edwin H. *Principles of Criminolgy.* New York: J. B. Lippincott Co., 1947.

Swigert, Victoria Lynn, and Ronald L. Farrell. "Normal Homicides and the Law." *American Sociological Review* 42 (February, 1977): 16–31.

Taylor, Shelley E. "Hospital Patient Behavior: Reactance, Helplessness, or Control?" *Journal of Social Issues* 35 (No. 1, 1979): 156–84.

Thomas, Adele. "Learned Helplessness and Expectancy Factors: Implications for Research in Learning Disabilities." *Review of Educational Research* 49 (Spring, 1979): 208–21..

Thomas, William I. *The Unadjusted Girl.* Boston: Little, Brown and Co., 1923.

Thornberry, Terence P., and Margaret Farnworth. "Social Correlates of Criminal

Involvement: Further Evidence on the Relationship between Social Status and Criminal Behavior." *American Sociological Review* 47 (August, 1982): 505–18.

Tissue, Thomas. "Response to Recipiency under Public Assistance and SSI." *Social Security Bulletin* 41 (November, 1978): 3–15.

Tittle, Charles R., Wayne J. Villemez, and Douglas A. Smith. "The Myth of Social Class and Criminality: An Assessment of the Empirical Evidence." *American Sociological Review* 43 (October, 1978): 643–56.

Turner, Jonathan H., and Leonard Beeghley. *The Emergence of Sociological Theory.* Homewood, Ill.: Dorsey Press, 1981.

U.S. Bureau of the Census. *Characteristics of Households and Persons Receiving Selected Noncash Benefits: 1981*, Series P–60, No. 136. Washington, D.C.: U.S. Government Printing Office, 1983.

——— "Characteristics of the Population Below the Poverty Level: 1980." *Current Population Reports,* Series P-60, No. 133. Washington, D.C.: U.S. Government Printing Office, 1982.

——— "Money Income of Households, Families, and Persons in the United States: 1980." *Current Population Reports,* Series P–60, No. 132. Washington, D.C.: U.S. Government Printing Office, 1982.

——— "Money Income and Poverty Status of Families and Persons in the United States, 1981." *Current Population Reports,* Series P–60, No. 134. Washington, D.C.: U.S. Government Printing Office, 1982.

——— *Statistical Abstract of the United States.* Washington, D.C.: U.S. Department of Commerce, 1981.

U.S. Chamber of Commerce. *White Collar Crime.* Washington, D.C.: U.S. Chamber of Commerce, 1974.

U.S. Department of Health, Education, and Welfare. *A Guide to Supplemental Security Income.* Washington, D.C.: U.S. Government Printing Office, 1979.

——— *Health Status of Minorities and Low Income Groups.* Washington, D.C.: U.S. Government Printing Office, 1978.

U.S. Department of Health and Human Services. *Aid to Families with Dependent Children: A Chartbook.* Washington, D.C.: U.S. Government Printing Office, 1980.

——— *Aid to Families with Dependent Children, 1977 Recipient Characteristics Study, Part I.* Washington, D.C.: U.S. Government Printing Office, 1980.

——— *Characteristics of State Plans for Aid to Families with Dependent Children: Need, Eligibility, Administration.* Washington, D.C.: U.S. Government Printing Office, 1981.

——— *Disposition of Public Assistance Cases Involving Questions of Fraud, Fiscal Year 1979.* Washington, D.C.: U.S. Government Printing Office, 1981.

——— *Research Tables Based on Characteristics of State Plans for Aid to Families with Dependent Children.* Washington, D.C.: U.S. Government Printing Office, 1980.

——— *Selected Health Characteristics by Occupation.* Washington, D.C.: U.S. Government Printing Office, 1980.

U.S. Department of Justice. *Criminal Victimization in the United States, 1978.* Washington, D.C.: U.S. Government Printing Office, 1980.

——— *Fraud and Abuse in Government Benefit Programs.* Washington, D.C.: U.S. Government Printing Office, 1979.

U.S. House of Representatives. "Administration of the AFDC Program." *Third Report by the Committee on Governmental Operations,* July 18, 1979. Washington, D.C.: U.S. Government Printing Office, 1980.

——— "Department of Labor and Health, Education, and Welfare Appropriations for 1979." *Hearings before a Subcommittee of the Committee on Appropriations,* Part 6. Washington, D.C.: U.S. Government Printing Office, 1979.

——— "Departments of Labor, Health and Human Services, Education, and Related Agencies Appropriations for 1982." *Hearings before a Subcommittee of the Committee on Appropriations,* Part 5. Washington, D.C.: U.S. Government Printing Office, 1981.

——— "Fraud and Racketeering in Medicare and Medicaid." *Hearing before Select Committee on Aging,* October 4, 1978. Washington, D.C.: U.S. Government Printing Office, 1979.

U.S. Senate. "Waste and Abuse in Social Security Act Programs: "Medicaid and Medicare Frauds." *Hearing before the Subcommittee on Long-Term Care of the Special Committee on Aging,* August 30, 1976. Washington, D.C.: U.S. Government Printing Office, 1977.

——— "Waste and Abuse in Social Security Act Programs." *Hearing before the Subcommittee on Public Assistance of the Committee on Finance,* November 16, 1979. Washington, D.C.: U.S. Government Printing Office, 1980.

Valentine, Charles A. *Culture and Poverty.* Chicago, Ill.: University of Chicago Press, 1978.

Vaz Pato, Manuel, and John Williamson. "Socioeconomic Achievement: The Case of the Working Poor." *Journal of Sociology and Social Welfare* 6 (March, 1979): 245–64.

Verba, Sidney, and Norman H. Nie. *Participation in America: Political Democracy and Social Equality.* New York: Harper and Row, 1972.

Walsh, Edward J. *Dirty Work, Race and Self-Esteem.* Ann Arbor, MI: Institute of Labor and Industrial Relations, 1975.

Webb, Rodman B. *Schooling and Society.* New York: Macmillan, 1981.

Weber, Max. *Economy and Society.* New York: Bedminster, 1968.

Wilensky, Gail R. *Government and the Financing of Health Care.* Washington, D.C.: National Center for Health Services Research, 1982.

Williamson, John B. "Beliefs about the Motivation of the Poor and Attitudes toward Poverty Policy." *Social Problems* 21 (June, 1974): 634–48.

——— "Beliefs about the Welfare Poor." *Sociology and Social Research* 58 (January, 1974): 163–75.

Willie, Charles Vert. *The Caste and Class Controversy.* Bayside, N.Y.: General Hall, 1979.

Wilson, William Julius. *The Declining Significance of Race,* 2nd ed. Chicago: University of Chicago Press, 1980.

Wright, Sonia. "Work Response to Income Maintenance: Economic, Sociological, and Cultural Perspectives. *Social Forces* 53 (June, 1975): 553–62.

Zipp, John F., Richard Landerman, and Paul Luebke. "Political Parties and Political Participation: A Reexamination of the Standard Socioeconomic Model." *Social Forces* 60 (June, 1982): 1140–53.

Zola, Irving K. "Culture and Symptoms: An Analysis of Patients Presenting Complaints." *American Sociological Review* 31 (October, 1966): 615–30.

Name Index

This index refers only to names mentioned in the text. For names cited in notes, see the bibliography.

Subject Index

About the Author

Leonard Beeghley received his Ph.D from the University of California at Riverside in 1974. His areas of specialization are social stratification and sociological theory.

In addition to *Living Poorly in America,* Dr. Beeghley has written two other books: *Social Stratification in America: A Critical Evaluation of Theory and Research* and *The Emergence of Sociological Theory* (with Jonathan H. Turner).